PLACES TO GO PEOPLE TO SEE THINGS TO DO ALL ACROSS CANADA

E. Joan Abeles

Scholastic Canada Ltd.

Scholastic Canada Ltd.
123 Newkirk Road, Richmond Hill, Ontario, Canada L4C 3G5

Scholastic Inc.
555 Broadway, New York, NY, USA 10012

Ashton Scholastic Limited
Private Bag 1, Penrose, Auckland, New Zealand

Ashton Scholastic Pty Limited
PO Box 579, Gosford, NSW 2250, Australia

Scholastic Publications Ltd.
Villiers House, Clarendon Avenue, Leamington Spa, Warwickshire, CV32 5PR, UK

The author has tried as far as possible to ensure the accuracy of the information in this book. If there are inaccuracies, or if anything has changed since publication, please inform the publisher so that corrections can be made in any subsequent editions.

Illustration: Mary Jane Gerber

Typesetting: Wendy Smith

Indexing: Creative Juices

Canadian Cataloguing in Publication Data

Abeles, Joan
    Places to go, people to see, things to do, all across Canada

ISBN 0-590-74550-6

1. Children - Travel - Canada - Guidebooks.
2. Canada - Guidebooks. I. Title.

FC38.A24 1994   917.104'647   C93-094398-8
F1009.A24 1994

Copyright © 1994 by E. Joan Abeles. All rights reserved.
No part of this publication may be reproduced or stored in a retrieval system, or transmitted in any form or by any means, electronic, mechanical, photocopying, recording, or otherwise, without written permission of the publisher, Scholastic Canada Ltd.

7 6 5 4 3 2 1   Printed in Canada   4 5 6 7 8/9

In memory of my father, Paul Abeles.

Contents

Foreword

Introduction

British Columbia 1

Alberta 39

Saskatchewan 67

Manitoba 93

Ontario 117

Quebec 201

New Brunswick 241

Nova Scotia 255

Prince Edward Island 271

Newfoundland and Labrador 283

Northwest Territories 297

Yukon 307

Index 317

Foreword

Paul Abeles came to Canada from Czechoslovakia in 1939 as a refugee from Hitler's death camps. He loved his adopted country, and until his death in 1989 remained grateful to Canada for saving his life. He travelled across the country and marvelled at its immensity, its beauty, and its diversity. "Canada is the best country in the world," he told his children. And of course, he was right.

As an adult, I had the opportunity to travel extensively and came to share his pleasure and his sense of wonder at the rich heritage of our country, expressed in so many different and unique ways. *Places To Go* . . . is a tribute to the many people who, through their ingenuity, perseverance and vision, have made it their vocation to interpret, preserve and present the varied history and culture of a land of geographic splendour.

Canada is indeed a country to discover and explore.

E. Joan Abeles

Introduction

All across the country there are exciting places to go, people to meet, things to do and see. But how do you find them? This family guide to Canadian places is the place to start. There is a lot of information in this book. Here are a few tips on how to find what you're looking for.

Looking for an interesting place to go?

> Check out the maps, then browse through the site descriptions. You can guess that large urban centres have plenty to do, but you can also find great day trips and outings off the beaten path.

Want to know what to do when you get there?

> This book is divided into chapters, each focusing on one province or territory. Sections start with a simple, numbered map. Just find the area you're visiting on the map, then use the numbers to guide you to the site descriptions in that section. It's as easy as 1, 2, 3!

Want to learn more about your favourite subjects?

> Go to the index. Besides alphabetical listings, the index includes subject headings such as Historical – Homes and Settlements, Famous People, Transportation, Marine and Wildlife, and even just plain Amusement.

Just a few words of advice before you set out:

- ☞ Our maps are only outlines; you also need a good road map of the area you are going to.
- ☞ Sometimes our listings give approximate locations or a street address, along with a postal address. A good road map will usually give you the exact location of important sites.
- ☞ We have not listed specific hours and/or days of operation for the various sites, because these things change frequently. Call before you visit to make sure you won't be disappointed.

If you're sitting in your armchair working out your vacation, happy planning. And if you're already on the train or in the car, bon voyage!

BRITISH COLUMBIA

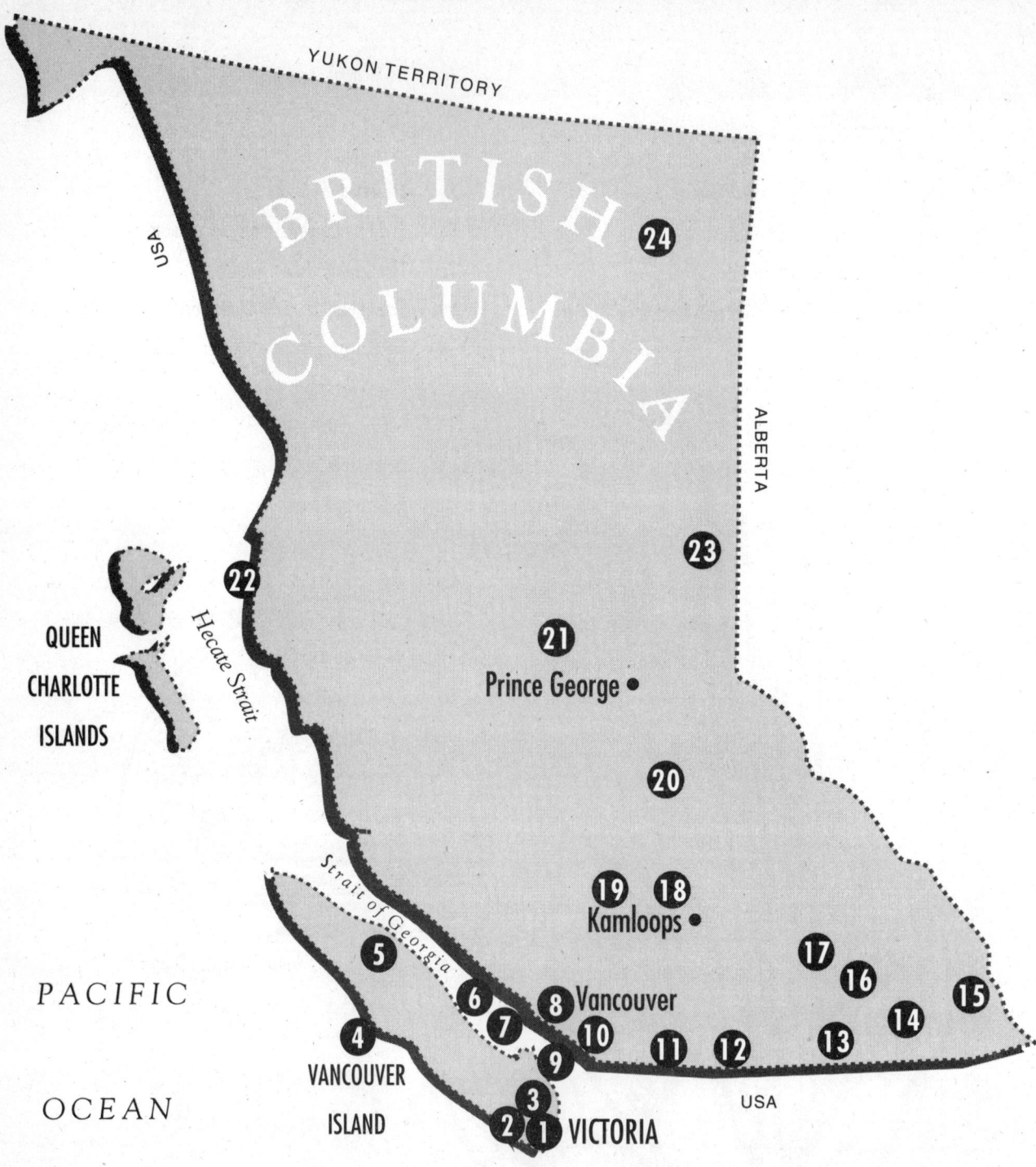

1a	Carr House	7m	Museum of Exotic World
1b	Dominion Astrophysical Observatory	8a	Capilano Suspension Bridge and Park
1c	Miniature World	8b	Lynn Canyon Suspension Bridge and Ecology Centre
1d	Royal London Wax Museum	9a	Steveston Museum
1e	British Columbia Legislature	9b	The Trev Deeley Motorcycle Museum
1f	Undersea Gardens of Victoria	9c	The Grocery Hall of Fame
1g	Canadiana Costume Museum and Archives of British Columbia	9d	The International Buddhist Society
1h	Emily Carr Gallery	10	Fort Langley National Historic Park
1i	Fort Rodd Hill and Fisgard Lighthouse National Historic Sites	11	Minter Gardens
1j	Butchart Gardens	12	The Grist Mill at Keremeos Provincial Historic Site
1k	Royal British Columbia Museum	13	Zuckerberg Island Heritage Park
2	The Sooke Region Museum	14	Canadian Museum of Rail Travel
3a	Native Heritage Centre	15	Fort Steele Heritage Town
3b	Duncan, City of Totems	16	The SS Moyie National Historic Site
3c	British Columbia Forest Museum	17	Sandon Historic Site and Museum
3d	Cowichan and Chemainus Valleys Ecomuseum	18	Hat Creek Ranch
4	Wickaninnish Interpretive Centre	19	Lillooet Museum
5	Comox Air Force Museum	20	Barkerville Historic Town
6	Little Qualicum Spawning Channel	21a	Kitwanga Fort National Historic Site
7a	The Pacific Space Centre	21b	Fort St. James National Historic Site
7b	University of British Columbia Botanical Gardens	22	North Pacific Cannery Village and Museum National Historic Site
7c	Vancouver Aquarium	23	Charlie Lake Cave
7d	Bloedel Conservatory	24	Fort Nelson's Welcome Visitor Program
7e	Science World		
7f	British Columbia Sports Hall of Fame and Museum		
7g	St. Roch National Historic Site		
7h	Museum of Anthropology		
7i	Dr. Sun Yat-Sen Classical Chinese Garden		
7j	Port of Vancouver Public Viewing Centre		
7k	Vancouver Museum		
7l	Canadian Craft Museum		

In the site descriptions, note that:

▲ indicates that second language services are available: English in Quebec and French elsewhere in Canada. Where "limited service" is given, it would be wise to call ahead for specifics

■ indicates that educational services are available

Carr House 1a

207 Government St., Victoria

✉

c/o Ministry of Small Business,
Tourism and Culture,
5th flr., 800 Johnson St.
Victoria, BC V8V 1X4

☎ (604) 387-3434

One of British Columbia's greatest contributions to Canadian culture is writer and artist Emily Carr and her stunning paintings of her native province. Carr House, the home where Carr was born, is an ideal place for children because the house was restored with interactive programs in mind; the period rooms contain hands-on displays. What a wonderful way to get acquainted with a national treasure!

■ on-site; elementary grades

Dominion Astrophysical Observatory 1b

5071 West Saanich Rd.
Victoria, BC V8X 4M6

☎ (604) 363-0012

At the Dominion Astrophysical Observatory, star-gazing is a popular pastime. On Saturday nights you can join the astronomers at their telescopes and look out at the universe. There are two major reflecting telescopes at the site; they are used to study some of the more arcane mysteries of the solar system. Binary stars, the foreboding-sounding black holes, star clusters, dark matter, and quasars, the brightest objects in the universe and the centres of distant galaxies — these are just a few of the mysteries that you can explore at the observatory. It is open daily in addition to the Saturday night viewing programs.

Miniature World 1c

Empress Hotel
649 Humboldt St.
Victoria, BC V8W 1A7

☎ (604) 385-9731

This Lilliputian world invites you to leave behind your everyday cares to step into a veritable fantasy. Start your tour at "Space 2201," an interactive display that puts you onto the observation deck of an interstellar spaceship in orbit above the planet Jupiter. Then do an about-face and march back into history in "The Fields of Glory" display. Here, nine dioramas take you through several historic events: the War of the Roses, Waterloo:1815, The American Civil War, World War II, and several more. In "Frontierland" you can relive the pioneer and frontier days of Canada and the United States, while "Fantasyland" invites you to relive some of the stories of your childhood: Santa's Workshop, Gulliver in the Land of Lilliput, and Once-Upon-A-Time Land. Literary types will enjoy "Titania's Palace" (for Shakespeare buffs) and "The World of Dickens," a series of dioramas from five popular Dickens stories. Some other displays are "The World of Dollhouses," "The Great Canadian Railway," and "The Greatest Show on Earth."

■ guided tours

Royal London Wax Museum 1d

470 Belleville St.
Victoria, BC V8V 1W9

☎ (604) 388-4461

The Royal London Wax Museum provides a lesson in what appears to be living history. The wax figures are so lifelike that you almost expect them to speak to you. The displays explore a number of important areas; there are extensive representations of royalty. "Pathfinders Park" highlights explorers; "Undefended

Border" features Canadian and American leaders; while the "Garden of Literature" presents some of our great authors. "Knoll of Knowledge," an inspiring exhibit, introduces inventors whose discoveries have made life easier or healthier for us. Other popular displays include "Sports Legends," "Storyland," the "Galaxy of Stars," and, of course, the "Chamber of Horrors." All in all, there are more than 200 people represented, each with a story to be told.

■ guided tours

British Columbia Legislature 1e

Parliament Buildings
Victoria, BC V8V 1X4

☎ (604) 387-3046

To get the best possible introduction to the British Columbia Legislature, wait until dusk. Then look. What appears to be a glittering, twinkling fairyland is really the Parliament Buildings outlined by 3000 tiny lightbulbs. It's a breathtaking sight. Wait until the next morning and then go for a tour. Note that, in the construction, special care was taken to use materials native to British Columbia. Of particular interest is the legislative library rotunda: against the background of the white-veined marble walls are many stained and art glass windows, including the Queen Victoria Diamond Jubilee window. The staircases leading to the lobby of the legislative chamber illustrate quotations from various writers and philosophers. (No doubt these are intended to prod the politicians into reflection!) Enhancing the front of the legislature building are numerous statues, including ones of Queen Victoria and Captain George Vancouver; a giant redwood tree, planted in 1863; a marble obelisk, raised in memory of Sir James Douglas; and the Knowledge Totem, a Coast Salish carving.

▲ ■

Undersea Gardens of Victoria 1f

490 Belleville St.
Victoria, BC V8V 1W9

☎ (604) 382-5717

At the height of their popularity, the Beatles sang of an octopus's garden at the bottom of the sea. That idea seems not at all far-fetched when you descend into the Undersea Gardens of Victoria. Through viewing windows, you can see more than 5000 marine specimens in their natural habitat. Begin your visit in the Undersea Theatre, where you will be introduced to life in the deep and particularly to the personage of Armstrong the giant octopus. Learn how giant barnacles feed, and get acquainted with the pacific salmon. But watch out for the ferocious wolf eels! All in all, the Undersea Gardens can provide a new appreciation of the ocean and its ecology.

■

Canadiana Costume Museum and Archives of British Columbia 1g

2818 Aldwynd Rd.
Victoria, BC V9B 3S7

☎ (604) 479-5102/384-6059/727-7072

One can learn about fashion all through the ages at the Canadiana Costume Museum, which houses a large collection of authentic clothing and accessories, and the supplies necessary to maintain and restore them. Of special interest is the annual exhibit, held during summer in an 1840s schoolhouse. Here one can view the garments and items common during the eras when the schoolhouse was in operation; particular attention is paid to children's clothing.

■ on-site; outreach

Emily Carr Gallery 1h

Art Gallery of Greater Victoria
1040 Moss St.
Victoria, BC V8V 4P1

☎ (604) 384-4101

Writer and artist Emily Carr — Klee Wyck, "laughing one," as she was named by the Coast Salish people who befriended her — is one of Canada's greatest artists. Her bold, colourful renderings of her native British Columbia, particularly its forests and towering totem poles, are unforgettable. The Emily Carr Gallery, a satellite of the Art Gallery of Greater Victoria, is housed in the Rithet Building, where Carr's father, Richard Carr, once sold dry goods to men starting out for the gold fields of the Klondike.

Fort Rodd Hill and Fisgard Lighthouse National Historic Sites 1i

603 Fort Rodd Hill Rd.
Victoria, BC V9C 2W8

☎ (604) 363-4662

Fort Rodd Hill, built by Britain in 1878 to guard its westernmost colony against an attack by sea, is a part of what was known as the Victoria-Esquimalt coast defences. Though it was actively garrisoned until 1956, when modern equipment such as long-range missiles replaced the original armaments, it never saw action. Visitors to the fort can see all the original buildings, which include the Guardhouse, the Underground Magazine, the Searchlight Engine Room and the Fortress Plotting Room. Move on to the Fisgard Lighthouse, built in 1860 — the first operational lighthouse on the west coast of Canada. It is now both a designated National Historic Site and a working lighthouse. Exhibits located inside the building relate the history of the west coast lighthouses. Be sure to take a few moments to admire the stunning view of the Strait of Juan de Fuca.

▲ ■ on-site; print materials

The Butchart Gardens 1j

✉ Box 4010
Victoria, BC V8X 3X4

☎ (604) 652-4422

No visit to Victoria would be complete without a leisurely stroll through the renowned Butchart Gardens. Begin your visit in the magnificent Sunken Garden, which lies at a depth of 15 m (50 ft.) in an old limestone quarry. Note the Ross Fountain and the wild character of the ivy-covered walls. Choose either the route past the Concert Lawn or the Rhododendron Grove and proceed to the Rose Garden to breathe the heavily scented air. Move on past the Dolphin Fountain and through the Torii Gate to the serene classical Japanese Garden. Next is the Star Pond and the Italian Garden decorated with touches of Florentine art. Displays of maps and brochures document the history of the Gardens. Staff in the Plant Identification Centre will be happy to answer any questions you may have.

Royal British Columbia Museum 1k

675 Belleville St.
Victoria, BC V8V 1X4

☎ (604) 387-3014

This unusual museum invites you to walk right through its displays. Begin your visit on the second floor. The exhibits here, entitled "Living Land" and "Living Sea," include an ice-age mammoth and various dioramas that bring to life the climatic regions of British Columbia. You can explore the ocean floor or stroll through a coastal forest and along the seashore. Proceed to the Modern History Gallery where you can walk the streets of a pioneer town, head north to the Klondike to see a working gold-rush water wheel, or pretend that you are an early adventurer aboard a replica of Captain Vancouver's ship *Discovery*. Walk into a Native longhouse, examine a reconstructed pit house, and gaze upward in the Totem Pole Gallery. In this museum, which contains more than a million artifacts, everyone can find something exciting. Be sure to see the totem poles in adjoining Thunderbird Park. If you visit during summer, you might also see a Native carver creating a new work of art.

■ on-site; elementary grades; outreach via broadcast; teaching materials

The Sooke Region Museum 2

Sooke Road

P.O. Box 774
Sooke, BC V0S 1N0

☎ (604) 642-6351

In the Sooke Museum, learn about the heritage and history of the peoples of the west coast. Various exhibits explore Native history, early settlers, the gold rush, logging, farming and fishing. Of particular interest are the old steam/donkey engine, the blacksmith shop, and the pioneer family cottage staffed by costumed interpreters. Enjoy the museum's entertaining and informative films. If you attend during summer, check the calendar before you go, so you can be sure to enjoy the museum's specialty: lawn barbecues featuring salmon and strawberry shortcake.

▲ limited service
■ on-site

Native Heritage Centre 3a

200 Cowichan Way
Duncan, BC V9L 4T8

☎ (604) 746-8119

For a unique experience that invites you to share in the history and culture of the Cowichan people of the Pacific Northwest, visit the Native Heritage Centre at Duncan. In the Longhouse Story Centre, you will be introduced to the ways and legends of the Cowichan band through a multimedia presentation. Move on to the Bighouse, fashioned after the traditional Northwest longhouse. Here you may dine on Native fare and enjoy cultural demonstrations of beadwork and moccasin making. In the huge Carving Shed, watch Native craftspeople create magnificent totem poles and canoes. Children have a special place here. While you tour the site, little ones can participate in a beading group, where staff will help them create beaded name badges on home-tanned moose hide, headbands, or friendship bracelets. And, if you time your visit right, you might be able to participate in a four-hour ceremonial feast. Before leaving, visit the Khowutzun Gallery, where Native crafts and jewellery are for sale.

■ on-site; all grades

Duncan, City of Totems 3b

c/o Duncan-Cowichan
Chamber of Commerce,
381 Trans Canada Hwy.
Duncan, BC V9L 3R5

☎ (604) 746-4636

Totem carving is an ancient and revered art among the tribes of the Pacific Northwest. By carving totems, Native people preserve their history and heritage and honour their tribal rituals and sacred spirits. Duncan's totem project began in 1985, when six local carvers were commissioned to create totem poles. Look closely at the figures on the poles. They represent characters in ancient legends, sacred spirits, and the hopes and aspirations of the carvers and their people. You will see many representations of the whale and the wolf. These are considered to be part of the same animal spirit. The eagle symbolizes the legendary Thunderbird, who saved the Salish tribe from starvation. Totem carving has a place in the present, too: this unique outdoor museum also displays a totem carved by a Maori in New Zealand and one honouring Rick Hansen, the Man in Motion. During the summer months, the town offers guided tours called Totem Walks.

▲

British Columbia Forest Museum 3c

2892 Drinkwater Rd., Duncan

✉
R.R. 4
Duncan, BC V9L 3W8

☎ (604) 746-1251

The British Columbia Forest Museum is really a park — a great idea for a museum about forestry. Extending over 40 ha (100 a.), the theme of the museum is "Man in the Forest" and it tells the story of forestry and humankind, from the time when the First Nations were the only inhabitants of B.C., through to the present. Walk the many trails to see the exhibits, or ride on the little train pulled by a genuine steam locomotive. See the equipment used by the early loggers in British Columbia and marvel at a cedar log estimated to be 1350 years old. A number of buildings from the Copper Canyon Logging Camp are on the site: bunkhouses, the kitchen mess, the surveyor's and engineer's repair shop, a pre-fab schoolhouse built in 1905, a post office, and many others. You may also visit a completely refurbished ranger station and a fully functioning sawmill.

▲ limited service

■ on-site; grades K–10; teaching materials

Cowichan and Chemainus Valleys Ecomuseum 3d

✉ P.O. Box 491
Duncan, BC V9L 3X8

☎ (604) 746-1611

Artwork by Linda Kirby, courtesy Cowichan and Chemainus Valleys Ecomuseum

What is an ecomuseum? Good question. It has no walls and covers 2600 km^2 (1000 sq. mi.). Its theme is the forest legacy, and its mandate is to identify and tell the story of the forests, which have played such a major role in the history, economy, and culture of the Duncan area. The museum includes the communities located within its boundaries, heritage sites, and various other attractions. Because it's so large, visitors are invited to design their own tours that will take them to the spots of particular interest to them. The Caycuse Camp is recognized as the oldest logging camp in North America. The Kaatza Museum tells the story of the first settlers and forestry workers in the area. The Cowichan Valley Demonstration Forests teaches forest management practices. Cliffside, Shawnigan Lake, was where Sir John A. Macdonald, then Member of Parliament for Victoria, drove the last spike in the transcontinental railway in 1886. The Koksilah River is spanned by the tallest wooden railway trestle in Canada.

Wickaninnish Interpretive Centre 4

Pacific Rim National Park
Ucluelet, BC

☎ (604) 726-4701

The theme of this interpretive centre, appropriately, is the Open Pacific Ocean. Here the Pacific is described and explained through exhibits, displays, murals, films, and talks by the centre's staff. Topics include the living ocean, physical oceanography, and human interaction with

the sea. Of special interest is a 24-by-6 m (80-by-20 ft.) mural portraying sea life to scale, a sea-bird mural, an underwater submersible display, and Nuu-Chah-Nuith (Nootka), an aboriginal whaling canoe.

▲ ■ on-site

Comox Air Force Museum 5

CFB Comox
Lazo, BC V0R 2K0

☎ (604) 339-8635

It's "off we go, into the wild blue yonder" at the Comox Air Force Museum. CFB Comox was established during World War II as a Royal Air Force aerodrome. In 1987, the museum opened. A number of squadrons are based here, including 407 Squadron, responsible for maritime surveillance on the Pacific coast; 414 Composite Squadron, which flies T-33 jets in support of naval training and also offers electronic warfare support; 442 Search and Rescue Transport Squadron; and 416/441 Squadrons, which operate along with CF-18 fighter-interceptor aircraft. The museum's permanent exhibits reflect the heritage, customs, and traditions of Canada's Air Forces by focusing on the history of aircraft that flew from CFB Comox as well as the air-operation support equipment used there — and the people who made it all happen. There are temporary exhibits as well, which display aviation art or highlight recent developments, and events such as the Gulf War.

▲ ■ on-site; all grades

Little Qualicum Spawning Channel 6

✉ c/o Department of Fisheries & Oceans
Little Qualicum Project
4745 Melrose Rd.
Qualicum Beach, BC
V9K 1V3

☎ (604) 752-3231

If you've ever enjoyed the singular pleasure of eating barbecued salmon, then visit the Little Qualicum Spawning Channel to learn more about this popular and important fish. The channel is 4.16 km (2.5 mi.) long and 7.5 m (25 ft.) wide; it can accommodate 50 000 spawning salmon. This stew results in 59 *million* fry (babies) annually. Whew! At the facility you will see a diversion fence, which staff erect each fall to divert spawning fish into the fishway. From the viewing room, you can watch the salmon ascend the fishway during the months of October, November, and December. In the laboratory/marking facility, the fry are marked with a wire code tag or fin clip before they are released. The adult chinook salmon are kept in holding/rearing channels until they fully mature and are ready to spawn. Fertilization and incubation occurs at the Big Qualicum Hatchery.

The Pacific Space Centre 7a

1100 Chestnut St.
Vancouver, BC V6J 3J9

☎ (604) 736-4431

This multi-use space simulation centre, formerly the H.R. MacMillan Planetarium and the Gordon M. Southam Observatory, provides a wide variety of entertaining, educational, and tourist-oriented programs in the fields of astronomy, space science, space technology, remote sensing, and earth management. Visitors will enjoy the "Canada in Space" hall, which celebrates Canadian achievements and aspirations in space science, the Challenger Learning Centre space mission simulator, and the "Hot Seat Experience," which is a simulated space ride/wide-screen film experience. Other attractions include the Star Theatre and a family space-science activity centre called "Space Station North."

▲ ■ on-site; outreach, including Starlab portable planetariums; all grades; teacher workshops

University of British Columbia Botanical Garden 7b

6804 S.W. Marine Dr.
Vancouver, BC V6T 1Z4

☎ (604) 822-9666

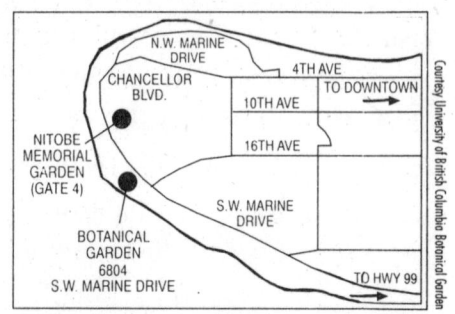

The tranquil University of British Columbia Botanical Garden is designed to suit Canada's temperate west coast climate. Stroll through the David C. Lam Asian Garden set in a coastal forest. Pass through the Moongate Tunnel to reach the Food Garden, a favourite with everyone, featuring vegetables, fruits, and nuts that can flourish in the local climate. During the hot summer months, find a cool spot to linger in the Arbour, and then visit the intriguing Physick Garden, which has been formally laid out to replicate a 16th-century Dutch engraving. Visit the Native Garden and the Lohbrunner Alpine Garden, with its displays of rare and beautiful plants. The Winter Garden features plants that bloom from November through March. For those seeking peace and tranquility, visit the lovely Nitobe Memorial Garden, an authentic Japanese garden just 3 km (2 mi.) north. A variety of courses and theme programs are offered all year long.

Vancouver Aquarium 7c

Stanley Park

✉

P.O. Box 3232
Vancouver, BC V6B 3X8

☎ (604) 682-1118

Courtesy Vancouver Aquarium

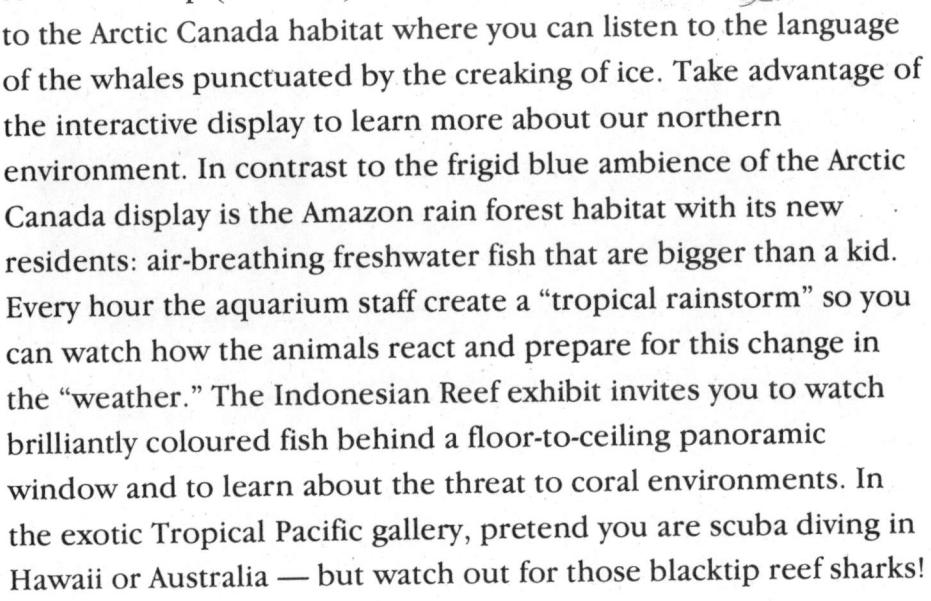

Dive right in to the Vancouver Aquarium. The water's fine and there's lots to see and do! Visit the Pacific Northwest display to watch sea otters at play and magnificent killer whales who are as curious about you as you are about them. Scuba divers descend into the halibut tank to feed the fish and to harvest kelp (seaweed). Move on to the Arctic Canada habitat where you can listen to the language of the whales punctuated by the creaking of ice. Take advantage of the interactive display to learn more about our northern environment. In contrast to the frigid blue ambience of the Arctic Canada display is the Amazon rain forest habitat with its new residents: air-breathing freshwater fish that are bigger than a kid. Every hour the aquarium staff create a "tropical rainstorm" so you can watch how the animals react and prepare for this change in the "weather." The Indonesian Reef exhibit invites you to watch brilliantly coloured fish behind a floor-to-ceiling panoramic window and to learn about the threat to coral environments. In the exotic Tropical Pacific gallery, pretend you are scuba diving in Hawaii or Australia — but watch out for those blacktip reef sharks!

▲ ■ on-site; off-site; all grades; teacher workshops

Bloedel Conservatory 7d

Queen Elizabeth Park
33rd and Cambie, Vancouver

✉

290 East 51st Ave.
Vancouver, BC V5X 1C5

☎ (604) 872-5513

Enter the climate-controlled environment of the Bloedel Conservatory to find yourself in an exotic world. There are three separate display areas representing tropical rain forest, warm temperate, and desert floristic regions. Enjoy over 500 plant species, including palms, tree ferns, orchids, gingers, tropical food-crop plants, and seasonal floral displays. In addition to the vegetation, there are 150 free-flying tropical birds, including five parrot species, a waterfall and a pond stocked with colourful Japanese Koi fish.

■ guided tours; all grades; post-secondary

Science World 7e

1455 Quebec St.
Vancouver, BC V6A 3Z7

☎ (604) 687-8414

The biggest problem facing visitors to Vancouver's Science World is deciding what to do first: see cosmic rays at work in the Cloud Chamber, or find out what a plasma ball is? Want to know how beavers build their dams? Step inside an honest-to-goodness beaver dam built by a real beaver to see the construction techniques first-hand. Walk through a working model of a camera. Enter one of the jamming rooms to compose your own computer-generated music. How perceptive are you? Visit the exhibits on illusions and fluid dynamics to see some of the quirks in human perception.

■ on-site; outreach; primary to middle grades; summer institutes for teachers

British Columbia Sports Hall of Fame and Museum 7f

BC Place Stadium
777 Pacific Blvd. S.
Vancouver, BC V6B 4Y8

☎ (604) 687-5520

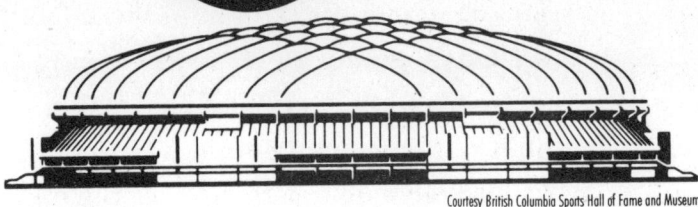

Courtesy British Columbia Sports Hall of Fame and Museum

For sports enthusiasts, the British Columbia Sports Hall of Fame and Museum is one exciting place to be; the emphasis is on doing, not just looking. Start your visit in the Hall of Champions, where touch-screen computers, photographs, and videos celebrate 200 of BC's outstanding athletes and teams. Move on to the Discovery Gallery to learn "what makes a champion"; take special note of the Terry Fox and Rick Hansen Galleries, the only permanent galleries in the country dedicated to these two Canadian heroes. In the Participation Gallery, test your skills in running, climbing, riding, and rowing via high-tech, hands-on technology. The History Galleries consist of 14 consecutive galleries that tell the story of the history of Canadian sport, from the early years of European settlement to the present. And don't forget to take a peek at the Erwin Singh Braich Temporary Exhibits Gallery to see what is on display the day you're there.

■ on-site; elementary grades

St. Roch National Historic Site 7g

1905 Ogden Ave.
Vancouver, BC V6J 1A3

☎ (604) 666-3201

Courtesy St. Roch National Historic Site

If a ship could be a hero, then the *St. Roch* would surely fit the bill. Built in 1928 in Vancouver, the *St. Roch*, a two-masted schooner, was the first ship to sail through the perilous Northwest

Passage and back again, braving howling winter gales, blizzards, and the ever-dangerous pack ice. Later, the *St. Roch* added another first to the records when it became the first ship to navigate the North American continent by sailing through the Panama Canal. In addition to these fabulous voyages, the *St. Roch* worked diligently for 26 years tending to Canada's interests in the Far North while serving as an Arctic supply and patrol vessel for the Royal Canadian Mounted Police. Visitors may board the *St. Roch* to recreate for themselves the exciting adventures from this schooner's past.

▲ ■

Museum of Anthropology 7h

University of British Columbia
6393 N.W. Marine Dr.
Vancouver, BC V6T 1Z2

☎ (604) 822-5087

Although UBC's stunning Museum of Anthropology contains artifacts and exhibits from around the world, it pays particular tribute to the First Peoples of the Northwest Coast. The entrance to the museum is actually a giant bent-cedar box carved by 'Ksan master carvers. Visitors find themselves in a mini-forest of towering totem poles. Imagine how the first Europeans must have felt on suddenly encountering their first totem pole! See the huge feast dishes; the exquisite carvings of gold, silver, argillite, and wood; and an array of ceramics. Step outside the museum building and look around. Look down at the sea below, over at the magnificent Rockies, up at the huge totems, and around at the Haida houses. This is the British Columbia of the First Nations. Before leaving the museum, be sure to see "Raven and the First Men," an acclaimed visual representation of the Haida creation myth, carved by Haida artist Bill Reid.

▲ ■ on-site; outreach teaching kits; all grades

Dr. Sun Yat-Sen Classical Chinese Garden 7i

578 Carrall St.
Vancouver, BC V6B 2J8

☎ (604) 662-3207

This is indeed a special place for the seeker of tranquility, the lover of nature, or the student of Chinese culture. From the moment you enter the garden, you are in a world apart. The garden is named after Dr. Sun Yat-Sen, considered by many to be the father of modern China. The garden, which is highly symbolic, was designed to convey the harmony between human beings and nature. Animal images — particularly bats — are intended to bring good fortune. Designers have incorporated the principles of balance between opposites — darkness with light, the ephemeral with the solid and permanent, "yin" with "yang." Enjoy the Central Courtyard, and then make your way along the Double Courtyard to the Jade Water Pavilion. Make your way to the Scholar's Study and on to the Lookout and the Moon Gate. Be sure to stop and admire the view from different angles, to breathe deeply of the scented air, and to relax into refreshment.

Port of Vancouver Public Viewing Centre 7i

1300 Stewart St.
Vancouver, BC V5L 4X5

☎ (604) 666-6129

In Vancouver, the Port of Vancouver Public Viewing Centre provides the best way to get down to the sea. Begin your visit with an informative and entertaining audio-visual presentation, and then proceed to the fourth-floor Observation Deck. Here you can see the various operations of the Vanterm Container Terminal and other port facilities, including the loading and unloading of ships. The education sector features interactive displays, and a life-sized container cutaway allows you to "see inside" the export and import industries. A Port People Puzzle highlights the various activities and occupations involved in a modern port. There is an audio tour and a port aerial map with activated lights.

▲ limited service

■ on-site; all grades; post-secondary; outreach teaching kits

Vancouver Museum 7k

1100 Chestnut St.
Vancouver, BC V6J 3J9

☎ (604) 736-5417

A visit to the Vancouver Museum is a magical journey through time and around the world. Begin your journey in the Fraser River delta some 8000 years ago to learn about the culture and heritage of some of the First Nations of the Pacific Northwest Coast. Put yourself into the position of a settler sailing to Canada; imagine the dreams and aspirations of the early Vancouverites. See how the artifacts on display document the growth of Vancouver from a small mill town to one of Canada's three largest cities in less than 100 years.

■

Canadian Craft Museum 7l

639 Hornby St.
Vancouver, BC V6C 2G3

☎ (604) 687-8266

The Canadian Craft Museum enjoys the distinction of being the only publicly-supported museum in Canada devoted exclusively to the recognition and appreciation of crafts. Containing in excess of 300 pieces made from clay, wood, metal, and fibre, it displays the work of nearly 200 artisans representing every province and territory. Enjoy such items as "A Nova Scotia Yarn" (a hand-knitted woollen sweater) and a small silver and brass representation of traditional diving suits, entitled "Le Nautilus."

■ on-site; outreach; teaching materials

Museum of Exotic World 7m

3561 Main St.
Vancouver, BC

☎ (604) 876-0073

Courtesy Museum of Exotic World

The Museum of Exotic World is the dream-come-true of retired Vancouver businessman Harold Morgan and his wife Barbara. It contains memorabilia of their travels to more than one hundred countries over a period of forty years. On display are pictures, bugs, masks, and more. Among the things to see are Burmese pagodas covered in gold, and precious gemstones and archaeological treasures excavated in Egypt and Peru and the lost cities of the Yucatan and Guatemala. Take a look at the photographs purported to be of a tribe of people with the shape of centaurs, called the Xam, and decide for yourself if seeing really is believing. Visitors are promised a glimpse of New Guinea cannibal tribes and their rituals, and, as an auditory experience, the sounds of a baboon fight recorded live in Kenya. Admission is free, and if Mr. Morgan is there, you are in for a real treat. A true raconteur, he will happily fill you in on the stories behind the items in his collection.

Capilano Suspension Bridge and Park 8a

3735 Capilano Rd.
North Vancouver, BC V7R 4J1

☎ (604) 985-7474

High above the Capilano River hangs the Capilano Suspension Bridge. Built originally in 1889, it is one of the highest suspension footbridges in the world. Suspended between the two walls of Capilano Canyon, the bridge is 140 m (450 ft.) long and

70 m (230 ft.) above the Capilano River. If you dare, stroll across the bridge and take in the magnificent scenery all around. Stop at the Totem Park, which has 25 authentic totem poles and life-sized statues, and then go on to the Nature Park to wander along its trails under towering trees and past deep pools.

▲ ■ site-tours; materials

Lynn Canyon Suspension Bridge and Ecology Centre 8b

3663 Park Rd.
North Vancouver, BC V7J 3G3

☎ (604) 987-5922

Lynn Canyon Ecology Centre

Artwork by Deborah Robertson, courtesy Lynn Canyon Ecology Centre

A visit to the Lynn Canyon Suspension Bridge and Ecology Centre offers an opportunity to learn about the environment in a beautiful setting. Although the park contains many hiking trails of various length and challenge, its most prominent attraction is the suspension bridge some 50 m (165 ft.) above Lynn Creek — that's 20 storeys. Be sure to visit the Ecology Centre as well. The centre has been divided into a series of wings, each with interactive displays, films, and print materials; these are the Plant Wing, the Animal Wing, the Human Wing, the Children's Wing, and the Film Wing. Guided tours are also available.

■ on-site; elementary grades

Steveston Museum 9a

3811 Moncton St.
Richmond, BC V7E 3A0

☎ (604) 271-6868

Steveston Museum recreates for the visitor the early days of one of the oldest continuing coastal fishing villages in the province. The museum is housed in a prefabricated building originally built in 1905 for the Northern Bank, a function it fulfilled until 1977. Begin your visit in what was once the bank manager's office. The office furniture and the business machines are mute testimony to the commercial history of the village. Staff regularly change the temporary exhibits in the display cases. Note that the main floor of the museum shares space with a working sub-post office operated by the Steveston Historical Society. Proceed to the second floor, which is intended to represent the living quarters of the earliest bank managers. The dining room and bedroom have been restored to the turn-of-the-century period.

■ on-site; outreach

The Trev Deeley Motorcycle Museum 9b

13500 Verdun Place
Richmond, BC V6V 1V4

☎ (604) 273-5421

For anyone who ever thrilled to the roar of the motorcycles in the film *Easy Rider*, a visit to the Trev Deeley Motorcycle Museum is a must. The Deeley family has been in the motorcycle business since 1914, and the collection includes some very rare machines. More than 200 classic motorcycles from 32 different manufacturers are on display, most of which have been restored to running order. The oldest bikes in the collection are a Harley and a Triumph dated 1915.

The Grocery Hall of Fame 9c

6620 #6 Rd.
Richmond, BC V6W 1C8

☎ (604) 278-0665

Food, glorious food! Where would we be without it? Artifacts commemorating the history of the food industry and food retailing in Canada are on display at the Grocery Hall of Fame. This unusual museum covers an entire hectare (about 2.5 a.) and in time will consist of a complete walk-through village. See

grocery memorabilia of every description. A turn-of-the-century grocery store includes a meat counter, candy, canned goods, and old-fashioned scales and cash registers. Note the biscuit tins adorned with the smiling faces of assorted monarchs. Children will wonder at barley sugar and treacle toffee, the treats of yesteryear. Imagine trying to keep food cold in the old ice box. Costumed mannequins are on hand to add to the realism. Also of interest is the food library containing a vast collection of resources and artifacts related to the food industry.

▲ ■ on-site; library resources

The International Buddhist Society 9d

9160 Steveston Hwy.
Richmond, BC V7A 1M5

☎ (604) 274-2822

Buddhism has been one of the world's great religions for 2600 years, preaching the virtues of kindness, benevolence, perseverance, self-discipline, and charity. Richmond's renowned Buddhist Temple is the most exquisite example of traditional Chinese architecture in all of Canada, resembling authentic Chinese temples on the shores of China's Yangtze River. The interior contains marvellous artifacts of sculpture, painting, carpentry, and embroidery. Note the magnificent statues of Buddha, the silk paintings, and the ceramic murals. The aura of tranquility and spirituality extends into the Temple's surroundings. Here, huge evergreens tower over diminutive bonsai plants, a tea garden, a rock landscape, and a decorative mural.

■

Fort Langley National Historic Park 10

✉
P.O. Box 129
Fort Langley, BC V0X 1J0

☎ (604) 888-4424

To understand the significance of Fort Langley is to learn about the role that the fur trade played in the history of Canada. In the early years of the 19th century, the Hudson's Bay Company was the main agent of commerce and controlled much of the fur trade. In 1827, the Hudson's Bay Company chose a site near the mouth of the Fraser River to construct Fort Langley, to be a major fur-trading and provisioning post. A few years later, agriculture was introduced, so the fort was relocated upstream to accommodate all the activities associated with agriculture. The era when fur trading and the Hudson's Bay Company ruled supreme in the area came to an end with the Fraser River gold rush in 1858. The original fort was dismantled and the land sold; however, its historic significance was recognized and it has since been reconstructed. The only original building at the site is the storehouse. The fort is staffed by interpreters dressed in period costume, who demonstrate the daily activities of life at Fort Langley; you can also view a slide show detailing the history and features of Fort Langley. A number of special events occur during the year.

▲ ■ on-site; teaching materials

Minter Gardens 11

52892 Bunker Rd., Rosedale
✉
46129 Hope River Rd.
Chilliwack, BC V2P 3P1

☎ (604) 794-7191

This exquisite garden has been described as a world-class show garden. With majestic Mount Cheam towering in the background, the 11 gardens provide a sensory delight for the visitor. In April, spring is welcomed by 100 000 tulips. Flowers of all description bloom in the summer, while fall is the season when the chrysanthemum reigns. Attractions include the rose garden, a maze to "lose" yourself in, a pond that hosts a variety of waterfowl, a water wheel, floral topiary (tree sculpture) ladies, a bonsai garden and magnificent peacocks. Take deep breaths of the scented air in the fragrance garden, watch the birds in the aviary — let the Minter Gardens work their magic.

The Grist Mill at Keremeos Provincial Historic Site 12

R.R. 1, Upper Bench Rd.
Keremeos, BC V0X 1N0

☎ (604) 499-2888

The Grist Mill at Keremeos has a varied past. Founded in 1877, it thrived until around 1890. In the years that followed, the general store became a private home and the mill served as an agricultural building and artist's studio, during which time the milling machinery lay dismantled on the lower floor. Miraculously, it suffered little damage and today the Grist Mill is the only remaining pioneer mill in the West with its original machinery and building intact. Reconstruction of the water wheel was based on archaeological findings, and involved digging through 20 cm (8 in.) of silt to uncover the original foundation timbers. Visitors proceed to the upper floor, where they can see how the milling process begins. On the lower floor, the grain is cleaned and ground. In the Exhibit Building (originally the store) you can follow the whole milling process through hands-on exhibits. The grounds include a number of additional points of interest: Heirloom Apple Orchard, Heritage Wheat Fields, Circle Gardens, and the Root Cellar. Before leaving, step into the Visitor Centre to pick up some freshly ground whole-wheat flour, whole-wheat porridge mix, or special garden seeds to take home with you. Freshly baked treats and light lunches are available in the Tea Room.

▲ limited services   ■ on-site

Zuckerberg Island Heritage Park 13

✉ c/o Castlegar and District
Heritage Society
400–13th Ave.
Castlegar, BC V1R 1G2

☎ (604) 365-6440

Members of a religious sect, the Doukhobors, emigrated to Canada from their native Russia in 1899 and settled in the Kootenays in 1908. The Doukhobors were frequently at odds with local authorities over issues such as education, military service, and their refusal to swear an oath of allegiance. Alexander Zuckerberg, a Russian aristocrat by birth, was an engineer by profession and a pacifist and a mystic by inclination; he was a self-taught cabinet maker and sculptor; but, above all, he was a teacher. He came to Castlegar in 1931 to teach Russian to Doukhobor children. On his little island at the confluence of the Kootenay and Columbia Rivers, he built the Chapel House that served as his art studio, classroom, and home. It has a Russian Orthodox onion dome, a tower room, and a curved entranceway; it is filled with artifacts and memorabilia. Outside, you can see two of Zuckerberg's sculptures: the stump lady (a seated woman emerging from a tree stump) and, in the little cemetery, Zuckerberg's second wife, Alicia (portrayed as a First World War nurse).

Canadian Museum of Rail Travel 14

✉ Box 400
Cranbrook, BC V1C 4H9

☎ (604) 489-3918

All aboard! Visitors' tickets are now available at the Canadian Museum of Rail Travel (formerly the Cranbrook Railway Museum) to tour Canada's own version of the fabled Orient

Express, the restored "Trans-Canada Limited." This luxurious train was built in 1929 at the cost of 1 million dollars. The train is arranged here in two long sections, with an enclosed viewing corridor in between. See the dining, sleeping, combination baggage-sleeper and famous solarium-lounge cars. Imagine what travel must have been like in such quarters! Also on display is a large collection of Canadian Pacific Railway china, glass, and silverware; other heritage railway cars; and the former Elko Station. Enjoy an audio-visual presentation, informative displays, and an operating model railway exhibit.

▲ limited services   ■ on-site; elementary grades

Fort Steele Heritage Town   15

Fort Steele, BC V0B 1N0
☎ (604) 426-6923

Like so many historic sites in British Columbia, Fort Steele Heritage Town has its origins in the Kootenay gold rush. Thousands responded to the lure of the precious yellow metal, driving up the need for goods and services. In 1864, a man named John Galbraith began operating a ferry service for miners and prospectors crossing the Kootenay River. For a time, this spot was known simply as Galbraith's Ferry. However, the threat of a Native uprising in 1887 brought a force of North-West Mounted Police under Superintendent Samuel Steele. In just over a year, Steele defused tensions and further conflict was averted. The town was subsequently named Fort Steele. Today, it has been totally restored to its boom-town days. With over 60 reconstructed homes and buildings to see, visitors are in for a wonderful experience. The site is staffed by interpreters in period costume. In addition to answering your questions and demonstrating the day-to-day activities of the period, they stage street dramas in which you will be encouraged to participate. Visit Mrs. Sprague's Confectionery for old-time treats, or select something from a wide variety of gifts and souvenirs in Kershaw's General Store. The Wildhorse Theatre stages professional entertainment twice daily. Fort Steele's operating steam railway will transport visitors along the bank of the river, and pieces of railroading equipment are on display. Horse-drawn wagon rides are also available. On the main floor of the Wasa Hotel, a museum illustrates the development of the East Kootenay region.

■ on-site; primary and elementary grades; teaching materials

The SS Moyie National Historic Site 16

c/o Kootenay Lake Historical Society
P.O. Box 537
Kaslo, BC V0G 1M0

☎ (604) 353-2525

SS *Moyie* is not only a provincial historic landmark, but also a National Historic Site. To better understand the special place this vessel occupies in the history of British Columbia and Canada, remember that in the final years of the last century, the Slocan area experienced a boom because of the discovery of silver there. The town of Kaslo grew quickly on the shores of Kootenay Lake, and in 1898 the *Moyie*, a sternwheeler, began serving the lake communities. At that time, sternwheelers were the only reliable means of transportation in these remote areas. The *Moyie* retired from service in 1957, with the longest service record of any sternwheeler in Canada. Not only that, the *Moyie* was the last passenger-carrying sternwheeled steamboat to operate in North America and is the only boat of its kind in the world to survive intact.

Sandon Historic Site and Museum 17

✉
c/o Sandon Historical Society
P.O. Box 52
New Denver, BC V0G 1S0

☎ (604) 358-2247

In the closing years of the 19th century, Sandon enjoyed the distinction of being the principal community in Canada's richest silver-mining area. Located deep in the mountains of British Columbia, this historic site consists of 52 heritage buildings. The city hall and general store are currently being restored. The museum here holds lots of interesting artifacts. Also open to visitors is the home of the village police officer; Silversmith Powerhouse, which is western Canada's oldest operating hydro-electric plant; the Tin Cup Cafe; and an operating silver mine.

■ guided tours

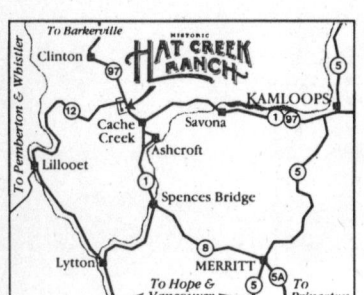

Hat Creek Ranch 18

✉
Box 878
Cache Creek, BC V0K 1H0

☎ (604) 457-9722

Historic Hat Creek Ranch invites you to step back in time to that period in our country's history when all eyes were trained to the North and the gold rush. The ranch itself, comprised of 24 historical buildings on 130 ha (320 a.), is located on one of the last remaining sections of the Old Cariboo Wagon Road. The buildings have been restored and costumed interpreters are on hand to bring the ranch's history to life. Hat Creek House is the last remaining roadhouse of its kind and one of the largest along the Cariboo Wagon Road. See the huge ranch kitchen, where hearty meals from the ranch's own harvest were prepared, and the stage-passenger waiting room. The BX Barn, built of massive logs, was used to stable the stagecoach horses of the B.C. Express Stage Line. The larger draft horses, used for hauling freight wagons, were stabled in the freight horse barn. Of course, no ranch of this type would be complete without a blacksmith shop — and in this one you can watch the blacksmith at his forge. Move on to the mower shed to admire the carefully restored genuine Concord stagecoach, as well as pieces of agricultural machinery from the pioneer era. Don't forget the pig barn and the sod-roofed chicken coop. There is a great deal to see at Hat Creek Ranch, and if you get tired of walking, there are wagon and saddle horses ready to carry you around.

▲ limited service

■ on-site

Lillooet Museum

Main St.

✉ P.O. Box 441
Lillooet, BC V0K 1V0

☎ (604) 256-4308/4556

Lillooet was a terminus point for boats traversing Harrison and Anderson lakes during the Cariboo Gold Rush. At that time, Lillooet was a very lively place indeed, with no less than 13 saloons and 25 other licensed premises. Lillooet is noted for its "Bridge of 23 Camels," which commemorates a group of camels brought in to serve as freight carriers on the Cariboo Trail, an unsuccessful experiment. The museum, housed in the former St. Mary's Anglican Church, has a number of period rooms, several displays of mining artifacts, an 1860s pump organ, Chinese and Interior Salish artifacts, and a printing press formerly owned by the intrepid Ma Murray, a pioneering newspaper owner and editor.

■ guided tours

Barkerville Historic Town

c/o Heritage Properties Branch
Northern Interior Region
Ministry of Tourism and Ministry
Responsible for Culture
Box 19, Barkerville, BC V0K 1B0

☎ (604) 994-3332

The shout rang out across the West in 1858 – "Gold!" – and thousands from other parts of Canada, the United States, Europe, and China flocked to the British Columbia interior to join the Cariboo gold rush. Barkerville was born when a prospector named Billy Barker made the richest strike anyone had ever seen. It quickly became a typical gold-rush boom town. It has now been restored to the 1870s era. You will step back in time to those wild days when gold was on everyone's lips and minds — and even in a few pockets. Walk into the shop of Mrs. Neate, the dressmaker, to see how the clothes of the time were made. Other walk-in exhibits with costumed interpreters working at their trades include Cameron & Ames Blacksmith Shop, Holt & Burgess Cabinetmaker's Shop, and the post office — British Columbia's eighth-oldest continually operating post office offering full postal service (the Barkerville postmark is something of a collector's item). Also visit the Wendle House, a boarding house, and the Williams Creek Schoolhouse. Follow your nose to the Barkerville Bakery, where you can buy freshly baked breads and pies. Find out what's news in the Cariboo *Sentinel* — you can even watch the presses in action. Dress up in period costume to have your picture taken at the Louis Leblanc Photo Studio. If you're hungry, step into one of the eateries offering typical period fare. Be sure to keep your eyes open for the dramatic street vignettes enacted several times a day. Participate in guided tours and various other programs designed to give visitors a realistic experience of life in a gold-rush town.

▲ ■ on-site; teaching materials

Kitwanga Fort National Historic Site 21a

Junction of Hwy. 16 and Hwy. 37

✉
c/o Fort St. James
National Historic Park
Box 1148, Fort St. James
BC V0J 1P0

☎ (604) 996-7191

Artwork by Marc Schofield, courtesy Parks Canada

Unlike other forts of historic importance in Canada, Kitwanga Fort has its roots and significance in the heritage and history of the First Nations of the Pacific Northwest. Kitwanga Fort was constructed by the Gitwangak Nation near an important trade route between the coast and interior tribes. Wars were fought for food, provisions, slaves, and control of the lucrative trade routes. The last and most famous defender was Nekt, a ferocious warrior who wore a suit of armour fashioned from the hide of a grizzly bear and lined with tablets of slate, and who wielded a magical club called Strike-Only-Once. Seven interpretive panels along the trail to the site retell the fort's history and the story of Nekt. Although the fort itself was destroyed by fire in battle nearly 200 years ago, it is believed that its primary defences consisted of a system of heavy logs that could be rolled down to crush approaching enemies.

▲

Fort St. James National Historic Site 21b

✉
P.O. Box 1148
Fort St. James, BC V0J 1P0

☎ (604) 996-7191

From the moment you enter Fort St. James, a Hudson's Bay Company fort restored to the year 1896, you feel like you're reliving history. Begin your visit in the visitor centre, where displays, artifacts, and a video presentation entitled "A Letter Home" set the stage. The wharf and tramway were used to unload and move cargo from the lake to the general warehouse and fur store. Here furs were baled before shipment to Victoria. In the fish cache, dried salmon and bacon were kept. Move on to the men's house, which served as a residence for company employees and visitors, and the trade store and office, where furs were traded for the goods within. Other sites include the officer's dwelling house, which was the residence for the manager in charge of the post; the dairy; the chicken yard; the garden; and the fields. During the summer months, the fort is staffed by interpreters in period costume, who demonstrate life at the fur trading post, answer questions, and help to make your visit a memorable experience.

▲ ■ guided tours

North Pacific Cannery Village and Museum National Historic Site 22

1889 Skeena Dr.
Port Edward, BC V0V 1G0

☎ (604) 628-3538

There is something fishy about the North Pacific Cannery Village and Museum! Much of the history and economy of British Columbia's north coast has traditionally been tied to the salmon. The North Pacific Cannery, built in 1889, continued to operate until 1968. Today the museum provides visitors with a lesson, not only in the fish-canning industry, but also in sociology. At its peak, the cannery employed 300 to 400 people from four distinct ethnic groups: Chinese, Japanese, Native, and European, usually between the months of May and September. Each group had its own area of expertise to contribute, and each had its own living area. Visitors may tour the cannery buildings, managers' houses, cannery store, and office. There are a number of interesting and informative exhibits illustrating the canning industry, fishery on the Pacific Northwest Coast, and cannery village life. Of special interest during the summer is a live performance presenting important incidents and personalities in the development of the industry.

▲ ■ on-site; all grades

Courtesy North Pacific Cannery Village and Museum National Historic Site

Charlie Lake Cave 23

c/o Fort St. John–
North Peace Museum
9323 –100th St.
Fort St. John, BC V1J 4N4

☎ (604) 787-0430

Because the Charlie Lake Cave is located on private property, archaeologists and spelunkers (cave explorers) will have to be satisfied with the display in the Fort St. John–North Peace Museum. The cave helps us piece together the prehistory of Canada because it appears to be one of the earliest sites occupied by human beings. Archaelogists have retrieved a fluted spear point, stone tools, various animal bones, and a simple stone bead estimated to have been crafted an incredible 10 500 years ago. These artifacts are housed at Simon Fraser University, but the museum presents an artist's conception of the country at that time, showing both the topography and animals.

Fort Nelson's Welcome Visitor Program 24

Bag Service 399
Fort Nelson, BC V0C 1R0

☎ (604) 774-2541

The Fort Nelson Welcome Visitor Program is a delightful home-grown presentation staffed entirely by local residents who volunteer their time. The program, which continues to be immensely popular with visitors to the Fort Nelson area, features audio-visual presentations, demonstrations, and speakers on a wide variety of topics of local interest. Representatives from Forestry and Westcoast Energy, trappers, hunters, teachers, artists, and RCMP officers are just a few of the different individuals who participate in this program to help introduce visitors to life in northern British Columbia.

▲ French language tours with advance notice only

Artwork by Dharma Design, courtesy Fort Nelson—Liard Regional District

Alberta

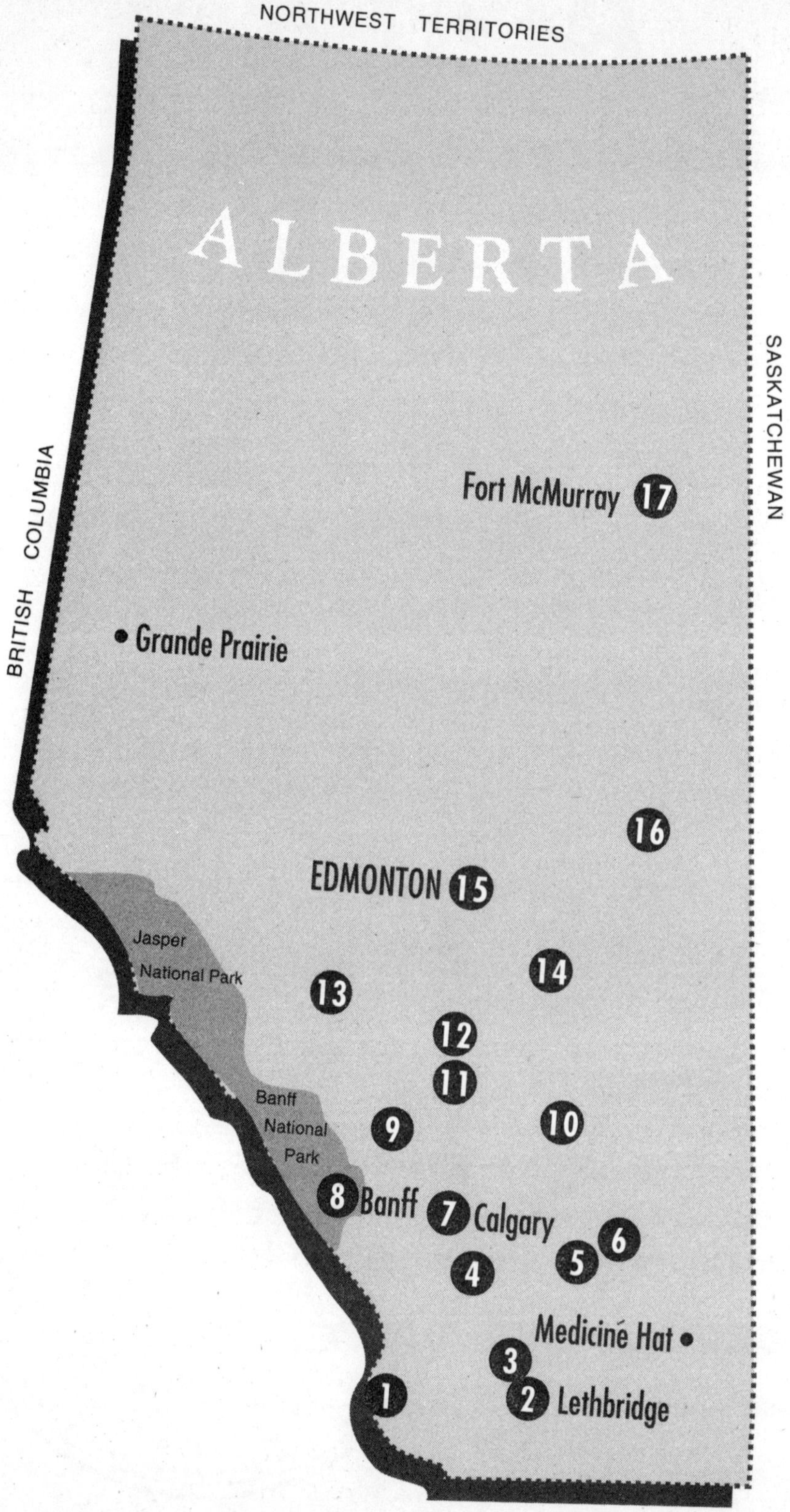

ALBERTA

NORTHWEST TERRITORIES

BRITISH COLUMBIA

SASKATCHEWAN

Fort McMurray ❼

• Grande Prairie

EDMONTON ❶❺

❶❻

Jasper National Park

❶❸

❶❹

❶❷

❶❶

Banff National Park

❾

❿

❽ Banff ❼ Calgary

❹

❺

❻

Medicine Hat •

❸

❷ Lethbridge

❶

USA

1	Frank Slide Interpretive Centre	12	Stephansson House Historic Site
2	Fort Whoop-Up Interpretive Centre	13	Rocky Mountain House National Historic Site
3a	Fort Macleod	14	Reynolds—Alberta Museum
3b	Head-Smashed-In Buffalo Jump	15a	West Edmonton Mall
4	Nanton Lancaster Air Museum	15b	Ukrainian Cultural Heritage Village
5	Brooks Aqueduct National Historic Site	15c	Fort Edmonton Park
6	Dinosaur Provincial Park	15d	Provincial Museum of Alberta
7a	Alberta Science Centre	15e	Old Strathcona Model and Toy Museum
7b	Heritage Park Historical Village	15f	Alberta Railway Museum
7c	Calgary Exhibition and Stampede	15g	The Edmonton Art Gallery
7d	Calgary Zoo, Botanical Gardens and Prehistoric Park	15h	Rutherford House Provincial Site
7e	Canadian Western Natural Gas, Light, Heat and Power Museum	16	Fort George—Buckingham House Provincial Historic Site
7f	Energeum	17	Fort McMurray Oil Sands Interpretive Centre
7g	Museum of Movie Art		
7h	Canada Olympic Park		
7i	Aero Space Museum		
7j	Glenbow Museum		
7k	Fort Calgary Historic Park		
8a	Cave and Basin National Historic Site		
8b	Columbia Icefield Athabaska Glacier		
9	Cochrane Ranche Provincial Historic Site		
10a	Atlas Coal Mine Museum		
10b	Royal Tyrrell Museum of Palaeontology		
11	Police Dog Service Training Centre		

In the site descriptions, note that:

▲ indicates that second language services are available: English in Quebec and French elsewhere in Canada. Where "limited service" is given, it would be wise to call ahead for specifics

■ indicates that educational services are available

Frank Slide Interpretive Centre

Hwy. 3

✉

Box 959
Blairmore, AB T0K 0E0

☎ (403) 562-7388

In 1903, the town of Frank, nestled in the shadow of Turtle Mountain, had reason to be optimistic about its future. Its main industry was coal mining in the mountain — and there was lots of coal to be had. Then, on April 29 at 4:10 A.M., in the space of 100 seconds, 90 million tons of limestone fell from the mountain, burying the southern edge of the town and killing 70 people. Remnants of the town still exist, and visitors may take a self-guided walking tour through the site. Displays in the Interpretive Centre highlight the history of the Crowsnest Pass, the slide, the Canadian Pacific Railway, European settlement, early underground coal mining, and life in the community. See the audio-visual presentation entitled "In the Mountain's Shadow." Don't miss the marvellous views of Frank and the Crowsnest Pass area.

▲

Fort Whoop-Up Interpretive Centre

Third Ave. S.

✉

P.O. Box 1074
Lethbridge, AB T1J 4A2

☎ (403) 329-0444

Fort Whoop-Up has its origins in the not-so-admirable actions of two American whisky traders, John Jerome Healy and Alfred Baker, who left Fort Benton, Montana, in December 1869 with 50 gallons of pure alcohol and brought it to what is now Lethbridge. Here they built a post — the first of 50 whisky trading posts to operate in southern Alberta between 1869 and 1874. The problems created by the whisky trade with the Natives resulted in the creation of the North-West Mounted Police, who soon brought law and order to the region. Tour the fort and participate in the interpretive programs. See if you can operate a fur press; taste freshly baked bannock. Enjoy the artifacts on display in the Interpretive Gallery and the informative audio-visual presentation.

■   on-site; grades 1–9; outreach; teacher workshops

Fort Macleod 3a

✉

Box 776
Fort Macleod, AB T0L 0Z0

☎   (403) 553-4703

Established in 1874, Fort Macleod was the first fort to be built by the North-West Mounted Police, and was named for Colonel James Macleod, commander of the detachment and commissioner of the mounted police from 1876 to 1880. A visit to Fort Macleod should certainly include a stop in the Fort Museum, where artifacts and displays highlight a number of pertinent themes: the work of the North-West Mounted Police, prison life, aboriginal culture, the Royal Canadian Mounted Police, and pioneering and ranching traditions. Proceed to the fort buildings to taste a little of what fort life was like in the era portrayed. A special attraction during the summer months is the Fort Museum's Mounted Patrol, whose members, dressed in 1878 North-West Mounted Police uniforms and mounted on dark bay horses, perform musical rides four times daily.

▲   limited services

Head-Smashed-In Buffalo Jump 3b

✉

Box 1977
Fort Macleod, AB T0L 0Z0

☎   (403) 553-2731 (Calgary line: 265-0048)

What is a buffalo jump? Think back in time to a period when the Europeans with their horses and guns had not yet arrived in America. In order to successfully hunt the large and powerful bison, Native people of the Plains devised a very sophisticated and effective method of driving the animals over a cliff. Head-Smashed-In Buffalo Jump has been designated a UNESCO World Heritage Site, recognizing its status as one of the largest and best preserved of these jump sites. The modern interpretive centre at Head-Smashed-In Buffalo Jump almost defies description. From the outside it looks small and a part of its surroundings; it was built into a hillside deliberately to achieve this effect. Inside, the centre is very large, extending over five informative and impressive levels. On Level 1 of the centre, the exhibit entitled "Napi's World" orients the visitor to the ecology of the prehistoric Plains. Proceed to Level 2, "Napi's People," to be introduced to the lifestyle of the Plains people. The buffalo jump itself is the focus of Level 3, and on Level 4, "Cultures in Conflict," we come face to face with the grim impact of Europeans on the Native population. On the fifth level, "Uncovering the Past," visitors learn about the archaeological work in progress at the site.

 on-site; all grades; outreach; teaching materials

Nanton Lancaster Air Museum 4

P.O. Box 1051
Nanton, AB T0L 1R0

☎ (403) 646-2243

Courtesy Nanton Lancaster Air Museum

At the Nanton Lancaster Air Museum, you can relive the dark days of the London Blitz and learn about the contributions made by Bomber Command to the Allies' World War II effort. The Lancaster, a Canadian-built aircraft, was the most successful bomber used because of its unparalleled speed, ceiling, and lifting power. The Lancaster on display is dedicated to the memory of Squadron Leader Ian Bazalgette (VC, DFC). Bazalgette was flying a Lancaster of the Pathfinder Force, marking the target of a rocket site at Troissy St. Maximin for the main bomber squadrons, when flak (gunfire from the ground) set the plane on fire. As the only Pathfinder still in the air, Bazalgette kept on course marking the target. After leaving the target area, he ordered the crew to bail out but remained on board himself with two wounded fliers. He died in the attempt to land the plane, and was awarded the Victoria Cross posthumously. Also on display at Nanton are simulators, gun turrets, engines, instrumentation, and equipment, as well as models, photographs, aviation art, and videos of Lancasters in action.

Brooks Aqueduct National Historic Site 5

Brooks

✉

Historic Sites Service
8820–112 St.
Edmonton, AB T6G 2P8

☎ (403) 362-4451

The word aqueduct conjures up visions of ancient Romans and crumbling ruins. The Brooks Aqueduct is much more modern than that; but like the Roman constructions, it is a marvel of engineering. The two-mile (roughly 3 km) long Brooks Aqueduct was the longest concrete structure of its type in the world at the time of its construction, 1915. It was also the first aqueduct in the world with its particular shape of flume and the first structure of such magnitude to be built with steel-reinforced concrete. Built to provide irrigation water, the Brooks Aqueduct was vital to the development of southeastern Alberta. Interpreters provide walking and driving tours of the site.

Dinosaur Provincial Park 6

✉

P.O. Box 60
Patricia, AB T0J 2K0

☎ (403) 378-4342

In 1979, the United Nations designated Dinosaur Provincial Park a UNESCO World Heritage Site because it is the most abundant source of fossils from the late Cretaceous period anywhere in the world. Paleontological excavations continue, and the Royal Tyrrell Museum in Drumheller maintains a field station, where recently excavated fossils are prepared for shipment to Drumheller. Visitors can take bus tours or self-guided walking and driving tours. There are also special programs: the Lab Tours, the Centrosaurus Bonebed Hike, and the Fossil Safari Hike. Be sure to drop into the Tyrrell Museum Field Station to see the dinosaur specimens on display. You can watch the preparation of the fossils and enjoy the interpretive programs, lectures, and videos that are available.

▲ limited services

■

Alberta Science Centre 7a

701–11 St. S.W.

✉

P.O. Box 2100, Station M, #73
Calgary, AB T2P 2M5

☎ (403) 221-3700

The Alberta Science Centre is an ever-changing kaleidoscope of exciting programs and exhibits made just for kids. Here, visitors are invited to "push, pull, open, look, talk, listen, and play!" Recent displays featured such popular topics as Dinomania, Brain Teasers, Marine Monster Mania (robotic sea creatures — both contemporary and prehistoric), and Backyard Monsters (massive robotic insects). While visiting the science centre, make a point of seeing the '65 Planetarium as well. Here you can travel to distant planets and constellations, or enjoy the spectacle of an exciting laser light and music show.

■ on-site; star shows; demonstrations; student competitions

Heritage Park Historical Village 7b

1900 Heritage Dr. S.W.
Calgary, AB T2V 2X3

☎ (403) 252-3528

With more than 100 restored buildings and exhibits, Calgary's Heritage Park enjoys the distinction of being Canada's largest historical village. The park has been designed to portray three different time periods: the 1860s fur-trading era, 1880s pre-railway settlement, and a typical western town of 1910; each has its own section in the park, and visitors may wander at will. Among the many attractions available are a bakery where you can buy treats right out of the oven, a ride on a train drawn by steam locomotive, a cruise on the Glenmore Reservoir aboard a sternwheeler, and an antique amusement park. Visit the Sam Livingston farm, one of the first homesteads in the area. Watch the blacksmith ply his trade and relive past days of education in the park's one-room schoolhouse. Costumed interpreters are on hand to help bring history to life for you.

▲ ■

Calgary Exhibition and Stampede 7c

1410 Olympic Way S.E.

✉

Box 1860, Stn. M
Calgary, AB T2P 2L8

☎ (403) 261-0101/(800) 661-1260

Courtesy Calgary Exhibition and Stampede

Summer visitors to Calgary generally try to plan their trip to coincide with Calgary's premier attraction, the Calgary Stampede. This is a show in the tradition of the Old West. The rodeo features saddlebronc and bareback riding, calf roping, steer wrestling, and the fearsome bull riding. On the lighter side are the Stampede clowns and events such as wild cow milking and the wild horse race. Thrill to the chuckwagon races, enjoy the many attractions of the International Stock Show, try your skill at the games on the midway, and then relax while you watch the fireworks display and the nightly show on the outdoor stage. Ride 'em cowboy!

Calgary Zoo, Botanical Gardens and Prehistoric Park 7d

St. Georges Island

✉

P.O. Box 3036, Stn. B
Calgary, AB T2M 4R8

☎ (403) 232-9300

The Calgary Zoo, Botanical Gardens and Prehistoric Park is surely a must on the itinerary of visitors to Calgary. The site houses over 11 000 species of animals and prides itself on its success in breeding endangered species such as the Sumatran orangutan, Sri Lankan elephant, and spectacle bear. The conservatory is an inviting spot for browsing among exotic plants, flowers, and birds. Be sure to stop by the butterfly house to admire these beautiful winged insects. The younger set will want to see the prehistoric park, which recreates Canada as it might have looked during the dinosaur ages. See 23 life-sized dinosaur models in their "natural" environment. As well, the zoo presents an exciting array of interesting and informative natural history programs daily to complement the exhibits.

▲ limited service

■ on-site; all grades; outreach; teaching materials

Canadian Western Natural Gas, Light, Heat and Power Museum 7e

Canadian Western Centre
909–11th Ave. S.W.
Calgary, AB T2R 1L8

☎ (403) 245-7157

This museum pays tribute to natural gas, one of Alberta's foremost resources and a major force in the province's economy. See displays of pipes, gasometers, and other items associated with the development of this industry.

Energeum 7f

640 Fifth Ave. S.W.
Calgary, AB T2P 3G4

☎ (403) 297-5290/4293

As the name suggests, the Energeum is a unique museum, committed to Alberta's number-one industry, energy. The 325 m^2 (3500 sq. ft) of the museum are packed with interactive displays, all related to exploring the world of energy. Learn how energy resources are discovered, and explore the early years of energy in Alberta. How is energy developed? Where does it go? These are some of the questions that will be answered on your tour. Could you be an oil tycoon? Try your hand at discovering oil at this interactive display. Pick up a telephone to hear tall tales of the early days. Note what has happened to automobiles as the fortunes of the oil industry have waxed and waned. Check out the fibre-optic map, where you can trace the history of Alberta's energy industry. Inspect the model rig. Examine the relationship between energy and the environment. Ponder the future of energy . . . and, finally, relax in the theatre while you watch an informative video.

■ on-site; outreach; teaching materials

Courtesy Canadian Western Natural Gas, Light, Heat and Power Museum

Museum of Movie Art 7g

Suite 9, 3600–21 St. N.E.
Calgary, AB T2E 6V6

☎ (403) 250-7588

This museum, made to order for film buffs, contains more than 3000 original movie posters from the 1920s to the present. It houses posters from the Feduruk Collection of the 1930s, movie posters from the old Gaiety Theatre in Vegreville, Alberta, and a set of King Kong lobby cards valued at $15 000. Movie posters are works of art. In the early days of the industry, they were produced by a complex and expensive procedure involving stones and colours, all of which had to be made and mixed by hand. The posters were produced in limited quantities, only to supply cinemas. Many were destroyed after the film's run, so those that have survived are quite valuable. Replica posters may be purchased in the museum's shop.

Canada Olympic Park 7h

Trans–Canada Hwy. at
Canada Olympic Dr. S.W.
Calgary, AB T2M 4N3

☎ (403) 247-5423

Who can ever forget the excitement and the glory of the 1988 Olympics, when the eyes of the world were focused on Calgary? Canada Olympic Park is an ongoing memento of that special time in the city's history. Visit the Olympic Hall of Fame and Museum, where you can experience an Olympic bobsleigh ride by means of a computerized simulator. See three floors of exhibits honouring

Olympic achievements since 1924. Drive up to the top of the 90-m ski jump to imagine the thrill of taking off into space with nothing but your own skill to guide you to the bottom. An added bonus is the breathtaking view from the site.

Aero Space Museum 7i

64 McTavish Place N.E.
Calgary, AB T2E 7H1

☎ (403) 250-3752

Fly up to Calgary's Aero Space Museum! See the many different kinds of aircraft that were flown by Canadians in both world wars; and those used in peacetime operations, both in Canada and elsewhere. The museum places special emphasis on the role of the western provinces in aviation industry. On display are various aircraft, such as the Sopwith Triplane, the Avro Lancaster MK X, the Sikorsky S-51 Helicopter, the speedy Beech SC17R Staggerwing, and many more. The museum also contains one of the largest collections of aviation engines in North America, and a comprehensive library and archives section. As you browse among the aircraft on display, note also the exhibits of equipment, uniforms, and other related memorabilia, and reflect on how the world has been transformed by flight in the 20th century.

Glenbow Museum 7j

130–Ninth Ave. S.E.
Calgary, AB T2G 0P3

☎ (403) 268-4100

Courtesy Glenbow Museum

One of the stellar attractions in all of western Canada is Calgary's Glenbow Museum. The Glenbow consists of 8370 m² (90 000 sq. ft.) of exhibition space spread over three floors, plus a new fourth floor. Begin your visit on the second floor, which presents both Glenbow-sponsored exhibitions and travelling exhibitions from around the world. The third floor is committed to the heritage of western Canada. Here you will see displays detailing the cultures of the First Nations, the arrival of the early settlers and the missionaries, and the growth of ranching, farming, and the energy industry. The history of the North-West Mounted Police is covered as well. The themes of new fourth-floor exhibits are the warrior in society, achievement in West Africa, and personal adornment around the world. The Glenbow's library and archives contain more than 800 000 images of pioneer life: records, diaries, journals, and letters of the early pioneers.

▲

■ on-site; all grades; teaching materials; videos; events for teachers

Fort Calgary Historic Park 7k

750–Ninth Ave S.E.

✉

P.O. Box 2100, Stn M
Calgary, AB T2P 2M5

☎ (403) 290-1875

Fort Calgary Historic Park consists of two sites: the Deane House and Fort Calgary itself. The North-West Mounted Police used the Deane House, built in 1906, as a residence for the superintendent, Richard Burton Deane. It has been restored, has a restaurant and is now available for various functions. Fort Calgary, built in 1875 by a troop of North-West Mounted Police, is the place where the city of Calgary was born. The fort preserves and interprets the city's past. The outlines of the original fort are visible in the 16-ha (40-a.) riverside park. In the interpretive centre, find a hands-on "discovery" room where visitors can touch artifacts of the past, and an informative audio-visual presentation.

▲ ■

Cave and Basin National Historic Site 8a

Banff National Park

c/o The Superintendent
Banff National Park
Box 900, Banff, AB T0L 0C0

☎ (403) 762-3324

The Cave and Basin is generally considered to be the birthplace of Canada's national parks. While prospecting for gold in the Rockies in 1883, brothers William and Tom McCardell and their partner, Frank McCabe, came across a mist-filled cave that contained hot springs. "Like some fantastic dream from the Arabian nights," was how William described their discovery. For many years, it was believed that bathing in the hot springs would cure a variety of ailments. Although these claims have been largely discounted, bathing in the hot springs is still an immensely popular pastime. In 1985, national parks' centennial year, Parks Canada rebuilt the swimming pool that originally existed on the site and returned the buildings to their 1914 appearance to celebrate the springs' halcyon days. A visit to the Cave and Basin is decidedly spooky. Enter a winding rocky tunnel; sniff the air, pungent with the odour of sulphur. Finally, you arrive in the cave; dip your hand in the water — how does it stay so warm? The Centennial Centre contains a number of informative displays to explain the development of the hot springs and their effect on the local flora and fauna, the role of the railway in the formation of the early national parks, and interactive exhibits for exploring the future of national parks. You can enjoy also a walk along the boardwalk interpretive trails.

▲ ■ guided tours

Columbia Icefield Athabaska Glacier 8b

Icefields Pkwy. (Hwy. 93)

✉

c/o Brewster Transportation & Tours
Box 1140, Banff, AB T0L 0C0

☎ (403) 762-6735

Imagine the thrill of walking on ice formed from snow that fell some 400 years ago. Then come and do it at the Columbia Icefield Athabaska Glacier. This is the largest of the three icefields visible along the Icefields Parkway. The best way to see the glacier is to hop on the Snocoach, a bus with immense tires, specially designed for glacier travel. You will traverse a steep lateral moraine (a long knife-edged ridge of broken rock piled at the side of the glacier) and then drive out onto the ice. When the Snocoach stops, get out and walk around, but be careful to stay within the bounds designated by your driver-guide. Note that this glacier is in retreat, and that its natural summer melt has been accelerated by the greenhouse effect. Walking around on a glacier is a unique experience, especially during the summer months. It is cold all year long, so remember to bring a warm jacket and appropriate footwear — and don't forget to bring your camera.

▲

Cochrane Ranche Provincial Historic Site 9

Junction of Hwy. 22 and Hwy. 1A

✉

Programme Coordinator
Cochrane Ranche/
Stephansson House Historic Sites
Historic Sites Service
Room 203, Provincial Building
P.O. Box 1522, Edmonton, AB
T0L 0W0

☎ (403) 932-2902 or (403) 932-3242 (summer only)

The Cochrane Ranche, established in 1881, was the first of the large-scale ranching ventures in what is now Alberta. In its early days, the ranch was plagued by a series of misfortunes. Nowadays, it functions as a historic site and welcomes visitors to its 61 ha (150 a.) of parkland. Stroll among the reconstructed and restored buildings: the corral, the manager's house, the bunkhouse, a log dugout, the blacksmith shop, and the stable. Don't miss the visitor centre, which has a slide show and displays of artifacts that were unearthed during archaeological excavations on the site of the original buildings. You can also visit the Western Heritage Centre, which provides a historical perspective on ranching.

■ on-site; elementary grades; teaching materials

Atlas Coal Mine Museum 10a

✉
Box 203
Drumheller, AB T0J 0Y0

☎ (403) 823-2171/822-2220

For many years, coal was a major source of energy, burned to provide heat and light and to power industry. The Drumheller area was a coal centre, and the Atlas Coal Mine Museum interprets the period from 1936 until the mine's official closing in 1984. Learn how the miners lived and worked. Tour the wash house, the mine offices, the houses, the lamp house, and the blacksmith shop. Examine the ore-sorting tipple — the only one of its kind in Alberta — and drop in to the visitor centre to see the displays and a video about coal mining.

■

Courtesy Atlas Coal Mine Museum

Royal Tyrrell Museum of Palæontology   10b

✉ Box 7500
Drumheller, AB T0J 0Y0

☎ (403) 823-7707
(Calgary line: 294-1992)

Courtesy Royal Tyrrell Museum/Alberta Community Development

Dinosaurs live at the Royal Tyrrell Museum of Palæontology! This unique, very modern facility houses more than 200 dinosaur specimens, the largest collection in the world. The overall theme of the museum is "A Celebration of Life," and it uses more than 800 specimens to explore the origin and diversification of life on earth from its beginnings to the present. The museum features 15 exhibit areas, the most popular of which, of course, is the dinosaur display. A number of interactive displays allow visitors to test their knowledge of a subject and even to create their own dinosaurs using a computer simulation. The site includes a preparation laboratory, where staff prepare fossils for exhibit. A telephone accesses the "Bone Line" where visitors can talk directly to the staff about the work they are engaged in. Although the dinosaurs are the central attraction, be sure to see the beautiful paleoconservatory, a large, bright, airy greenhouse that contains 110 species of plant life, many of which are related to, or have evolved from, those that grew in the Alberta area during the time of the dinosaurs.

■ on-site; all grades; teaching materials; newsletters; teacher workshops

Police Dog Service Training Centre   11

✉ Royal Canadian Mounted Police
Box 6120
Innisfail, AB T4G 1S8

☎ (403) 227-3346

For anyone who has ever thrilled to the exploits of Rin Tin Tin (or just loves dogs), a visit to the Police Dog Service Training Centre in Innisfail should prove most interesting. Here, selected German shepherds, along with their handlers, are put through weeks of arduous training before being assigned to duty. Police dogs respond to tone of voice: one to issue commands, one to praise, and one to reprimand. In spite of their fearsome appearance, the dogs only hold on to a suspect; they never attack to injure. Dogs are trained for tracking duties, to apprehend suspects, and to locate explosive devices and narcotics. They also provide excellent support in search-and-rescue activities.

Stephansson House Historic Site 12

Markerville

✉

Historic Sites and Archives Service
Cochrane, AB T0L 0W0

☎ (403) 728-3929
(summers); (403) 932-2902

Stephansson House is the family home of Icelandic poet Stephan G. Stephansson, who was born in Iceland in 1853. Stephansson emigrated to the United States in 1873, and then to Alberta in the 1880s. Stephansson farmed by day, experimenting with crops and raising sheep and dairy cattle. By night he wrote poetry in his native language. With over 2000 pages of verse, he is one of Canada's most prolific poets. The house has been restored and furnished in the style of 1927, the year he died, although most items date from the turn of the century. The site is staffed by costumed interpreters who provide guided tours and demonstrate the activities of pioneer life, such as spinning, baking, household chores, and, of course, poetry reading.

■ on-site; elementary grades

Rocky Mountain House National Historic Site 13

Box 2130
Rocky Mountain House, AB T0M 1T0

☎ (403) 845-2412/(403) 845-3948

To fully appreciate the historic importance of Rocky Mountain House National Historic Site, you must think back to the year 1799, when the Hudson's Bay and North West Companies were competing to dominate the West and the fur trade. Rival posts were established at Rocky Mountain House. The site proved something of an anomaly, however: it had been chosen to foster trade with the Kootenay Indians, but the Kootenays were never around much. Then it was intended to act as a base for exploration, especially to find a way through the Rocky Mountains. That route was eventually found, but much farther north than the forts. Rocky Mountain House is committed to an accurate portrayal of fur-trade history. Begin your visit in the visitor orientation centre, and then stroll out to the fort sites. At points along the trail, solar-powered audio guides will provide information about life at the forts. As well, see the outdoor exhibits, one about buffalo and others that feature teepees and replicas of a York boat and a Red River cart.

▲ ■ on-site; educational materials

Reynolds–Alberta Museum 14

Hwy. 13

P.O. Box 6360
Wetaskiwin, AB T9A 2G1

☎ (403) 361-1351

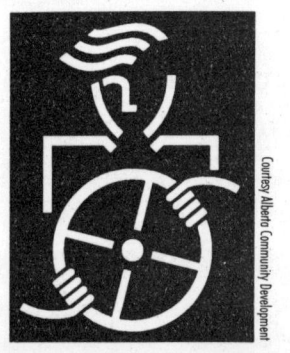

REYNOLDS-ALBERTA MUSEUM

The Reynolds–Alberta Museum invites you to celebrate the "Spirit of the Machine" from Alberta's transportation,

agricultural, and industrial past. The museum concentrates on the
period from 1900 to the 1950s because it was during this time that
mechanization replaced horse-drawn equipment. Within each
theme — the spirit of the machine, the spirit of the collector, the
spirit of the community, the spirit of restoration and conservation,
and the spirit of tomorrow — the exhibits focus on the stories
behind the pieces on display. They explore the technological
changes that took place, the adaptation to local conditions, the
purpose of various pieces of equipment, and their replacements.
Visitors are encouraged to roll up their sleeves and get involved
through creative, interactive exhibits, on-site artifact
demonstrations, exciting interpretive programs, and audio-visual
presentations. The museum now houses Canada's Aviation Hall of
Fame as well.

■ on-site; all grades

West Edmonton Mall 15a

✉ Suite 2872, 8770–170 St.
Edmonton, AB T5T 3J3

☎ (403) 444-5200

Covering half a million m^2 (5.2 million sq. ft.) and the
equivalent of 48 city blocks, the West Edmonton Mall defies
description. No visit to Alberta's capital would be complete
without at least a peek inside. The largest complex of its type in
the world, this mall combines under one very large roof more
than 800 shops and retail outlets, an amusement park, a wave
pool, a miniature golf course, tropical fish, exotic birds, a
perpetual motion machine, the famous submarine ride, a hotel, a
casino, restaurants, and much, much more. If your timing is right,
you can even see the Edmonton Oilers at practice at the ice
palace. And through it all, you can shop, eat, and relax.

Ukrainian Cultural Heritage Village 15b

8820–112 St.
Edmonton, AB T6G 2P8

☎ (403) 662-3273

The Ukrainian Cultural Heritage Village honours, portrays, and preserves the unique heritage and contribution to Alberta of immigrants from the western Ukraine. The site consists of close to 40 buildings, most of them staffed by costumed interpreters who can provide information, answer questions, and demonstrate typical daily activities associated with the time period and the function of the buildings. Visitors, too, are invited to participate in the activities. There are reconstructions of family homes from a period spanning 15 years (from 1906 to 1920). Several traditional barns and farmsteads illustrate the the shift from traditional Ukrainian farming practices to methods more suited to western Canada. See various styles of granaries built to store wheat. In the rural community area, the buildings on display include shops, a sawmill, schools, churches, a market, a hall for cultural events and meetings, and a police post. Tour the site on foot or take a ride in a horse-drawn grain tank.

■ on-site; grades K–7

Fort Edmonton Park 15c

Fox Dr. and The Whitemud Frwy.

✉
P.O. Box 2359
Edmonton, AB T5J 2R7

☎ (403) 496-8787

Indulge your curiosity about the days of the Wild West in an authentic frontier town. The original Fort Edmonton was constructed in 1795 by the fur-trade giant The Hudson's Bay Company, but it changed location five times. Visitors to the fort can choose whatever era they wish to explore. Start your visit in the fort itself, reconstructed to represent how it looked in 1846, when it was the headquarters for the Saskatchewan district of the HBC. Costumed interpreters are hard at work — some repairing the York boat, others trading furs, and still others baking bannock. Around the fort, each of several "streets" present a different period of time. Just outside the fort gates, see the teepee village. You can learn the craft of beading and enjoy the tales of the Native storytellers. Move on to 1885 St., the era of the horse and buggy, general stores, and homesteading. Enjoy a stagecoach ride, shop at the bakery, and join the fun in a street dance. On 1905 St., which celebrates the arrival of the railway and the designation of Edmonton as the capital of Alberta, you can tour the home of Alberta's first premier, Alexander Rutherford, have your palm read, and go for a ride on a streetcar. 1920 St. presents the development of Edmonton. Check out the Ukrainian bookstore, the brickyard, and the greenhouses, and enjoy an old-fashioned ice-cream soda at the drugstore. There are plenty of eateries for refreshments, and a 1919 Baldwin steam train transports visitors around the site.

▲

Provincial Museum of Alberta 15d

12845–102 Ave.
Edmonton, AB T5N 0M6

☎ (403) 453-9100

Visitors to the Provincial Museum of Alberta are invited to step into the province's history by means of a series of lifelike dioramas, displays, and hands-on programs for children. The Habitat Gallery recreates actual locations from Alberta's four main natural regions: prairie, aspen parkland, mountain, and boreal forest. Explore the arrival of the first human beings. Exhibits trace the heritage of Alberta's Native peoples and their way of life from prehistory, through to the arrival of the Europeans and the fur trade, and into the 20th century. Collections of clothing, toys, musical instruments, religious artifacts, a reconstructed harness shop, and displays of early agriculture present the contributions and lifestyles of immigrants from all over the world. Examine the geological formation of the province in exhibits of rocks, minerals, fossils, and the ever-popular dinosaur skeletons. Of special interest is the display of the Manitou Stone, a 145-kg (319-lb.) meteorite, venerated by the Natives, which looks like a face.

■ on-site

Courtesy Old Strathcona Model and Toy Museum

Old Strathcona Model and Toy Museum 15e

8603–104 St.
Edmonton, AB T6E 4G6

☎ (403) 433-4512

A visit to the Old Strathcona Model and Toy Museum is a special experience. This small, private museum displays more than 400 scale models of famous buildings, planes, and historical and contemporary subjects representing many countries and cultures. What sets this museum apart from other model and toy museums is that all the displays are constructed from paper, and most have been created lovingly and painstakingly by curators Bob and Gerry Bell as a hobby over the years of their marriage. See recreations of such sites as Shakespeare's Globe Theatre, the Eiffel Tower, the fabled Schloss Neuschwanstein, the Taj Mahal, Canada's own CN Tower, and much more. Also see a collection of caricatures of Canadian prime ministers that Bob Bell undertook, and a representation of the Mounties on their famous Musical Ride. Because of the unique nature of this museum, children under the age of eight must be accompanied by an adult. The displays are strictly for viewing: there are no hands-on or interactive displays.

■ on-site; workshops

Alberta Railway Museum 15f

24215–34 St., Edmonton

✉

Londonderry Postal Outlet #70014
Edmonton, AB T5C 3R6

☎ (403) 472-6229

For train buffs and anyone who ever loved *The Little Engine That Could*, the Alberta Railway Museum offers an exciting look at railroading history in Canada and in Alberta in particular. Three main buildings stand at the site: a railway station that includes the museum itself, built in 1909 at St. Albert; the water tower standing almost 10 m (32 ft.) high and built in 1919 at Gibbons; and the 21-m (70-ft.) CPR turntable constructed in 1912. As well, see a number of steam and diesel locomotives, and various passenger and freight cars. Of particular note is Intercolonial Baggage Car 736, the oldest railway passenger train car existing in Canada today; the NAR Dawson Creek, of all-wood construction and representative of 19th-century North American railroad car interior decoration; and NAR Bunk, Recreation and Shower Car 18104, which served at one time as Henry Ford's private business car.

■ on-site

The Edmonton Art Gallery 15g

2 Sir Winston Churchill Square
Edmonton, AB T5J 2C1

☎ (403) 422-6223

A thing of beauty is a joy forever at the Edmonton Art Gallery. Here on 1953 m^2 (21 000 sq. ft.) of exhibition space, the museum displays and stores in excess of 3500 pieces of art. These include Canadian and international works, contemporary and historical art, drawings, prints, photographs, sculpture, and mixed-media pieces. The gallery's outreach program circulates 50 exhibits annually throughout the province.

■ on-site; all grades

Rutherford House Provincial Site 15h

11153 Saskatchewan Dr.
Edmonton, AB T6G 2S1

☎ (403) 427-3995/(403) 427-2022

Step inside Rutherford House, the Edwardian-style mansion that belonged to Alexander Rutherford, Alberta's first premier, and enter an era of gracious living. The house has been meticulously restored to the 1915 period when Rutherford entertained the political and social notables of the day. Note the gleaming silver, warmly polished wood, and elegant furnishings. The house is staffed by costumed interpreters who demonstrate household activities, dramatize important events in Rutherford's life, and lead guided tours.

■ elementary grades

Fort George–Buckingham House Provincial Historic Site 16

✉
General Delivery
Elk Point, AB T0A 1A0

☎ (403) 724-2612

Situated on the north bank of the North Saskatchewan River near the town of Elk Point, Fort George–Buckingham House offers the visitor an opportunity to experience the early days of the fur trade in Alberta. In the 1700s, when they were rivals for supremacy, the North West Company and the Hudson's Bay Company both opened posts at this site. Although Fort George and Buckingham House competed for the same resources in furs and provisions, they were neighbours, faced with the same challenges and struggles to survive in an isolated and harsh land whose indigenous population was powerful and volatile. Listen to "Louis," a voyageur, recount his dreams, or learn the thoughts of William Tomison, the Chief Factor of Buckingham House. See the impact of the fur trade and the rivalry between the two commercial giants on the Natives. Walk along the interpretive pathways to the sites of both establishments.

▲ ■

Fort McMurray Oil Sands Interpretive Centre 17

515 MacKenzie Blvd.
Fort McMurray, AB T9H 4X3

☎ (403) 743-7167

Courtesy Alberta Community Development

In energy-conscious Alberta, the process of extracting oil from the sands is a fascinating subject indeed. The displays in the modern interpretive centre have been designed to demystify that process. The best place to begin is the exhibit that acts as an introduction, explaining the history and geology of the sands and their industrial development. Proceed to the displays about the mining, processing, engineering challenges, and marketing of the oil. Other displays recount the growth of Fort McMurray and discuss its future directions. Move to the interactive area where you can participate in such hands-on activities as model building, demonstrations, and games, or watch an entertaining and informative multimedia presentation in the centre's theatre. Did you know that Alberta produces 82 percent of Canada's domestic oil? Or that enough recoverable oil sand exists to keep a Syncrude-sized mining plant operating for the next 500 years?

▲

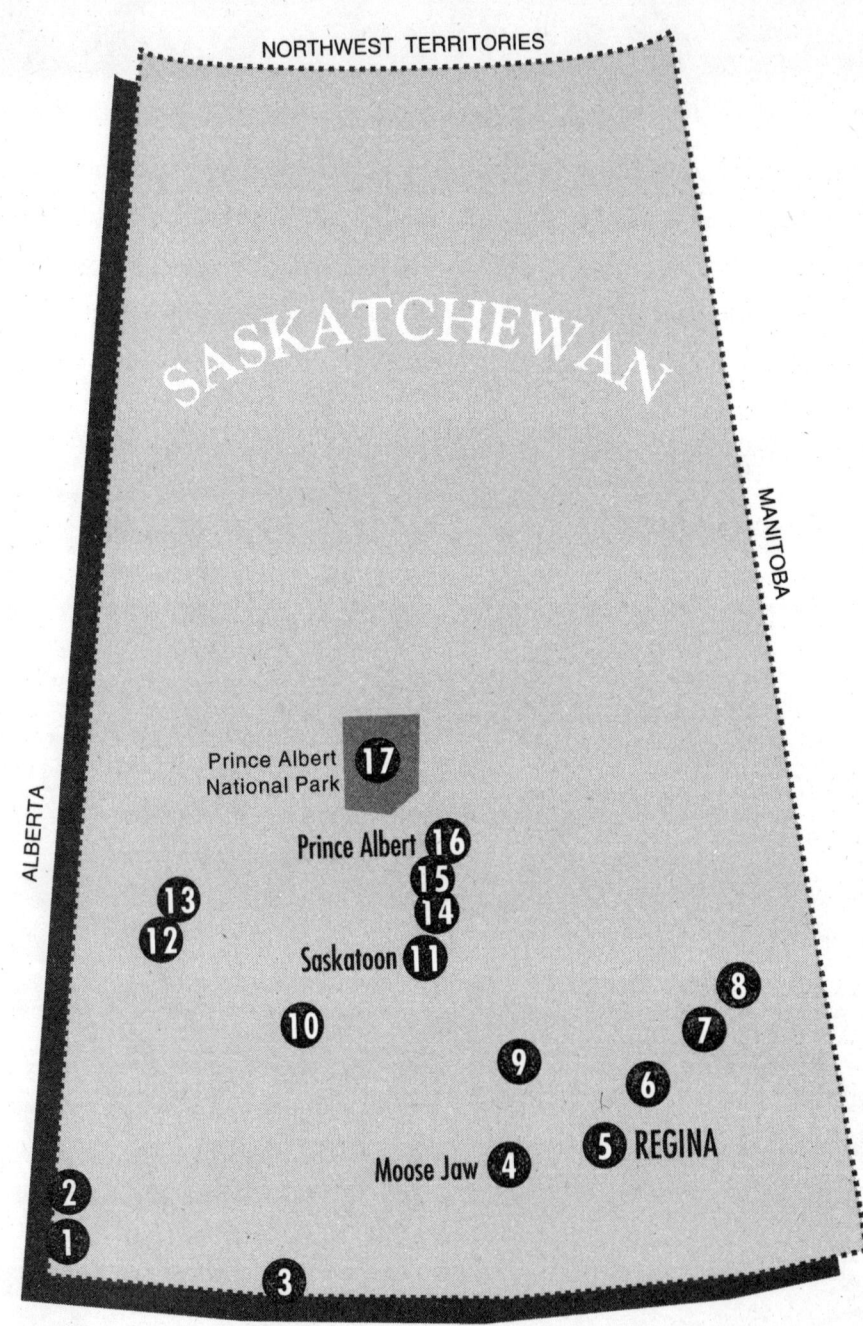

1	Fort Walsh National Historic Site	11h	Saskatoon Western Development Museum
2	Cypress Hills Massacre National Historic Site	12	Fort Battleford National Historic Park
3	Grasslands National Park	13	North Battleford Western Development Museum
4a	Wood Mountain Provincial Historic Park	14	Batoche National Historic Park
4b	Moose Jaw Western Development Museum	15	Duck Lake Regional Interpretive Centre
5a	MacKenzie Art Gallery	16a	The Right Honourable John G. and Olive Diefenbaker Museum
5b	Saskatchewan Science Centre		
5c	Royal Canadian Mounted Police Centennial Museum	16b	Fort Carlton Historic Park
5d	Royal Saskatchewan Museum	17	Prince Albert National Park
5e	Diefenbaker Homestead		
5f	Cumberland House Provincial Historic Park		
5g	Steele Narrows Provincial Historic Park		
5h	Cannington Manor Provincial Historic Park		
6	Motherwell Homestead National Historic Park		
7	Yorkton Western Development Museum		
8	National Doukhobour Heritage Village		
9	Last Mountain House Provincial Historic Site		
10	Harris & District Museum		
11a	Wanuskewin Heritage Park		
11b	Ukrainian Museum of Canada		
11c	Mendel Art Gallery and Civic Conservatory		
11d	The Right Honourable John G. Diefenbaker Centre Museum and Archives		
11e	The Little Stone School		
11f	Museum of Antiquities		
11g	Western Development Museum		

In the site descriptions, note that:

▲ indicates that second language services are available: English in Quebec and French elsewhere in Canada. Where "limited service" is given, it would be wise to call ahead for specifics

■ indicates that educational services are available

Fort Walsh National Historic Park

Box 278
Maple Creek, SK S0N 1N0

☎ (306) 662-2645

Following the tragedy at Cypress Hills in 1873 (see below), the North-West Mounted Police were dispatched to the area to put an end to the whisky trade and to establish law and order. In 1975, Fort Walsh was constructed as a North-West Mounted Police post 2.4 km (1.6 mi.) north of the spot where the Farwell and Solomon trading posts were located. These traders were involved in supplying whisky to the Natives and thus were partly to blame for the massacre. The two trading posts have been reconstructed on their original sites, and Farwell's Post is open to the public. Here you will see the goods that were traded for furs, and a costumed interpreter will show you how the liquor given to the Natives was prepared. The visitor centre contains a large display area to introduce the fort to visitors. The displays are supplemented by programs and films. Also on the site are the non-commissioned officers' quarters, the workshop, the stable, the blacksmith and carpenter shops, the guardhouse, the armoury, and the commissioner's residence. Many of these buildings are now open to the public and are interpreted by staff in period costume.

▲ ■ all grades; on-site; teaching materials

Cypress Hills Massacre National Historic Site

Fort Walsh National Historic Park

Box 278
Maple Creek, SK S0N 1N0

The Cypress Hills Massacre was decidedly one of the darker moments in our nation's history. In 1873, a horse belonging to a white man disappeared from Farwell's whisky trading post at Cypress Hills. This caused a drunken battle to erupt between a small group of white wolf-hunters and an Assiniboine encampment. The fight raged through the night. In the morning, when it was all over, 20 Natives were dead. It was this incident that resulted in the creation of the North-West Mounted Police, spelling the end of the notorious whisky trade. The historic site is a part of the Fort Walsh National Historic Park.

Grasslands National Park

P.O. Box 150
Val Marie, SK S0N 2T0

☎ (306) 298-2257

Welcome to the prairie as it looked before the arrival of settlers and homesteaders. Grasslands National Park has been created to preserve an area of undisturbed mixed-grass prairie. Unique in North America, it has much to offer its visitors. In addition to the mixed grass ecosystem protected here, you may see several species of wildlife, 12 of which are endangered or otherwise very scarce. The park has been host to a great deal of "precontact" (before the arrival of Europeans) history. Staff have identified more than 500 prehistoric sites, including bison drive lanes and jumps, campsites with teepee rings and vision-quest sites. And, from a later period, there are ranch and homestead sites. Many artifacts representing 5000 years of prehistory have been found; reproductions are available for visitors to see. Interpretive trails, guided hikes, and audio tapes are available to help make a visit to Grasslands a memorable and meaningful experience.

▲ ■ May and June only; on-site

Wood Mountain Provincial Historic Park 4a

✉

c/o Saskatchewan Natural Resources
110 Ominica St. W.
Moose Jaw, SK S6H 6V2

☎ (306) 787-2700/(306) 694-3659

Wood Mountain Post was established by the North-West Mounted Police in 1874 because of its proximity to the American border and the importance of controlling the whiskey that flowed north into Canada. In 1876, the famous Battle of the Bighorn was fought in Montana between General Custer's cavalry and the Sioux. Although the Sioux won the day, the proverbial writing was on the wall for the future of the Sioux nation, and so Sitting Bull and 4000 of his people came north to Wood Mountain. Their presence caused great difficulty for the North-West Mounted Police, since neither the American nor the Canadian governments was willing to accept responsibility for them. In 1881, their encampment ravaged by sickness and starvation, Sitting Bull and the Sioux agreed to be settled on reserves, and policing at Wood Mountain returned to normal. Wood Mountain Post has been reconstructed, and visitors are invited to tour the buildings. Of particular interest are the recreated barracks and mess hall, which contain displays about the history and daily life of the post. Interpretive programs help bring history to life.

■

Moose Jaw Western Development Museum 4b

50 Diefenbaker Dr.

✉ Box 185
Moose Jaw, SK S6H 4N8

☎ (306) 693-5989

The focus of the Moose Jaw branch of the Western Development Museum is the History of Transportation, particularly in Saskatchewan. This topic is addressed through displays on air, rail, water, and ground transportation. Of particular interest is the new Snowbirds Gallery and Cinema 180 Theatre. Here visitors can learn the behind-the-scenes story of Canada's famous aerobatic, precision-flying Snowbirds, all the better to appreciate their skill. In the Cinema 180 Theatre, take to the air with the Snowbirds by means of the feature film, *Fly With the Snowbirds*.

■ on-site; elementary grades; teaching materials

MacKenzie Art Gallery 5a

3475 Albert St.
Regina, SK S4S 6X6

☎ (306) 569-8191

The MacKenzie Art Gallery maintains a collection of more than 1600 works of art, including Canadian historical and contemporary pieces with a special focus on western Canadian art. The Prairie Artist Series is a popular feature that provides an opportunity for prairie artists to present their work and for established artists to show new or experimental works. During the month of August, a re-enactment of the trial of Louis Riel is staged in the gallery's Shumiatcher Theatre.

▲ ■ on-site; all grades

Saskatchewan Science Centre 5b

Winnipeg St. and Wascana Dr.

✉
P.O. Box 5071
Regina, SK S4P 3M3

☎ (306) 791-7900

SASKATCHEWAN SCIENCE CENTRE
The Powerhouse of Discovery

Courtesy Saskatchewan Science Centre

For budding scientists, the Saskatchewan Science Centre offers a playground filled with an endless variety of things to do and learn. The site is housed in the building that once functioned as Regina's powerhouse, hence its nickname: the Powerhouse of Discovery. A breathtaking prairie panorama greets you as you enter the building, with sky scenes and subterranean and underwater images. Inside, more than 70 hands-on exhibits introduce visitors to the basics of science, using such themes as Patterns Around Us, The Living Body, Our Planet Earth, and Beyond Earth. Press a button on a bunsen burner to watch a hot-air balloon soar three storeys into the air; watch chicken embryos developing; or try out the centre's ham radio station. Another feature of this popular place is its ultra-modern IMAX theatre, which presents exciting and relevant films, such as *Blue Planet* (environment), *The Dream Is Alive* (space flight), and *To the Limit* (limits of the human body). The centre also hosts a number of visiting exhibits.

▲ limited service   ■ on-site; all grades

Courtesy Royal Canadian Mounted Police Centennial Museum

Royal Canadian Mounted Police Centennial Museum 5c

11th Ave.

✉
c/o RCMP Training Academy
P.O. Box 6500, Regina, SK S4P 3J7

☎ (306) 780-5900

Come to the Royal Canadian Mounted Police Centennial Museum, where you can trace the history and exploits of the force that "always gets their man." Here you will see artifacts, photographs, and memorabilia from 1874, when 300 recruits from Manitoba and eastern Canada were assigned to the Canadian Northwest to establish law and order. You will see an original mortar and field gun from the trek west, a recruiting officer's room from the late 1800s, uniforms, documents, and other artifacts. The chronicles of Chief Sitting Bull are recounted here, as well. Also on display are posters from movies featuring the RCMP. Nearby is the RCMP Training Academy. A popular feature is the Sergeant-Major's Parade, performed each weekday. Senior recruits give a public demonstration of foot drill accompanied by the martial music of the Academy Band.

▲ ■ on-site

Royal Saskatchewan Museum 5d

College Ave. and Albert St.

✉ 2445 Albert St., Wascana Park
Regina, SK S4P 3V7

☎ (306) 787-2815

Come and explore the world at the Royal Saskatchewan Museum (formerly the Saskatchewan Museum of Natural History). The Earth Sciences Gallery is a major attraction. Walk through the gallery to trace geological time through exciting dioramas. These days the Paleo Pit is the place to be — meet the dinosaurs and other prehistoric creatures that roamed the earth long before the first human being made an appearance. The new Native Peoples Gallery with its emphasis on Canada's First Nations, their history and their heritage, is also a must.

▲ ■ on-site; all grades; teaching materials

Diefenbaker Homestead 5e

Lakeshore Dr.

✉ c/o Wascana Centre Authority
Box 7111, Regina, SK S4P 3S7

☎ (306) 522-3661

Canada's 13th prime minister, John G. Diefenbaker, was born on September 18, 1895, in Neustadt, Ontario. In 1903, the family moved to Saskatchewan and lived on a homestead near Borden until 1910. John, aged 11, helped his father to build the home. In 1910, the family moved to Saskatoon to provide better educational opportunities for John and his brother Elmer. In 1967, the Diefenbaker homestead and the cabin, which had belonged to Diefenbaker's Uncle Ed, were relocated to Wascana Centre; it had been discovered that young John had slept in his uncle's home owing to space limitations in his own. The homestead has been restored as accurately as possible to the period when young John lived there, and it welcomes visitors. Most of the furnishings have been donated by outside organizations and individuals, but some pieces are from the Diefenbaker family.

▲ ■

Cumberland House Provincial Historic Park 5f

✉ c/o Saskatchewan Natural Resources
3211 Albert St.
Regina, SK S4S 5W6

☎ (306) 787-2700

Cumberland House enjoys the distinctions of being both the first Hudson's Bay Company post in the interior of Canada and Saskatchewan's oldest settlement. Its origins stretch back to

1774, when the Hudson's Bay Company realized that it needed a major trading and provisioning post in the interior in order to combat intense competition from independent traders who were paddling canoes laden with goods right into Native encampments and trading there. Cumberland House was constructed and, although it was never a terribly successful trading post, it had far-reaching effects. It laid the foundations for a solid inland trade route, and Saskatchewan's first permanent settlement was born. Located on Pine Island in the Saskatchewan River delta area, Cumberland House received a new lease on life in 1874 with the arrival of the first steam-powered sternwheeler. From then on it became a transportation centre, and it functioned in this capacity until 1925 when the railway replaced the steamboats. Visitors to Cumberland House Historic Park can see remnants of the 1890s post and a sternwheeler, both of which have been preserved.

Steele Narrows Provincial Historic Park 5g

✉

c/o Saskatchewan Parks, Recreation and Culture
3211 Albert St.
Regina, SK S4S 5W6

☎ (306) 787-2700/9573

This was the site of the last engagement of the Northwest Rebellion, a major event in the history of Saskatchewan. The Rebellion erupted in 1885, out of the uneasy relations between the three major cultures in the area, the Natives, the Métis, and the whites. A skirmish took place at Frenchman Butte, and then another at the ford between Makwa Lake and Sanderson Bay on June 10, 1885. This battle lasted three hours; four Cree died and three NWMP scouts were injured. The Cree escaped, but two weeks later they surrendered. In 1962, the ford was named Steele Narrows after Superintendent Samuel B. Steele, who led the detachment of NWMP in pursuit of the Cree warriors. Interpretive panels at the site give details of this battle.

Cannington Manor Provincial Historic Park 5h

c/o Saskatchewan Natural Resources
3211 Albert St.
Regina, SK S4S 5W6

☎ (306) 577-2131 or (306) 787-9573

The vision of the Canadian government in the 1880s of a British agricultural society on the prairies was the motivating factor behind the establishment of Cannington Manor. It was a vision that failed when confronted with reality. Life on the prairies was often harsh, demanding more hard work and grim determination than imagined by the Victorian gentlemen who came to settle. Although initially many built themselves fine, large homes, in accordance with the lifestyle they envisioned, most lacked the funds to maintain them, and eventually went off to pursue wealth and/or adventure elsewhere — in the Yukon, as gold prospectors, or in Africa as soldiers in the Boer War. By 1900, much of the village had been abandoned. Today, many representative buildings have been restored or reconstructed. A visit should begin in the visitor centre, where the displays will orient you to the village. See the Le Mesurier House, typical of the dwellings inhabited by young bachelors who came to Cannington Manor to make their fortunes. Important places in the town were the carpenter's shop, the blacksmith's shop, and, of course, the flour mill. A popular meeting place was the Mitre Hotel and the Moose Mountain Trading Company Store, which was a link to the outside world. Be sure to see the school and the teacherage — a building one doesn't often see any more — which, as the name suggests, was a dwelling provided to the village teacher and his family. Cannington Manor is staffed by interpreters who demonstrate period activities.

Motherwell Homestead National Historic Park 6

✉ Box 247
Abernethy, SK S0A 0A0

☎ (306) 333-2116

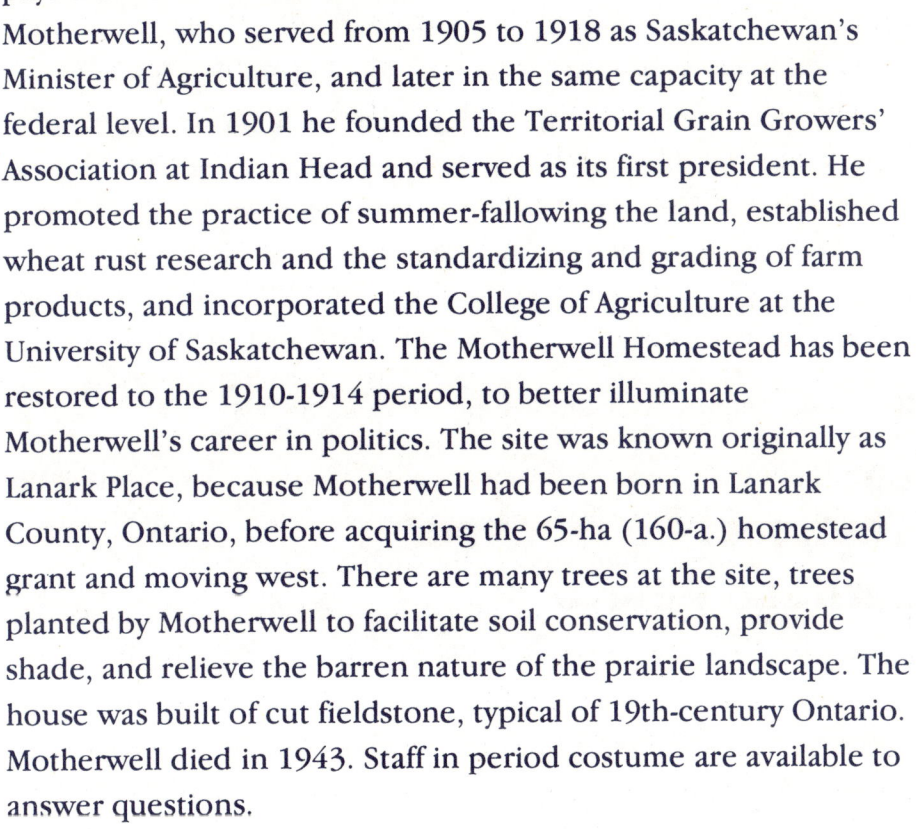

Motherwell Homestead National Historic Park pays tribute to William Richard Motherwell, who served from 1905 to 1918 as Saskatchewan's Minister of Agriculture, and later in the same capacity at the federal level. In 1901 he founded the Territorial Grain Growers' Association at Indian Head and served as its first president. He promoted the practice of summer-fallowing the land, established wheat rust research and the standardizing and grading of farm products, and incorporated the College of Agriculture at the University of Saskatchewan. The Motherwell Homestead has been restored to the 1910-1914 period, to better illuminate Motherwell's career in politics. The site was known originally as Lanark Place, because Motherwell had been born in Lanark County, Ontario, before acquiring the 65-ha (160-a.) homestead grant and moving west. There are many trees at the site, trees planted by Motherwell to facilitate soil conservation, provide shade, and relieve the barren nature of the prairie landscape. The house was built of cut fieldstone, typical of 19th-century Ontario. Motherwell died in 1943. Staff in period costume are available to answer questions.

▲ ■ on-site; grades K–9

Yorkton Western Development Museum 7

Hwy. 16 W.

✉

Box 98,
Yorkton, SK S3N 2V6

☎ (306) 783-8361

In this branch of the Western Development Museum, people dominate. The Story of People outlines the history of immigration to Saskatchewan, and the traditions and cultures of the immigrants. The displays include many items that the immigrants brought with them to Saskatchewan. A special feature of the museum is the exhibit of two mannequins carved from a single tree. The carver had to leave his love behind in the Ukraine and never saw her again. He carved the two mannequins, in his and her likenesses, from the trunk of a tree on his new homestead.

■ on-site; elementary grades; teaching materials

National Doukhobour Heritage Village 8

✉

Box 99
Verigin, SK S0A 4H0

☎ (306) 542-4441

The National Doukhobour Heritage Village consists of 11 buildings, but most are reconstructions. Only the Verigin Prayer Home (named for Peter V. Verigin and his son Peter P. Verigin, both Doukhobour leaders) and a machine shed still exist of the original buildings. Visitors are welcome to the village, which is an interesting and informative peek at the life of the Doukhobours, a Christian sect that emigrated to Canada in search of religious freedom at the end of the 19th century. The early homes portray the lifestyles and habits of the pioneer

Doukhobours. See the *peche*, a brick oven where the baking was done, the *banya* (bathhouse), the granary, the blacksmith shop, and the barn. Also on display is a statue of renowned Russian author Leo Tolstoy, who supported the Doukhobour move to Canada by donating the proceeds of his novel *Resurrection*. The brick prayer home displays several artifacts and handicrafts worthy of note.

■ on-site

Last Mountain House Provincial Historic Park 9

c/o Saskatchewan Natural Resources
Box 370, Strasbourg, SK S0G 4V0

☎ (306) 787-2700/725-4423

In 1869, Last Mountain House was constructed as a trade and provisioning post for the Hudson's Bay Company. The post enjoyed only a short existence. In 1871, it burned and was abandoned. Although its life was a brief one, it serves to remind us of just how important the bison were to the survival of the traders and pioneers. Life at the fort was mundane. Daily activities centred around groups who came to trade or obtain provisions. One of these was pemmican, a nutritious and long-lasting blend of meat, fat, and berries that was a staple of the Native and fur-trader diets. One of the key activities was the buffalo hunt from which hides, meat, and other products would be obtained for trade. However, the animals were becoming scarce. As they moved farther west, beyond the reach of the Last Mountain hunters, and their numbers declined, the post could no longer supply the needed pemmican, so was no longer useful. Much of the post has been reconstructed and is open to visitors. Interpretive staff are on hand to supply information and answer questions.

Harris & District Museum 10

Box 263,
Harris, SK S0L 1K0

☎ (306) 656-2172

In 1914, quartz thought to contain rubies was discovered, sparking a "Ruby Rush." The original Ruby Rock which caused all the excitement is on display at the museum. But there is a great deal more than the Ruby Rock to see. The office of Dr. N.T. George (1881–1947), an early country doctor, has been set up here, as well as a 1930s vintage country store with a candy display case. See also the re-creation of a pioneer kitchen and imagine preparing meals with the implements and equipment you see. Of special note is an archaeology display featuring a 10 500-year-old clovis point, among other artifacts.

Wanuskewin Heritage Park 11a

R.R. 4
Saskatoon, SK S7K 3J7

☎ (306) 931-6767

Wanuskewin Heritage Park

Courtesy Wanuskewin Heritage Park

The English translation of the Cree word "Wanuskewin" is "seeking peace of mind." It is an apt name for Wanuskewin Heritage Park, a special place steeped in the history and spirituality of the Northern Plains Indians. The history of Wanuskewin extends back in time up to 8000 years ago. Nineteen precontact (before the arrival of Europeans) historic sites have been discovered, all clustered within one square kilometre (less than half a square mile). Begin your visit at the interpretive centre. In the main exhibit hall, three main themes tell the story of the Northern Plains people: The Buffalo and his Brothers (people and animals); The Earth, Our Mother (people and plants); and The Nation's Hoop: A Nest of Many Nests (many peoples). Interactive technology brings the displays to life. An activity area provides you with an opportunity to learn a number of new skills: to build a teepee, bake bannock, tan a hide, or use a travois. An interpretive trail system brings you to many interesting sites, and the University of Saskatchewan's on-site laboratory has an observation area where visitors can participate in some of their activities.

■ on-site

Ukrainian Museum of Canada 11b

910 Spadina Cr. E.
Saskatoon, SK S7K 3H5

☎ (306) 244-3800

The Ukrainian Museum of Canada has a number of branches across the country, but the Saskatoon location is the largest. Housed in a building designed to resemble the exterior of a Ukrainian pioneer home on the prairie at the turn of the century, the museum presents temporary and permanent exhibits, all related to the Ukrainian community in Canada. The permanent exhibit tells the story of the immigration and settlement of Ukrainian pioneers, and describes their family, community, and religious life through photographs, text, and artifacts. Displays of textiles, domestic and agricultural implements, folk art, and religious artifacts all help convey the story. The Museum also presents demonstrations and workshops of traditional Ukrainian crafts, such as *pysanka* (Easter eggs), writing, ritual bread baking, straw weaving, glass painting, and embroidery. Videos are also shown.

■ on-site; all grades; teaching materials

Mendel Art Gallery and Civic Conservatory 11c

950 Spadina Cr. E.
P.O. Box 569
Saskatoon, SK S7K 3L6

☎ (306) 975-7610

The residents of the city of Saskatoon treasure the beautiful Mendel Art Gallery and Civic Conservatory, with its collections of art and plants, as the gem of their city. It has even served as the setting of a mystery novel, *Murder at the Mendel*. The permanent collection of more than 3000 pieces, which are primarily Canadian in origin, focuses on both the history of art and current art making, in Saskatchewan as well as in western Canada. Stroll through the current exhibits, and then relax in the peaceful conservatory, whose air is redolent with the perfume of plants and the rich smell of earth.

■ on-site; all grades

The Right Honourable John G. Diefenbaker Centre Museum and Archives 11d

University of Saskatchewan
Saskatoon, SK S7N 0W0

☎ (306) 966-8384

The Diefenbaker Centre pays tribute to the man who was prime minister of Canada from 1957 to 1963. Visit an exact replica of the prime minister's office and cabinet room as they have looked throughout most of the 20th century. Also included is a full-scale replica of the privy council chamber, along with exhibits on Diefenbaker's long career in politics, his years as a young prairie lawyer, and his time as our 13th prime minister. See the collection of his personal memorabilia, including buttons, badges, gifts from visiting heads of state, place settings, and a gown worn by his wife Olive. This is a remarkable testament to the life of the man who once said, "He who does not know the past can never understand the present, and he certainly can do nothing about the future."

■ on-site; all grades

The Little Stone School 11e

University of Saskatchewan
Saskatoon, SK S7N 0W0

☎ (306) 966-8385

Relive "school days, school days, dear old golden rule days" at the Little Stone School. Constructed in 1887, the Little Stone School is Saskatoon's oldest public building. In 1911, it was taken apart stone by stone, moved to the University of Saskatchewan's campus and reassembled. The school has been restored to reflect the 1904 era, complete with a costumed "school mistress" who interprets the site. Come back to school and refresh your knowledge of "reading, 'riting and 'rithmetic."

▲ ■ on-site; elementary grades; teaching materials

Museum of Antiquities 11f

University of Saskatchewan
Saskatoon, SK S7N 0W0

☎ (306) 966-8385

Where can you see ancient Greek and Roman coins? Why, at the University of Saskatchewan's Museum of Antiquities, of course. But coins aren't the only things on display here. See, as well, full-scale replicas of ancient Greek and Roman sculptures dating back as far as 3000 B.C. Among the replicas, many of which were created in the Louvre and the British Museum, you will find the Rosetta Stone, Parthenon Frieze, the Charioteer of Delphi, "Hermes with the Infant Dionysus" and the Aphrodite of Melos. Of special interest is a priceless 18th-century bust of Hannibal, the Carthaginian general who crossed the Alps with his elephants to invade Italy, and whose exploits were chronicled by the author Homer.

■ guided tours

Western Development Museum 11g

c/o Provincial Service Centre
P.O. Box 1910, 2935 Melville St.
Saskatoon, SK S7K 3S5

☎ (306) 934-4467

Although the Western Development Museum gives Saskatoon as its central location, the museum spans all of Saskatchewan, and has branches in four places, each with its own focus.

Saskatoon Western Development Museum 11h

Courtesy Saskatoon Western Development Museum

2610 Lorne Ave. S.
Saskatoon, SK S7J 0S6

☎ (306) 931-1910

Called "1910 Boomtown," the Saskatoon Western Development Museum tells the story of Saskatchewan's history and heritage. The museum contains the longest indoor museum street in Canada, recreating the atmosphere and style of 1910, a period of growth and immigration to the province. The photo studio and blacksmith shop are operational, so step in and enjoy watching the interpreters at their crafts. In addition to the street, you can view a large collection of agricultural equipment and transportation vehicles.

■ on-site; elementary grades; teaching materials

Fort Battleford National Historic Park 12

Box 70
Battleford, SK S0M 0E0

☎ (306) 937-2621

Courtesy of Fort Battleford National Historic Park

In 1876, a detachment of North-West Mounted Police was dispatched to the Battleford area to establish a post. This was a strategic location because large numbers of Cree people wintered here. About this time, the government was attempting to settle Natives on reserves, and anticipated some resistance; it was felt that a strong police presence would help. Life for the Native population in the 1880s was difficult. They had surrendered much of their land, and an unfortunate combination of harsh winters, crop failures, and nearly-obliterated buffalo herds had brought them close to starvation. In 1885, a number of frustrated and desperate Cree warriors, under the leadership of Chief Poundmaker, attacked the fort. In the summer, after the fighting ended, the warriors who had been involved in the siege of Battleford and the Frog Lake Massacre were found guilty of treason and were hanged. After that time, Fort Battleford remained peaceful. It was abandoned in 1924, but in 1951 the government declared it a national historic park. The fort, which has been meticulously restored to the 1880s period, is staffed by costumed interpreters who demonstrate life as it was at the time. Note the 20 kg (9-lb.) muzzle-loading rifle. Be sure to visit the ornately furnished commanding officer's residence. In the officers' quarters, see several vintage musical instruments, which would have been used by the NWMP band. During the summer months, a number of special activities will enhance your visit to the site.

▲ ■ on-site

North Battleford Western Development Museum 13

Junction of Hwy. 16 and Hwy. 40

✉

Box 183
North Battleford, SK S9A 2P1

☎ (306) 445-8033

The North Battleford Western Development Museum emphasizes Saskatchewan's agricultural heritage, its focus being Heritage Farm & Village. The outdoor museum features a village with over 30 homes and businesses of the 1920s. Many of the buildings are original structures moved from farms and towns around the province. Pay special attention to the farmstead at the edge of the village, where visitors can participate in farm life, planting and harvesting crops and caring for farm animals, all using the tools and methods of the 1920s. The site is next to the perfect symbol of its theme: a wheat pool grain elevator.

■ on-site; elementary grades

Batoche National Historic Park 14

✉

P.O. Box 999
Rosthern, SK S0K 3R0

☎ (306) 423-6227

As the fur trade spread west, French-Canadian voyageurs found wives among the Native women. Their children became known as the Métis. The Métis were an independent group for a long time, trading, freighting, raising cattle, and farming. By 1885, all three groups in the Northwest, the white, the Natives, and the

Métis, had serious grievances and were frustrated by government inaction. Firebrand leader Louis Riel declared a provisional government at the Métis settlement of Batoche. This brought a quick reaction. A Northwest Field Force was assembled and dispatched under Major General Frederick Middleton. The Battle of Batoche raged for three days, until the remaining Métis, outnumbered by Middleton's men and with little remaining ammunition, surrendered or fled. The Batoche site has been restored to the 1885 era. Stop first at the visitor centre where an informative audio-visual presentation, supplemented by a display of artifacts, will introduce you to the history of Batoche. Proceed to the Jean Caron, Sr., Farmhouse constructed in 1895 to replace the original destroyed by Middleton's troops. Of particular interest is the "zareba"; built by Middleton's force out of wagons pulled into a circle and reinforced by supply boxes, it served as an attack point by day and a defensive position by night. Don't miss the Métis Rifle Pits — the Métis stronghold during the siege. The cemetery outside the church contains the graves of Métis leader Gabriel Dumont, several of the Métis killed in the battle, and many of the original settlers. See as well the River Lot Farms and the remains of Batoche Village. Guides in period costume interpret some of the buildings on the site.

▲ ■

Duck Lake Regional Interpretive Centre 15

✉
Box 328
Duck Lake, SK S0K 1J0

☎ (306) 467-2057

On March 26, 1885, the first battle of the Northwest Rebellion was fought at Duck Lake, between the Métis under Gabriel Dumont and Louis Riel and the North-West Mounted Police. The battle lasted only 30 minutes, and the Métis were the clear winners in this first skirmish. The rebellion lasted until May, when the North-West Mounted Police put an end to the uprising at Batoche. The Duck Lake Regional Interpretive Centre interprets the history of the area. Visitors to the centre proceed through the exhibits in a circular pattern, which is intended to reflect the teepee, medicine wheel, and sun dance of the Native people. The first exhibits tell of the origins and ways of the Native people. The next set reflects the 19th century with its emphasis on settlement and survival, followed by displays that focus on religion and education, and then on the establishment of law and order, which dominated the late 19th and early 20th centuries. Proceed through a thematic exhibit on economics and commerce, to end up at the Heart of Canada's Old Northwest display area. Interactive technology helps bring the displays into focus. The gold watch and chain of Gabriel Dumont and a shotgun said to have belonged to Louis Riel are notable features. Be sure to see the tiny jail that stands next to the museum, and hear the story of Almighty Voice, one of the jail's most famous inmates.

▲ ■

The Right Honourable John G. and Olive Diefenbaker Museum 16a

246–19th St. W.

✉

c/o 1084 Central Ave.
Prince Albert, SK S6V KP3

☎ (306) 922-7320/922-9641

In 1924, a young lawyer moved to Prince Albert where he established a law practice. That young lawyer was John G. Diefenbaker, and in 1957 he became Canada's 13th prime minister, a post he held until 1963. Throughout his lengthy political career, he maintained a strong connection with his many friends and supporters in Prince Albert, and in 1975 he and his second wife,

Olive, transferred ownership of their home to the city, to be established as a museum. Many items on display are on loan from the John G. Diefenbaker Centre at the University of Saskatchewan; these exhibits are changed periodically.

■ guided tours

Fort Carlton Historic Park 16b

✉

c/o Saskatchewan Natural Resources
Prince Albert District, Box 3003
Prince Albert, SK S6V 6G1

☎ (306) 953-2322/787-2700

If you would like to take a trip back to the 19th century, then come to Fort Carlton. This was the era when the Hudson's Bay Company, with its seemingly insatiable demand for furs, held sway over western Canada, and the screech of Red River carts filled the air. The fort has been restored to the 1870s period, at which time it functioned as a major provisioning and transportation post for the Hudson's Bay Company. Begin your visit in the fort's visitor centre, with its informative displays; then proceed into the fort itself. See the shop where sails and harnesses were mended. In the fur and provisions store, the furs were graded, priced, and packed. The European goods, which were traded for furs, were kept in the trading shop. It was a most unpleasant place in the winter: because gunpowder was stored there, the clerks could not have a fire for warmth. Note the warehouse, the factor's house, and the quarters where the various employees were housed. For a time the North-West Mounted Police used the fort as a post, so their non-commissioned officers' quarters have also been restored. Interpretive staff are on hand to assist.

■ on-site

Prince Albert National Park 17

Box 100
Waskesiu Lake, SK S0J 2Y0

☎ (306) 663-5322

This park is noted for its pristine beauty and tranquility, but its most memorable feature is a one-room log cabin on the shores of Ajawaan Lake. This was the home of the famous naturalist and author known to many as Grey Owl. Grey Owl's original name was Archie Belaney. He was an Englishman who had emigrated to Canada in 1906 and adopted Native ways and a Native name for himself. It was here at Ajawaan Lake that he and his wife raised Jellyroll and Rawhide, the beaver pair featured in his writings, and it was here that he wrote of Native people, nature and wildlife, warning of the destruction that the relentless progress of European civilization would bring. Prince Albert Park is also the site of the graves of Grey Owl, his wife Anahareo, and their daughter Shirley Dawn.

Courtesy Prince Albert National Park/Parks Canada

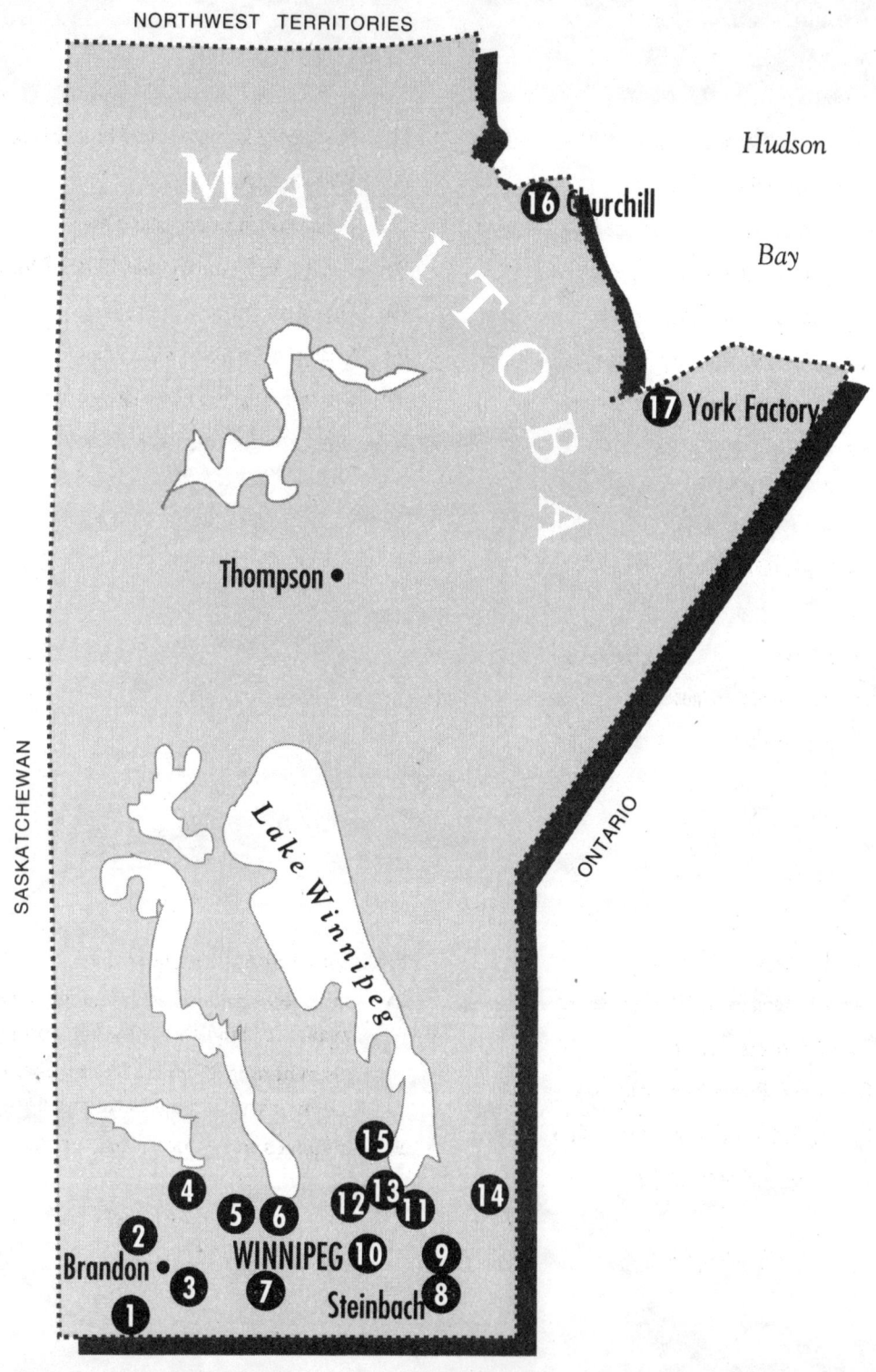

1	International Peace Garden	13c	St. Andrew's Rectory National Historic Park
2	Pheasantview Game Farm	14	Whiteshell Laboratories
3	Spruce Woods Provincial Heritage Park	15	Narcisse Wildlife Management Area
4	Margaret Laurence Home	16a	Prince of Wales Fort National Historic Park
5	Manitoba Agricultural Museum	16b	Cape Merry National Historic Site
6	Fort La Reine Museum and Pioneer Village	16c	Sloop's Cove National Historic Site
7	World's Largest Smoking Pipe	16d	Churchill, Manitoba "Polar Bear Capital of the World"
8	Mennonite Heritage Village	17	York Factory National Historic Site
9	Philip's Magical Paradise Museum of Magic and Illusion		
10a	Dalnavert Provincial and National Historic Site		
10b	The Forks		
10c	Fort Whyte Centre for Environmental Education		
10d	Manitoba Children's Museum		
10e	Living Prairie Museum		
10f	Manitoba Museum of Man and Nature		
10g	Leo Mol Sculpture Garden		
10h	Grant's Old Mill		
10i	Gabrielle Roy House		
10j	Riel House National Historic Park		
10k	Centre Culturel Franco-Manitobain		
11	Dugald Costume Museum		
12	Quarry Park Provincial Heritage Site		
13a	Lower Fort Garry National Historic Park		
13b	Marine Museum of Manitoba		

In the site descriptions, note that:

▲ indicates that second language services are available: English in Quebec and French elsewhere in Canada. Where "limited service" is given, it would be wise to call ahead for specifics

■ indicates that educational services are available

International Peace Garden

Box 419
Boissevain, MB R0K 0E0

Straddling the Canada-United States border, the International Peace Garden in Boissevain is the largest garden in the world dedicated to peace. The garden features beautiful formal gardens, an electrically operated floral clock, and breathtaking landscape. You can find a number of picnic areas as well. The Peace Chapel has three encircling stone walls, all engraved with quotations by great persons committed to the cause of peace. The Peace Tower represents people from the four corners of the globe. See the musical and dramatic performances in June and July. The beauty of the International Peace Garden may encourage us all to quietly consider the concept of peace.

Pheasantview Game Farm

Kenton, MB R0M 0Z0

☎ (204)838-2216

Old Macdonald's farm was never like this. Here, on 49 ha (120 a.), you can see exotic birds, llamas, donkeys, seven different kinds of sheep — including the rare four-horned Jacob sheep — pygmy goats, wild boars, many different breeds of rabbits, and much more. Picnic facilities are available. Come and make friends with a llama!

■ on-site

Spruce Woods Provincial Heritage Park 3

✉ Box 900
Carberry, MB R0K 0H0

☎ (204) 827-2543/834-3223

To experience some of the unique ecosystems of Manitoba, spend some time at Spruce Woods Provincial Heritage Park. Notable features of the park include the desertlike Spirit Sands. This tract of sand dunes covers 25 km² (10 sq. mi.) and is surrounded by hills. Here you will find lizards, snakes, and cacti indigenous to the area. See also the fancifully named Devil's Punch Bowl, a sunken pit created by the action of an underground stream. Enjoy a ride in a horse-drawn, covered wagon to these sites.

Margaret Laurence Home 4

312 First Ave.
Neepawa, MB R0J 1H0

☎ (204) 476-5157

In a tribute to Margaret Laurence on the occasion of her death in 1987, one admirer praised her as one of our national treasures. Margaret Laurence has earned herself a permanent and prominent place in the history of Canadian letters and, indeed, world literature. This beloved author was born in Neepawa on July 18, 1926, to Robert and Verna Wemyss. When Laurence was nine, her father died and the family moved to the house on First Ave., the home of her maternal grandfather. Laurence grew up in that house, staying in Neepawa until she graduated from high school and went to Winnipeg to attend university. The town of Manawaka, which is the setting of several of her novels, is patterned after Neepawa, and a film entitled *Our Kinda Talk: An Introduction to Margaret Laurence* makes clear the relationship between Neepawa and Manawaka. In the house are the Margaret

Laurence Room and the Margaret Laurence Reading Room, where a great selection of reading materials and videos are accessible to visitors.

Manitoba Agricultural Museum 5

P.O. Box 10
Austin, MB R0H 0C0

☎ (204) 637-2354

The Manitoba Agricultural Museum celebrates the strong agricultural heritage of the prairie provinces. This museum has the largest collection in North America of the huge "steam tractor engines," which were used to break up the prairie sod. See a number of buildings that preserve and present the past. The Ayr School, built originally in 1883, has been reconstructed complete with slates, teacher's platform, and a 150-year-old teacher's desk. The Westbourne Post Office (1902) displays postal artifacts from the turn of the century. Of particular interest is the Homesteaders' Village on the site. The village contains two churches reflecting two different styles of worship. Three residences show the progression of life on the prairies, from early log cabin to elegant manor with stained glass windows and adjoining living and dining rooms that could be converted into a ballroom. The Homesteaders' Village also contains a livery stable, an operational blacksmith's shop, and a grist mill. Every year the museum hosts the Threshermen's Reunion and Stampede, where participants demonstrate the agricultural practices of the past.

Fort la Reine Museum and Pioneer Village 6

✉ Box 744
Portage la Prairie
MB R1N 3C2

☎ (204) 857-3259

This museum is committed to the preservation of local heritage — and it was designed to be rustic. The main museum building houses artifacts of the local Native people and of the pioneers from local farms and villages. You can view a number of interesting displays and buildings in the pioneer village. See a log homestead, county church, schoolhouse, fort, and trading post, a York boat, Red River cart, fire hall and barn. As well, see the railway exhibit, which includes a caboose and a watchman's shack, as well as the Van Horne Car. This was the official business car of Sir William Van Horne, the builder of the CPR.

■ on-site

World's Largest Smoking Pipe 7

✉ c/o Gabrielle Cote, President
St. Claude Historical Society
38 Birch Ave.
Box 525
St. Claude, MB R0G 1Z0

☎ (204) 379-2228

St. Claude is home to the biggest smoking pipe in the whole world. And though it's roughly 6 m (20 ft.) long and 1.5m (5 ft.) high, it actually does smoke — real tobacco! It was built to commemorate the early settlers of the area, who came from St-Claude au Jura in France, a town whose main industry was the manufacture of pipes.

Mennonite Heritage Village 8

✉ Box 1136
Steinbach, MB R0A 2A0

☎ (204) 326-9661

In Manitoba, the Mennonite community numbers around 60 000. The Mennonite faith has its roots in 16th-century Switzerland, where a group of Christians sought to reform practices that they felt were not in keeping with the tenets of the Christian faith — such as killing someone as a means of settling a dispute. Steinbach's Mennonite Heritage Village is a living testimony to the culture and traditions of the Mennonites and their contribution to the development of Manitoba. You can visit 29 different sites in the village. A good place to begin is the village centre and artifacts building, which houses a number of informative displays telling the story of the Mennonites from the 1500s to the present. See a number of representative dwellings of the community: from the Semlin (the early sod and wood homes) to the log houses that followed and the traditional 18th-century combination house and barn. See as well the public school, the church, the windmill, the Agricultural Display Building and the Reimer Store. If you get hungry, the Livery Barn restaurant serves traditional Mennonite fare. Members of the Mennonite community staff the village.

■ on-site; elementary grades

Philip's Magical Paradise Museum of Magic and Illusion 9

✉ Box 63
Giroux, MB R0A 0N0

☎ (204) 326-1219

Abracadabra! Hocus Pocus! Giroux, Manitoba, is the site of western Canada's only museum of magic and illusion. This museum invites people to touch the displays, many of which have been donated by magicians from around the world. See the 50-cent piece that once belonged to the great Harry Houdini, and the Water-Torture Cell that was used by Doug Henning. Be prepared to have the museum's static machine make your hair stand on end, see the transformation in the Blue Room, and look through peep holes. Mannequins model well-known acts. Philip's Magical Paradise is the fulfilment of the final wish of young Philip Hornan, who died of cancer at the age of 15. Philip was a talented young magician who performed a number of escapes from jail cells across Canada. Be sure to see the RCMP cell from which Philip and his friend, magician Dean Gunnarson, once escaped. Although the museum does not collect an admission charge, donations are accepted, which will be given to children's charities.

Courtesy Philip's Magical Paradise Museum of Magic and Illusion

■ on-site

Dalnavert Provincial and National Historic Site 10a

61 Carlton St.
Winnipeg, MB R3C 1N7

☎ (204) 943-2835

Built in 1895, Dalnavert was the family home of Sir Hugh John Macdonald, premier of Manitoba in 1900, and the only son of Canada's first prime minister, Sir John A. Macdonald. Today Dalnavert is a peaceful and elegant museum, testimony to the lifestyle of the wealthy during the Victorian period in Winnipeg. The artifacts and furniture were donated by Manitoba families; as well, a number of original Macdonald family items were recovered and are on display. There is a curious point of interest in the basement: marks on the walls and in an enclosed corner. As police magistrate for the city of Winnipeg in 1911, Sir Hugh had a reputation for kindness and fairness, and it is said that he often brought vagrants home for a night's lodging. The marks might have been made by small beds. Dalnavert was named both for Sir Hugh's father's home in Toronto and his maternal grandmother's birthplace in Scotland.

■ on-site; outreach; all grades; teaching materials; guided tours

The Forks 10b

c/o The Forks Renewal Corporation
310–25 Forts Market Rd.
Winnipeg, MB R3C 4S8

☎ (204) 943-7752

The Forks' history extends back well over 6000 years. At this natural meeting place where the Red and Assiniboine rivers come together, Native tribes would come together to talk, to trade, and sometimes to fight. They were followed by French and Métis fur traders. The next wave to discover The Forks was Scottish settlers who established a community here. Called the Red River Settlement, in time it would become the city of Winnipeg. Interpretive displays, historical pageants and special events combine to make this one of the most exciting places to visit in Manitoba.

The Wall through Time. The Wall through Time is a graphic, linear display of events at The Forks through the centuries. Donated by the International Union of Bricklayers and Allied Craftsmen, Local No. 1, the Wall depicts great floods, battles, the era of the fur trade, and even the age of the dinosaurs for all to see. The displays are supplemented by interpretive text in English, French, and Cree.

Public Archaeology Program at The Forks. Come and be an amateur archaeologist for a day. Many interesting artifacts — from fur-trade artifacts to bones and fish scales that are about 6000 years old — have been uncovered here, and the work continues. Under the supervision of a team of professional archaeologists, you can participate in such activities as excavating, artifact cleaning, artifact identification, and computer operation. Who knows what stunning discovery you might make!

▲

Fort Whyte Centre for Environmental Education 10c

1961 McCreary Rd.

✉

P.O. Box 1241
Winnipeg, MB R3Y 1G5

☎ (204) 989-8358

Courtesy Fort Whyte Centre for Environmental Education

The Fort Whyte Centre for Environmental Education is "Open to Interpretation!" Take them up on their offer: come learn all about the world around you. Begin your visit in the interpretive centre. In the Aquarium of the Prairies, two distinct aquatic habitats are presented in Manitoba's largest freshwater aquarium. Move on to the Kiwanis Touch Museum, which invites you to "please touch" the coats of wolves, weasels, and waterfowl. When you enter the waterfowl room, be prepared for a cacaphony of sound — an assortment of quacks and honks will greet you. Here you will see some very busy bees (not to worry — the hive is enclosed by glass) and a number of three-dimensional prairie landscape exhibits. And maybe, just maybe, you'll be able to admire some newly hatched ducklings. If the weather is fine, continue your visit outside on the many trails, floating boardwalks through the marshes, and the marvellous waterfowl gardens, where Manitoba's different wetland habitats are animated with the waterfowl indigenous to each.

▲ ■   on-site; all grades

Manitoba Children's Museum   10d

Before April, 1994:
109 Pacific Ave.
Winnipeg, MB R3B 0M1

From June 1, 1994:
The Forks

✉

c/o The Forks Renewal Corporation
310–25 Forts Market Rd.
Winnipeg, MB R3C 4S8

☎ (204) 957-0005

It's definitely a kid's world at the Manitoba Children's Museum! Here, children are encouraged to touch, to try, and to explore the many different facets of our world. This will continue on an even bigger scale when the doors open to the new Manitoba Children's Museum at The Forks, June 1, 1994. Preschoolers can make discoveries about animals in their natural habitats, the weather and the seasons in The Tree and Me Gallery. Kids can jump on a 1952 vintage diesel locomotive, with its operating cab controls and live hook-up with the local railway yards. In the Sun Gallery, light and energy, art and mythology are waiting to be explored. If television is their medium, kids will love the television studio, equipped with cameras, monitors, a control desk with switcher/mixer, newsdesk, lighting, and audio controls — all updated and expanded in the new museum at The Forks. There's even a spaceship's bridge complete with 12 networked computers, star chart, solar energy exhibit, and a five-foot diameter topographic world globe. The permanent displays are supplemented by a number of temporary exhibits and special programs designed to appeal to the under-15 crowd.

▲ ■ on-site; grades K–9

Living Prairie Museum 10e

2795 Ness Ave.
Winnipeg, MB R3J 3S4

☎ (204) 832-0167

Courtesy Living Prairie Museum

You'll feel at home on the range at Winnipeg's Living Prairie Museum. Here, you will find a piece of what is known as Tall Grass or True Prairie, untouched since seen by La Verendrye, the first European explorer to come this far west. Learn how prairie is not just flat land but an ecosystem comprised of 151 native plant species (grasses and flowers) and wildlife. The reception centre has displays on prairie history and ecology. See the informative slide show and visit the observation deck. Naturalists are on hand to answer your questions, and guided hikes are offered.

■ on-site; grades K–9; teacher workshops

Manitoba Museum of Man and Nature 10f

190 Rupert Ave.
Winnipeg, MB R3B 0N2

☎ (204) 956-2830

Courtesy Manitoba Museum of Man and Nature

Can you imagine what life at the bottom of the ocean might have looked like 450 million years ago? Or what it would have been like to be one of the early explorers sailing into Arctic waters 300 years ago? Or perhaps you would have liked to be a buffalo hunter in the days when huge herds of the shaggy beasts roamed freely over the prairies. The Manitoba Museum of Man and Nature lets you explore these possibilities (and then some) through its galleries and interactive technology. The Orientation Gallery presents you with the fundamental theme of the museum: the interrelationship between people and the environment. Try the Arctic/Sub-Arctic Gallery to be introduced to the traditional ways of the Inuit and the Chipewyan people, or the Boreal Forest Gallery, which shows how a different ecology supports a different way of life. Visit the Urban Gallery to learn how Winnipeg has developed into a modern, thriving city. What does the future hold? Explore science, technology, art, and illusion in the Touch the Universe Science Gallery. Be sure to visit the planetarium as well. Its Star Theatre always has exciting and interesting presentations.

Leo Mol Sculpture Garden 10g

Assiniboine Park, Winnipeg

☎ (204) 986-3130

Artist Leo Mol's work has been commissioned by the governments of Canada, Manitoba, and Alberta — as well as the Vatican. The sculptures in the garden, cast in bronze, are organized into four thematic groups: religious leaders, prominent people, wildlife, and the human form. A gallery on the site contains a collection of Mol's porcelain, smaller sculptures, stained glass, and sketches. The beauty and tranquility of the sculpture garden is enhanced by a large reflecting pool and fountain in front of the garden gallery.

Grant's Old Mill 10h

2777 Portage Ave.
Winnipeg, MB R3K 1C5

☎ (204) 837-5761

Cuthbert Grant, a Métis leader, built Grant's Mill in 1829. It was the first water mill built in Manitoba. The mill has been reconstructed and today operates as it did in Grant's day, grinding grains such as triticale, rye, buckwheat, and red spring wheat into flour, which you may purchase. Staff conduct tours of the mill.

▲ ■ guided tours

Gabrielle Roy House 10i

375, rue Deschambault

✉ c/o La Société Historique de St-Boniface
C.P. 125, St-Boniface, MB R2H 3B4

☎ (204) 233-4888

Unfortunately for Gabrielle Roy's many admirers, the Gabrielle Roy House is under private ownership and therefore not open to the public. Roy, one of Canada's best-known and best-loved francophone authors, was born in St-Boniface in 1909 and spent her childhood in the rue Deschambault house. Her novels — *Bonheur d'Occasion (The Tin Flute), La Petite Poule d'Eau (Where Nests the Waterhen), Rue Deschambault (Street of Riches),* among others — reflect many of her experiences. Roy died in 1983 at the age of 74.

Riel House National Historic Park 10j

330 River Rd.

✉ Box 73
St-Vital, MB R2M 4A5

☎ (204) 257-1783

Louis Riel, the firebrand leader of the Northwest Rebellion in 1885, has been described as one of the most tragic and least understood figures in Canadian history. For a long time, the Métis, people of mixed Native and French ancestry, had lived peacefully in what is now Manitoba and Saskatchewan. When preparations began for the transfer of the Red River Settlement to Canada, the Métis felt that their way of life was in jeopardy. Louis Riel set up a provisional government to negotiate with Canada. He later led the uprising at Batoche, Saskatchewan, but when the rebellion was snuffed out, he was charged with treason and hanged. Riel never lived in the Riel house, which belonged to his mother. His body was brought back here after his death, and here it lay in state for two days before burial. The house, a frame farm house, has been restored and refurnished to its 1886 appearance, six months after Riel's death. Interpretive staff provide guided tours and explain the way of life of the Métis at that time.

▲ ■ all grades; on-site; teaching materials

Centre Culturel Franco-Manitobain 10k

340 boule. Provencher
St-Boniface, MB R2H 0G7

☎ (204) 233-8972

As a site that celebrates French history and heritage in Manitoba, the Centre Culturel Franco-Manitobain has become a centre for artistic exhibits and presentations of all kinds. Check the schedule, and then come to see art exhibits by regional artists, theatre, or concerts. The restaurant, Le Foyer, serves French-Canadian fare. Be sure to stop in the gift shop to look for souvenirs; you will find a variety of art and craft items for sale.

▲ French and English

Dugald Costume Museum 11

✉

Box 38
Dugald, MB R0E 0K0

☎ (204) 853-2166

Fashion provides an interesting commentary on society and custom, especially when preserved and displayed, as at the Dugald Costume Museum. At present, the collection consists of 20 000 artifacts from 1765 to the present. Each display has been

organized around a theme and
presented in a "tableau" where
mannequins are posed in a realistic
activity. See the clothing and fashion
accessories of men, women, and children.
Tour the museum's pioneer home,
which provides a glimpse into the
past of a local family, and take a
look at the visual storage room,
where plexi-covered drawers
and cases allow visitors to
see other items in the museum's
collection.

■ on-site

Courtesy Dugald Costume Museum

Quarry Park Provincial Heritage Site 12

Box 250
Stonewall, MB R0C 2Z0

☎ (204) 467-5354

The focal point of Quarry Park is the giant lime kilns found there. These kilns are almost 100 years old. While at the park, visit the museum and interpretive trails. The interpretive building on the site presents exhibits and a slide show that relates the human and natural history of the area and the importance of the quarries.

Lower Fort Garry National Historic Park 13a

Box 37, Group 343, R.R. 3
Selkirk, MB R1A 2A8

☎ (204) 482-6843 (Winnipeg line: 983-3600)

Lower Fort Garry is the oldest intact stone fur-trade post in North America. The fort was constructed by the Hudson's Bay Company in 1830 to meet the need for a major trading and provisioning outpost near the head of the Red and Assiniboine rivers. The fort did not do well, one reason being that it was easier for the inhabitants of the region to conduct business and trade at The Forks, which was the traditional meeting place. An industrial complex was developed in 1865, which boosted the fort's importance for a few years, but the decline of the fur trade in the 1870s spelled the end of any meaningful role for Lower Fort Garry. The fort, which has been restored with period furniture and other accoutrements, welcomes visitors. The visitor reception building contains a number of exhibits plus an audio-visual presentation in its theatre. The park itself contains 20 sites of importance, including the Big House (residence for the fort's governor and his family), a retail store, a fur loft, the doctor's office, and an industrial complex. The fort is interpreted by animators in period costume. Don't be surprised if you see the governor himself strolling about the grounds, ready to greet you and discuss the affairs of the settlement.

▲ ■

Marine Museum of Manitoba 13b

Box 7
Selkirk, MB R1A 2B1

☎ (204) 482-7761

Courtesy Marine Museum of Manitoba

You might be surprised to find a marine museum on the prairies, but the Marine Museum of Manitoba is testimony to the importance of freshwater navigation and related activities to Manitoba's history. SS *Keenora*, Manitoba's oldest steamship, is only one of the several ships featured; others are the *Granite Rock*, the historic icebreaker CGS *Bradbury*, the passenger ship and freighter MS *Chickama II*, the fish freighter MS *Northland Lady Canadian*, and MS *Peguis II*, a lake and river tug.

You can see the Black Bear Lighthouse (1898), as well as a York boat. York boats, powered by sail, were used extensively by fur traders to navigate the inland waterways to western Canada. A video presentation enhances your understanding of freshwater navigation and its accoutrements.

■ on-site

St. Andrew's Rectory National Historic Park 13c

Lower Fort Garry National Historic Park

✉

Box 37, Group 343, R.R. 3
Selkirk, MB R1A 2A8

☎ (204) 482-6843 (Winnipeg line: 983-3600)

In 1829, the same year that the site for Lower Fort Garry was selected, Presbyterian Church Missionary Society minister William Cockran arrived with his family to establish a new mission post. A skilled builder, Cockran soon had his mission station completed and went on to construct a multipurpose building: one room was set aside for worship; another was intended to be used for teaching; and an addition contained a kitchen, a store, and a dairy. By the summer of 1831, Cockran, along with his parishioners, began work on the first church. A fiery orator, Cockran's sermons were popular and he attracted worshippers from Lower Fort Garry, as well his own parish of St. Andrew's. In the meantime, he expanded the mission farm and gardens, and opened a day school "for the improvement of the religious, moral and industrial habits of the vicinity." In 1844, to accommodate his ambitious objectives, Cockran and his volunteer craftsmen and artisans began work on the stone church that stands today. St. Andrew's continues to be an active parish. Visitors are invited to see the church and to view the exhibits on the rectory's main floor.

▲

Whiteshell Laboratories 14

Atomic Energy of Canada Limited (AECL)
Pinawa, MB R0E 1L0

☎ (204) 753-2311

Whiteshell Laboratories, like its AECL partners in Ontario, welcomes visitors to its site, and offers a comprehensive tour to introduce you to nuclear energy. Learn how we use nuclear energy in the treatment of cancer; how food irradiation prolongs the shelf life of our food by destroying the bacteria and insects that make our fruits, vegetables, and other foodstuffs go bad; and how Canada has become a world leader in the development of nuclear energy for peaceful purposes.

▲ ■ on-site; films and teaching materials

Narcisse Wildlife Management Area 15

✉

c/o Department of Natural Resources
Box 6000
Gimli, MB R0C 1B0

☎ (204) 642-6078

Snakes alive! The snake dens of Narcisse in Manitoba's Interlake area draw scientists and naturalists from all over the world. Here, every spring, thousands upon thousands of red-sided garter snakes emerge from hibernation for their annual mating ritual. Scientists are particularly interested in these snakes because of their ability to withstand and adapt to extremes of temperature. Come to view the snakes at the end of April or early in May; a warm, sunny day brings them to the surface. Platforms over the snake pits have been constructed so you can view the snakes easily without disturbing them. Although there appears to be an endless supply of snakes here, these gentle, non-poisonous reptiles are seriously threatened. Snakeskin is still a popular fashion item, and "pickers" harvest as many of the creatures as they can in spite of the Manitoba government's attempts to stop them. Another hazard is the thoughtless interference of some of the many people who come to Narcisse to view the spring mating. The Narcisse Snake Dens, a natural wonder, are well worth a visit, but please respect the fragile ecosystem and obey the directives from the Department of Natural Resources.

■ on-site

Prince of Wales Fort National Historic Park 16a

c/o Parks Canada
Box 127
Churchill, MB R0B 0E0

☎ (204) 675-8863

In the 18th century, the Hudson's Bay Company, ever-hungry for new sources of trade, cast its eyes to the north and saw opportunities for whaling, exploration and trade in furs with the Inuit, Dene, and Chipewyan. Accordingly, construction on what would become Prince of Wales Fort began in 1717, but the job would not be complete for another 40 years. When finished, the fort was state-of-the-art, a star-shaped stone flanker. With the harsh climate and the isolation of the site, life at the fort was hard. Nonetheless the company persevered to establish and maintain trade with the northern Natives. The fort was destroyed in 1782 by a French naval force led by the Comte de la Perouse. Now partially restored and boasting the only full complement of original cannon in North America, the fort welcomes visitors to contemplate this remnant of an important chapter in our history. Guided tours are offered.

▲ limited service

Cape Merry National Historic Site 16b

c/o Parks Canada
Box 127
Churchill, MB R0B 0E0

☎ (204) 675-8863

Located across the river mouth from Prince of Wales Fort, Cape Merry was intended to supplement the defences of the fort. It accommodated six cannon that could blast any hostile ships approaching on the Churchill River. Built in 1746, it was named after Captain John Merry, governor of the Hudson's Bay Company from 1712 to 1728. Visitors to the site can see the stone battery, a cannon, and part of a powder magazine. Bird watchers and naturalists will find much to delight them as well; in June and July, beluga whales frequent the river.

▲ limited service   ■ guided tours

Sloop's Cove National Historic Site 16c

c/o Parks Canada
Box 127
Churchill, MB R0B 0E0

☎ (204) 675-8863

Sloop's Cove is located just 2 mi. (3 km) upriver from Prince of Wales Fort. During the heyday of the Hudson's Bay Company, Sloop's Cove served an important function. As a natural harbour, it could provide shelter from ice ridges and storms, so HBC personnel came there to moor and repair the small craft (sloops) they used for northern whaling and trading expeditions with the Inuit. Be sure to take note of the signatures, etched into the rock, of Hudson's Bay Company employees — including Samuel Hearne, who journeyed from Fort Prince of Wales to the Arctic Ocean in search of the Northwest Passage in the late 1700s. Naturalists also find Sloop's Cove interesting. Here they see an excellent example of what is called land uplift. The melting of the glaciers of the last ice age removed a tremendous weight from the earth's surface, and the land has been rising steadily since. Thus the cove, a beach in the 1700s, is now too far out of the water to be useful to boats as a landing place.

▲ limited service

Churchill, Manitoba
"Polar Bear Capital of the World" 16d

✉

c/o Environment Canada Parks Service
Box 127
Churchill, MB R0B 0E0

☎ (204) 675-8863

Churchill is located far enough north to be in polar bear country, and a visit to Churchill can provide you with an opportunity to sight one of these magnificent white creatures. This area has the densest concentration of polar bears in the world. The best time for sightings is the late fall. With the onset of winter, bears begin to move north along the coast of Hudson Bay, where they wait for the water to freeze. They can then go out on the ice to hunt seal. Do not go off in search of polar bears by yourself; polar bears, if hungry, may attack human beings. Go on one of the many fine organized tours available out of Churchill, conducted in heated, bear-proof "Tundra Buggies" and led by experienced naturalists.

York Factory National Historic Site

c/o Parks Canada
Box 127
Churchill, MB R0B 0E0

☎ (204) 675-8863

York Factory, built in 1670, was the grand storehouse of the Northwestern fur trade. It was fought over for many years by the French and English. But you might find it hard to believe that this place, once described as "a monstrous blot on a swampy spot, with a partial view of the frozen sea," was the cause of several sea battles until 1713, when the Treaty of Utrecht ceded it to the British. What had begun as a fur trading post then evolved into a manufacturing centre and the administrative centre of the Hudson's Bay Company. At its peak, York Factory was quite elegant, containing more than 50 buildings, including a doctor's house, an Anglican church, a hospital, a school, a photographic room and a library. Of this major trading centre, only the "Kichewaskahikun," the depot or great house, is still intact.

▲ limited service

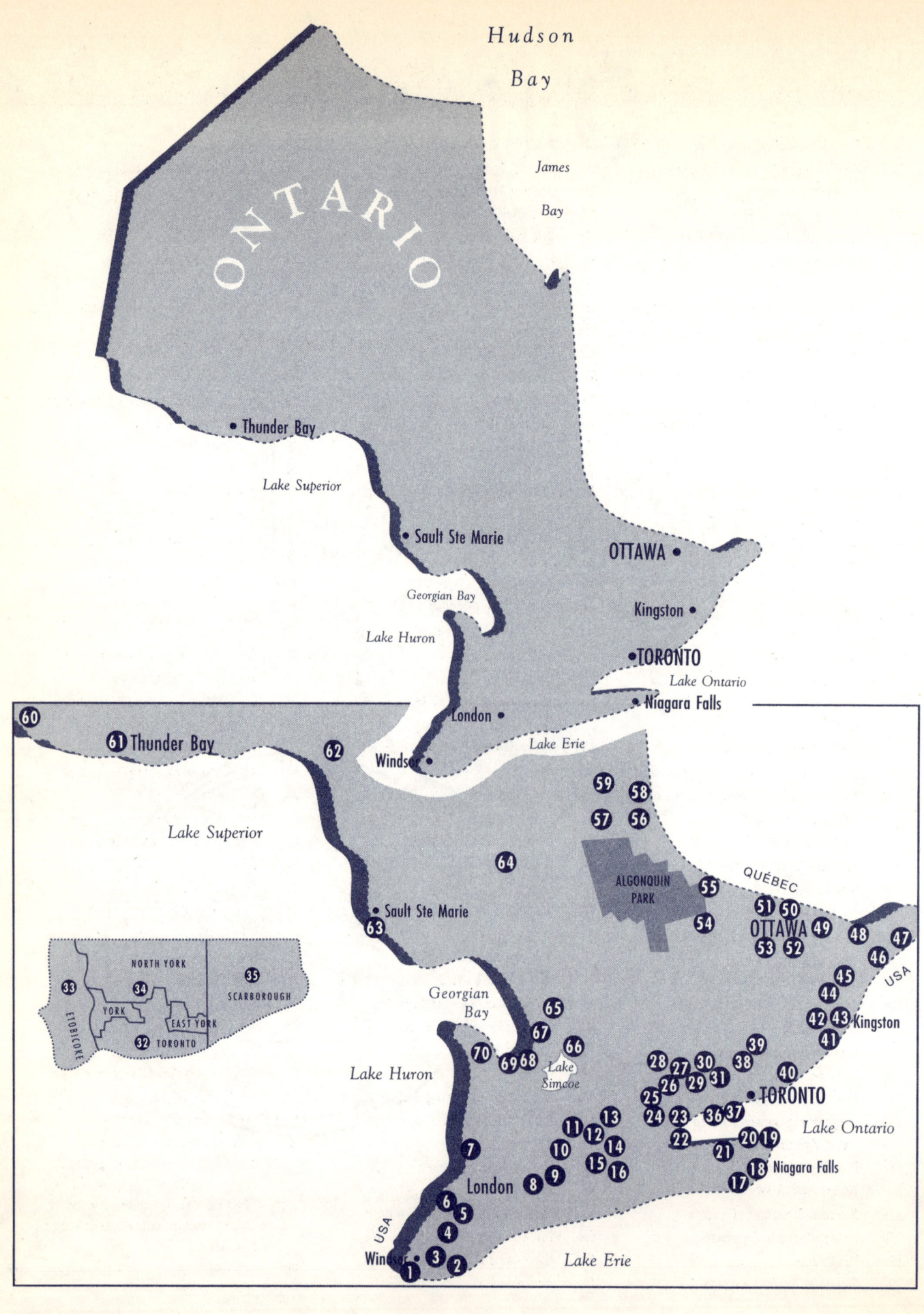

1a	Fort Malden National Historic Site	30	David Dunlap Observatory	49a	Bytown Museum
1b	North American Black Historical Museum and Cultural Centre	31	Thornhill Antique Clock Museum	49b	The Canadian Museum of Caricature
		32a	Addiction Research Foundation Museum	49c	The Bank of Canada's Currency Museum
2	Point Pelee National Park	32b	Art Gallery of Ontario	49d	Canadian Museum of Nature
3	John R. Park Homestead and Essex Region Conservation Authority	32c	Bata Shoe Museum	49e	Canadian Ski Museum
		32d	Black Creek Pioneer Village	49f	The Canadian War Museum
4	Uncle Tom's Cabin	32e	Canada's Sports Hall of Fame	49g	Central Experimental Farm
5	Oil Museum of Canada	32f	Casa Loma	49h	Laurier House National Historic Site
6	The Petrolia Discovery	32g	CN Tower	49i	Museum of Canadian Scouting
7	Huron Historic Gaol	32h	Colborne Lodge	49j	National Aviation Museum
8a	Banting Museum and Education Centre	32i	George Brown House	49k	National Gallery of Canada
8b	Fanshawe Pioneer Village	32j	Historic Fort York	49l	National Museum of Science and Technology
8c	The London Regional Children's Museum	32k	Hockey Hall of Fame	49m	Royal Canadian Mint
9	Ingersoll Cheese Factory Museum	32l	Mackenzie House	49n	Parliament Hill
10	Stratford Festival	32m	Marine Museum	50	Storyland
11	The Maple Syrup Museum	32n	Norman Elder Museum	51	Bonnechere Caves
12a	Woodside National Historic Site	32o	Ontario Place	52	Bon Echo Provincial Park
12b	Doon Heritage Crossroads	32p	Royal Ontario Museum	53	Petroglyphs Provincial Park
12c	Joseph Schneider Haus	32q	SkyDome	54	Algonquin Park
13	McCrae House	32r	Spadina	55a	Atomic Energy of Canada Limited Research Laboratories
14	African Lion Safari	32s	Toronto's First Post Office		
15	Bell Homestead	32t	The Toronto Stock Exchange	55b	Petawawa National Forestry Reserve
16	Six Nations Tourist Sites	33	Montgomery's Inn	56	Samuel de Champlain Provincial Park
17a	Mildred M. Mahoney Silver Jubilee Doll's House Gallery	34a	Ontario Science Centre	57	The Dionne Quints Museum
		34b	Holocaust Education and Memorial Centre of Toronto	58	Cobalt's Northern Ontario Mining Museum
17b	Historic Fort Erie			59	Underground Gold Mine Tour
18a	Lundy's Lane Historical Museum	34c	Todmorden Mills Heritage Museum and Arts Centre	60	White Otter Castle
18b	Marineland			61a	Amethyst Mine Panorama
18c	Niagara Falls Imax Theatre and Daredevil Gallery and Museum	35	Metro Toronto Zoo	61b	Old Fort William
		36	Cullen Gardens and Miniature Village	62	Winnie-the-Pooh Statue
18d	Tivoli Miniature World	37	Darlington Generating Station	63	Fort St. Joseph National Historic Site
19	Mackenzie Heritage Printery	38a	Lang Pioneer Village	64	Science North
20a	Shaw Festival	38b	Serpent Mounds Provincial Park	65	Bethune Memorial House
20b	Fort George	39	Hutchison Park	66	Steven Leacock Museum
21	St. Catharines Museum and Welland Canal Viewing Complex	40	Fort Kente	67	Huronia Museum and Huron Indian Village
		41	The Loyalist Cultural Centre	67b	Historic Naval and Military Establishments
22a	Art Gallery of Hamilton	42	Historic Babcock Mills	67c	Ste-Marie Among the Hurons
22b	Canadian Football Hall of Fame and Museum	43a	Bellevue House National Historic Site	68	Simcoe County Museum
22c	Dundurn Castle	43b	Canadian Forces Communications and Electronics Museum	69	Nancy Island Historic Site
22d	Hamilton Children's Museum			70	The Billy Bishop Museum
22e	Hamilton Museum of Steam and Technology	43c	Fort Henry	71	Fathom Five National Marine Park
23	Royal Botanical Gardens	43d	MacLachlan Woodworking Museum		
24a	Crawford Lake Conservation Area	43e	Marine Museum of the Great Lakes at Kingston		
24b	Ontario Agricultural Museum				
25	Peel Heritage Complex	44	Kingston Mills Blockhouse		
26	Wildcare Wildlife Rehabilitation Centre	45	Old Stone Mill		
27a	McMichael Canadian Art Collection	46a	The Battle of the Windmill Historic Site		
27b	Kortright Centre for Conservation	46b	Fort Wellington National Historic Site		
28	Puck's Farm	47	Upper Canada Village		
29	Paramount Canada's Wonderland	48	Watson's Mill		

In the site descriptions, note that:

▲ indicates that second language services are available: English in Quebec and French elsewhere in Canada. Where "limited service" is given, it would be wise to call ahead for specifics

■ indicates that educational services are available

Fort Malden National Historic Site 1b

100 Laird Ave.

✉

P.O. Box 38,
Amherstburg, ON N9V 2Z2

☎ (519) 736-5416

Determined to defend Canada from any incursions by the upstart Americans, in the 18th century the British built a string of forts at strategic points in Upper Canada (now Ontario). Fort Malden, originally called Fort Amherstburg, was built in 1796 near the mouth of the Detroit River, and became a centre for British operations during the War of 1812. It was destroyed by the British themselves when they were forced to retreat in 1813. Subsequently, the Americans briefly occupied the fort and began the task of its reconstruction. The fort once again served as a redoubt during the 1837 Upper Canada Rebellion. Its glorious military past was clouded, however, when it was converted to the Malden Lunatic Asylum in 1859, and later to a lumberyard and planing mill. Visitors to the reconstructed Fort Malden are given a good understanding of life in a British fort in the early years of the 19th century, as well as a glimpse at some of the buildings that serviced the fort during its later incarnations. The Hough House, for example, served as a laundry and bakery for the insane asylum. The Military Pensioner's Cottage has been fully restored, as has the Brick Barrack. In many other cases, the outlines, remnants, and excavations are clearly visible.

▲ including teaching materials

■ on-site; all grades; information kits and teaching materials for post-visit lessons and classroom activities

North American Black Historical Museum and Cultural Centre 1b

277 King St.

✉

P.O. Box 12
Amherstburg, ON N9V 2C7

☎ (519) 736-5433

Before the American Civil War put an end to slavery in the United States, the words of a popular folk song, "Follow the drinkin' gourd," were recognized by slaves as a code for the escape route to freedom: north to Canada. Between 1800 and 1860, 30 000 to 60 000 slaves travelled by the Underground Railroad to freedom in Canada. Many of the fugitives entered by way of the Detroit River into Amherstburg. Many members of the black community in this area are descendants of the original freedom-seekers who travelled this always uncertain, frequently treacherous route. The museum and centre has a permanent display of the Underground Railroad, as well as many items and artifacts that are testimony to the contributions of the black community to the area over the years.

■ site-tours; outreach speakers

Point Pelee National Park 2

Hwy. 77

✉

R.R. 1
Leamington, ON N8H 3V4

☎ (519) 322-2365

A birder's and naturalist's delight, Point Pelee enjoys the distinction of being the southernmost tip of Canada's mainland, in the same latitude as northern California. The park contains a unique combination of forest, marsh, beach, and field.

An important stopover for migrating birds, the park attracts many human visitors as well, who enjoy walking along the extensive boardwalk over the marshes. Look carefully for the many species of bird, frog, and other wildlife. Little propane-powered "trains" are available to transport you to the tip of the park, where you can sit on the sandy beaches or swim in Lake Erie. The currents can be treacherous, so take care to stay within the designated areas. If at all possible, try to time your visit to Point Pelee for the fall, when the annual migration of monarch butterflies occurs. The butterflies stop at Point Pelee, transforming the park into an autumn panorama of black and orange.

▲ ■ on-site; all grades; on-site teacher's activity kits; teacher workshops for senior high programs

John R. Park Homestead & Essex Region Conservation Authority

360 Fairview Ave. W.
Essex, ON N8M 1Y6

☎ (519) 776-5209

In the early 1820s, an American, John R. Park, and his older brother Thomas emigrated to Upper Canada. They were later joined by a third brother, Theodore, and together they built up a very successful shipping and trading business. Thomas and Theodore moved to Amherstburg, but John married and remained in Essex to manage the store, farm, and sawmill. The homestead has been restored to its 19th-century appearance, reflecting the way of life of the Parks. Visitors may visit the house, built in the Classical Revival style, and taste baking from the kitchen fireplace. The sawmill, powered by a working 1885 steam engine, cuts lumber, while the blacksmith shop attends to small repairs. Your visit should include a stop at the working smokehouse, the icehouse, the barn, and the stable to see the farm animals.

■ grades 1–10; on-site at both the John R. Park Homestead and Essex Region Conservation Area

Uncle Tom's Cabin 4

Kent County Rd. 40

✉

R.R. 5
Dresden, ON N0P 1M0

☎ (519) 683-2978

Uncle Tom's Cabin, Harriet Beecher Stowe's classic novel of black slavery in the United States, recounts the life of Reverend Josiah Henson. Born in the state of Maryland, Henson, a Methodist minister, escaped to Canada in 1830 by way of the Underground Railroad to settle near Dresden, Ontario, with his wife and children. The site consists of six buildings, including the Josiah Henson House (Uncle Tom's Cabin), a church, a sawmill, a museum, and a building that was used to house fugitive slaves. Artifacts on display in the museum remind us of the cruelty and intolerance of a not-so-distant era: see handcuffs, cast-iron manacles, bullwhips, and neck harnesses. And if Canadian visitors are tempted to point accusing fingers at the United States, they should note the Toronto newspaper advertisement offering a black woman and her son for sale. The clipping is dated February 10, 1806.

Oil Museum of Canada 5

Kelly Rd.

✉

R.R. 2, Box 16
Oil Springs, ON N0N 1P0

☎ (519) 834-2840

In 1862, oil gushed and flowed at Oil Springs near Sarnia, and the people were jubilant! For the first time, "black gold" was discovered in Canada; Oil Springs would become the site of the first oil well in North America. The Oil Museum of Canada is located at the site of William's Well, the first well to produce oil commercially. Outside the museum building, on its beautifully landscaped grounds, William's Well has been reconstructed. See the other working wells on display, and the exhibits explaining the process of extracting oil from the earth. Inside the museum building, displays portray the history of oil from its geological formation to the present. This comprehensive museum also gives visitors the opportunity to understand the evolution of equipment used in the industry, the development of the refinement process, the importance of oil internationally, and what life was like in an oil town during the 1860s.

The Petrolia Discovery 6

Tank St.

Box 1480
Petrolia, ON N0N 1R0

☎ (519) 882-0897

As the name suggests, the town of Petrolia owes its existence to the oil and gas industry. In 1865, Captain Bernard King discovered a huge oil field near Petrolia; the resulting boom lasted more than 30 years. The Petrolia Discovery takes a fascinating look at an industry that has been responsible for individual wealth, global rivalries and tensions, and technology in the 20th century. Displays at the site feature a boom town and explanations of oil-production technology and methods, including gum bed, cribbed well, spring pole, Canadian Rig, and jerker line system. Be sure to stop at the Fitzgerald Rig. Built in 1903 and still the largest pumping rig in the world, it has been pumping continuously for almost 100 years.

- audio-visual presentation; guided tours

Huron Historic Gaol 7

110 North St.
Goderich, ON N7A 2T8

☎ (519) 524-6971

Go directly to Jail! Do not pass Go! Do not collect $200!
The lines from a favourite board game come to mind when visiting the Huron Historic Gaol (pronounced jail). Though it's an interesting place to visit, one wouldn't want to take up residence as an inmate. Built between 1839 and 1842, the structure has an unusual octagonal shape with walls 60 cm (2 ft.) thick and 5.5 m (18 ft.) high, enclosing exercise yards and gardens. A tour of the gaol includes various day rooms and cell blocks, the turnkey's quarters, the infirmary for examining and treating prisoners, the holding cells, and the gaoler's office. A passage leads to the governor's residence, whose luxurious appointments contrast sharply with the bleakness of the gaol. Among the gaol's residents over the years was one James Donnelly of nearby Lucan, Ontario's "Black Donnellys."

Banting Museum and Education Centre
8a

442 Adelaide St. N.
London, ON N6B 3H8

☎ (519) 673-1752

On July 7, 1989, Her Majesty Queen Elizabeth, The Queen Mother, lit the Flame of Hope, which burns brightly in Sir Frederick G. Banting Square as a beacon of hope and inspiration for the millions of diabetics around the world who owe their lives to a London physician, Sir Frederick G. Banting. Adjacent to the square, find the Banting Museum and Education Centre, the house where Banting lived and practised medicine in the early 1920s before he and his colleague, Dr. Charles Best, discovered insulin. The museum includes a restored 1920s doctor's office and a recreated World War I battlefield casualty area. Banting had served in the Great War and was awarded a Military Cross for valour. Other displays explain the discovery of insulin, the many contributions of Banting and his colleagues, and the times in which they lived. It is a fitting tribute to the Canadian physician, who once said of his discovery, "Insulin doesn't belong to me; it belongs to the world."

▲ ■ guided tours

Fanshawe Pioneer Village 8b

Fanshawe Park Rd., R.R. 5
London, ON N6A 4B9

☎ (519) 457-1296

Set on 16 ha (40 a.) in the Fanshawe Conservation Area, Fanshawe Pioneer Village is like a time capsule preserved from the 19th century. Inhale the exhilarating fragrance of herbs from an authentic herb garden that provided seasonings and spices for baking and cooking. Listen to the ring of the blacksmith's hammer. Note the costumed interpreters engaged in the daily tasks and routines of another era, and, if you feel so inclined, try your hand at broom making or candle dipping. See the replica of the original building where *The London Free Press* — one of Canada's last independent daily newspapers — was first published, as well as the Peel House, the boyhood home of artist Paul Peel. Children will be fascinated by the replicas and restorations of schools in the village.

■ on-site

The London Regional Children's Museum 8c

21 Wharncliffe Rd. S.
London, ON N6J 4G5

☎ (519) 434-5726

The London Regional Children's Museum presents children with a wonderful opportunity to explore their world through interactive displays in seven exciting galleries. In the Street Where You Live, you can climb down into a sewer or deliver a letter. Costumes and crafts help to bring dinosaurs to life, while budding scientists can practise making their hair stand on end. Explore the world of the Inuit by playing Inuit games and by learning to write your name in Inuktitut. Future Marc Garneaus and Roberta Bondars can take their very own minivoyage into outer space. Children are invited to visit the whole museum and to stay as long as they want. In addition to the galleries, the museum offers special exhibits and a calendar of special events.

▲ ■ on-site; outreach; museum resource kits

Ingersoll Cheese Factory Museum 9

P.O. Box 340
Ingersoll, ON N5C 3V3

☎ (519) 485-0120

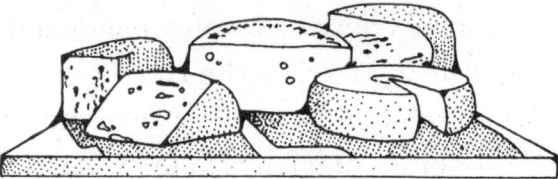

Regardless of how you like your cheese — wedges of tart cheddar to complement an apple pie, or melted mozzarella smothering a juicy pizza — the Ingersoll Cheese Factory Museum helps you to understand how cheese comes into being. This reconstructed cheese factory houses antique cheese-making equipment from area businesses, and outlines the important role cheese production has played in Oxford County. Other buildings on the site include an agricultural barn with farm-machinery displays, a blacksmith shop, and a community museum.

■ guided tours and demonstrations; cheese-making video

Stratford Festival 10

55 Queen St.

✉

P.O. Box 520
Stratford, ON N5A 6V2

☎ (519) 271-4040 (administration);
ext. 278 (archives);
ext. 319 (education dept.)

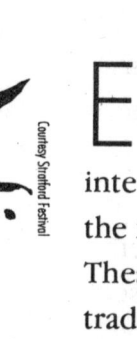

Every year, hundreds of thousands of tourists from all over North America flock to the pretty hamlet of Stratford, with the intention of soaking up some culture. From May until November, the festival's three theatres (the Festival Theatre, the Avon Theatre, and the Tom Patterson Theatre) offer a selection of traditional and avant-garde drama, including, of course, pieces by the Bard himself, William Shakespeare. Many local attractions, such as the art gallery, the exhibit of costumes, and other events, make a visit to Stratford a comprehensive and enriching experience.

■ guided tours; school visits; teaching materials

The Maple Syrup Museum 11

Spring St. S.
St. Jacobs, ON N0B 2N0

Each year in the early spring, when the sun starts to feel warm, the annual ritual of "sugaring off" begins. At the Maple Syrup Museum in the quaint Mennonite village of St. Jacobs, the history of the maple syrup industry is on display, along with the equipment used from early times to the present. Don't be surprised if pancakes and maple syrup turn up on your weekend breakfast table!

Woodside National Historic Site 12a

528 Wellington St. N.
Kitchener, ON N2H 5L5

☎ (519) 742-5273

Built in 1853 by James Colquhoun, a British barrister, Woodside was occupied by the King family from 1886 until 1893, making it the boyhood home of Canada's 10th prime minister, William Lyon Mackenzie King. Every effort has been made to recreate the setting in which Mackenzie King grew up. Each of the rooms has been fully restored and contains many of the original King family possessions. The basement of the house contains a theatre, as well as displays relating to the life of Mackenzie King and life during the Victorian era in Kitchener (called Berlin at that time). Costumed interpreters on hand will answer questions, provide interesting information, and help animate the many special events that occur at Woodside during the course of the year.

▲ ■ on-site; all grades; resource materials

Doon Heritage Crossroads 12b

Corner of Homer Watson and Huron Rds.

✉

R.R. 2
Kitchener, ON N2G 3W5

☎ (519) 748-1914

Described quite accurately as a "living history village," Doon Heritage Crossroads invites the visitor to "walk along a country lane across a covered bridge to join the villagers and farmers at the start of the twentieth century." Mennonites originally settled the area, and their influence is evident. As you wander through the village, note the railway station, the Peter Martin farm, the weavery, the dry goods and grocery store, the Baechler sawmill, and many other interesting sites. Stop and chat with the costumed interpreters, who are happy to answer questions and explain what they are doing. Demonstrations of pioneer crafts and ways and a calendar of special events help to make a visit to Doon an enriching experience.

▲ limited service   ■ on-site; all grades

Joseph Schneider Haus 12c

466 Queen St. S.
Kitchener, ON N2G 1W7

☎ (519) 742-7752

Joseph Schneider's large family is generally thought to have been the first Mennonite family to settle in the Kitchener area. Restored, with replicas of 1850s furniture made by local craftspeople, the haus invites visitors to get a real taste of life on a Pennsylvania German farm. Visitors are welcome to help out in the kitchen or to watch the costumed interpreters at their seasonal activities: butchering, sheep shearing, quilting, corn husking and so on, or to examine the displays.

▲ limited service   ■ on-site; all grades; resource kits

McCrae House 13

108 Water St.
Guelph, ON N1G 1A6

☎ (519) 836-1482

Since 1918, generations of Canadian schoolchildren have remembered the end of World War I on November 11 with a recitation: "In Flanders' fields the poppies blow/Between the crosses, row on row . . . ." John McCrae, a Canadian physician, wrote the poem while a member of the Canadian Army Medical Corps. McCrae House, now a museum and National Historic Site, is his birthplace and the house where he grew up. Displays trace the life and career of John McCrae, and the adoption of the poppy as a symbol of remembrance. Of particular interest are the many species of poppy that bloom in the surrounding gardens and memorial park. McCrae died of double pneumonia in France on January 28, 1918. He is buried in Boulogne.

■ lectures; slide presentations; guided tours

African Lion Safari 14

Safari Road, R.R. 1
Cambridge, ON N1R 5S2

☎ (519) 623-2620

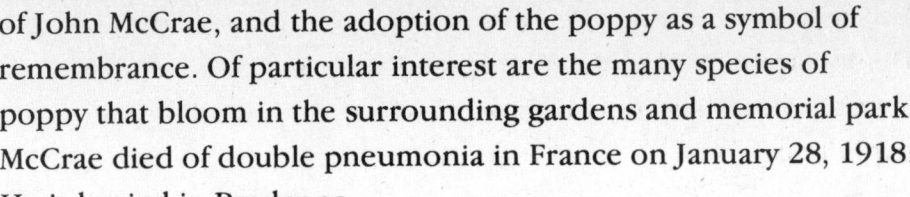

Courtesy African Lion Safari

The only shooting you'll do on this safari is with a camera. Whether you travel in your own car or in the Safari's own special buses, you'll want to have lots of film and a good vantage point for this unique close-up of some of the world's most exotic wildlife. Drive at a leisurely pace so as not to miss the family of lions snoozing to one side or the bears lumbering around the corner. Keep the windows closed or a nosy giraffe may stick his head in to inspect your passengers. The noise you hear on the roof is a mischievous gang of monkeys looking to check you out! If you time your visit right, you can enjoy some of the special events, such as the Birds of Prey Flying Demonstration, the Parrot Paradise Show, and the Elephant Bathing.

■ on-site; study guides

Bell Homestead 15

94 Tutela Heights Rd.
Brantford, ON N3T 1A1

☎ (519) 756-6220

On August 10, 1876, with the simple words, "To be or not to be," Alexander Graham Bell, inventor of the telephone, single-handedly launched the era of telecommunications at his parents' home in Brantford, Ontario. In a peaceful, woody setting overlooking the Grand River, the Bell Homestead has been preserved as a National Historic Site. Much of the original furniture is in place, and costumed interpreters guide visitors through the rooms of the charming white stucco house. Next to the homestead is the Henderson House, site of the first telephone business office. On display are several examples of telephone equipment dating from Bell's day to the present.

■ guided tours; teacher's tour-planner kit; newsletter

Six Nations Tourist Sites 16a

c/o General Delivery
Ohsweken, ON N0A 1M0

☎ (519) 445-4528

De Dwa Yea Nah ("Come Join Us") is the welcome extended by the Six Nations of the Grand River to several historic sites located near Brantford, Ontario.

Chiefswood Mansion is a literary shrine and museum dedicated to the memory of Emily Pauline Johnson, the celebrated Mohawk princess and poet. Pauline's father, Mohawk Chief George H.M. Johnson, built Chiefswood Mansion in 1835 as a wedding gift for his English bride, Emily Susan Howells.

St. Paul's, Her Majesty's Chapel of the Mohawks has the dual distinction of being the oldest Protestant church in Ontario and the only royal chapel outside the United Kingdom. Buried at the site are the remains of Captain Joseph Brant, leader of the

Mohawks, for whom the city of Brantford is named. Next to Brant's tomb see a memorial to the Native poet and princess Pauline Johnson. Visitors will enjoy the spectacular view of the ox-bow in the Grand River, where the Natives disembarked from their canoes before attending services, and the eight stained-glass windows. Each window depicts an event in the history of the Six Nations people.

Woodland Cultural Centre 16b

184 Mohawk St.

✉

P.O. Box 1506
Brantford, ON N3T 5V6

☎ (519) 759-2650

This museum and gallery invites the visitor to explore the history and culture of the Six Nations people, beginning with the Iroquoian and Algonquian prehistoric past, through the arrival of the Europeans, to the present. Note the replicated interior of a 19th-century longhouse, and the Indian Hall of Fame. Stop in the museum shop to purchase crafts created by Canada's First Nations artisans. Check the calendar of events for special programs, such as the annual Snowsnake Tournament in February.

■ themed and seasonal programs; guided tours

Mildred M. Mahoney
Silver Jubilee Dolls' House Gallery 17a

657 Niagara Blvd.
Fort Erie, ON L2A 3H9

☎ (905) 871-5833

When she was little, Mildred Mahoney dreamed of owning a dollhouse, a perfect little home and playground for the imagination. Her first dollhouse was an orange crate, acquired with pride during the Depression. Today, she presides over a collection of dollhouses valued at nearly $2 million. When you visit the Dolls' House Gallery, you enter a realm that stimulates and delights the imagination. There are many displays; Mahoney's favourite is the five-storey Marygate House, based on an 1810 English manor house, complete with authentic German Biedermeier furniture, tiny hand-blown wine bottles, and miniature musical instruments. The 17th-century Louis XIV *Cage d'oiseau*, built of wood and iron and modelled on Versailles, boasts 44 stained-glass windows. A Dutch dollhouse, an 1840 sea captain's house, has a hoist for lifting goods directly off barges and into the third-floor rooms, and a tiny washroom hidden under the stairs. The keystone of Mahoney's collection is a replica of the Ancient House of Ipswich. The original 16th-century building hid King Charles II of England after his return from exile in France more than 450 years ago. It features a 4 cm (1 1/2 in.), 24-karat gold statue of Queen Elizabeth II riding sidesaddle. The largest dollhouse, a miniature general store 2 m (6 ft.) long, has a 5000-item inventory.

Historic Fort Erie 17b

Niagara Pkwy. Fort Erie

c/o The Niagara Parks Commission
P.O. Box 150
Niagara Falls, ON L2E 6T2

☎ (905) 356-2241

Fort Erie was one of the forts built by the British to safeguard Upper Canada from an American incursion. The site of a bloody siege that ended in the defeat of the British forces, much of the fort has been restored and is open to visitors. As you walk about the site, note the monument, set atop a mass grave, to honour those who defended the fort. To capture a sense of what it was like to live during those critical days, visit the period rooms, exhibits, and demonstrations by costumed historical interpreters.

- all grades; history and social sciences; on-site; special overnight programs; outreach

Lundy's Lane Historical Museum 18a

5810 Ferry St.
Niagara Falls, ON L2G 1S9

☎ (905) 358-5082

All Ontario schoolchildren can tell you about the War of 1812-14. And much of that memorable conflict took place in and around Niagara Falls! Lundy's Lane Historical Museum is located on the site of the Battle of Lundy's Lane, the fiercest altercation of the war, fought between the Americans and the British on July 25, 1814. But the War of 1812 was not the end of Niagara's role as a battleground. In 1866, Fenians (members of the Irish Revolutionary Brotherhood, who felt that the best way to rid Ireland of British occupation was to attack her colonies, such as Canada) crossed the Niagara River and captured Fort Erie. The British eventually drove the Fenians back to American soil, and the attacks stopped. The colourful history of Niagara has been preserved at Lundy's Lane Historical Museum. Be sure to visit the first floor, which interprets the early settlement and tourism of Niagara Falls, and features the War of 1812 and the Fenian Raids. The second floor features a Victorian parlour, travelling exhibits, and seasonal displays.

■ guided tours; educational kits

Marineland 18c

7657 Portage Rd. S.
Niagara Falls

✉
8375 Stanley Ave.
Niagara Falls, ON L2E 6X8

☎ (905) 356-8250/2142

Kandu, Nootka and Kiska, Marineland's orcas (killer whales), and their friends the dolphins, the seals, and the playful sea lions are all waiting to strut their stuff for you at Marineland.

✏️ Seasoned performers and natural hams, these entertaining and intelligent creatures are fascinating to watch. But you can see many other attractions at Marineland. Buy some delicious deer treats to feed the gentle fallow and sika deer that live in the park, or treat the bears with their favourite snacks. Other attractions include an amusement park with rides to provide lots of thrills and chills.

■ on-site; materials

Niagara Falls IMAX Theatre and Daredevil Gallery and Museum 18c

6170 Buchanan Ave.
Niagara Falls, ON L2G 7T8

☎ (905) 358-3611

Thrill to an IMAX film adventure! Watch a film on a seven-storey-high screen, while sound booms at you from all around through six-channel stereo. Then visit the Niagara Daredevil Gallery and Museum. The displays here feature the various stunters who have attempted to cross the river or the falls by wire, boat, or barrel. The focal point of the museum and its exhibits is one question: "What makes stunters stunt?"

▲ ■ guided tours

Tivoli Miniature World 18d

5930 Victoria Ave.
Niagara Falls, ON L2G 3L7

☎ (905) 357-4100

It's a small, small world at the Tivoli. During a visit to this unique theme park, you'll travel around the world and back in time simultaneously. The little train that circles the site will take you to more than 90 of the world's most famous landmarks, all meticulously recreated in miniature and surrounded by landscaping designed to show them to best advantage. See the Acropolis in Athens, the Vatican, the Great Pyramids of Egypt,

Jerusalem's Wailing Wall, and Toronto's own CN Tower. Visit the Tivoli workshop to see the artists and craftspeople at work building the miniatures.

Mackenzie Heritage Printery

Queenston

✉
The Niagara Parks Commission
P.O. Box 150
Niagara Falls, ON L2E 6T2

☎ (905) 682-7203

The history of Upper Canada is a turbulent one, and one red-haired Scottish immigrant, William Lyon Mackenzie, fomented much of the unrest that characterized the 19th century. Unhappy with the way politics were practised in his adopted land, Mackenzie made his views known to the public in his own newspaper. On May 18, 1824, the first issue of *The Colonial Advocate and Journal of Agriculture, Manufacture and Commerce* was printed in the charming limestone building now known as the Mackenzie Heritage Printery. Visitors to this important site in Canada's history and its journalistic tradition will find an impressive collection of working hand presses and an interpretive display on the history of printing. Volunteer historian printers will demonstrate the operation of the presses. Of particular interest is the Roy Press, which was operated by Louis Roy, printer to Governor John Graves Simcoe. Roy printed *The Upper Canada Gazette*, which was first published at Newark (Niagara-on-the-Lake) in 1793.

■ guided tours

Shaw Festival 20a

P.O. Box 774
Niagara-on-the-Lake, ON L0S 1J0

☎ (905) 468-2153; Toronto direct line: (416) 690-7301

Every year, the tiny picturesque village of Niagara-on-the-Lake welcomes thousands of tourists and theatre buffs to the Shaw Festival. See any number of plays at the modern Festival Theatre, the Courthouse Theatre, or the Royal George Theatre. For academics and Shaw fans, the Academy of the Shaw Festival offers a series of Shaw seminars led by noted Shaw scholars and members of the company.

■ performances; posters; study guides; videos

Fort George 20b

Niagara Pkwy., Niagara-on-the-Lake

Niagara National Historic Parks
Niagara Courthouse, 26 Queen St.
Niagara-on-the-Lake, ON L0S 1J0

☎ (905) 468-3938 or 468-4257

Step out of the brilliant sunshine of a summer's day and into the dim interior of the visitors' centre at Fort George, and you could almost believe that you have been transported back in time to 1812, to a busy British fortification on the eve of hostilities with the Americans. As you wander about the fort, one of the largest built by the British for the defence of Canada, let the skilled guides, animators, and interpreters help you recapture the flavour of life at the fort. Note the luxurious quarters of the senior officers before you peek into the "black hole," a sparse, dark, and forbidding holding area for soldiers awaiting punishment. Listen to the stirring military airs played by the fort's popular Fife and Drum Corps, peer through the loopholes at the Niagara River, and munch on a "snickerdoodle," a fort favourite baked on-site.

St. Catharines Museum & Welland Canal Viewing Complex (Lock 3) 21

Canal Rd., St. Catharines

✉

St. Catharines Chamber of Commerce
11 King St., P.O. Box 940
St. Catharines, ON L2R 6Z4

☎ (905) 685-3711

One of Canada's greatest engineering feats was the building of the Welland Canal system, part of the St. Lawrence Seaway. This route gives ocean-going vessels access to the interior of Canada through the Great Lakes. Visitors to the St. Catharines Museum and Welland Canal Viewing Complex (Lock 3) can watch ships passing through the lock at such close range that you can speak with the sailors on board the ships. One of the complex's most popular features is a built-to-scale working model of a ship passing through a lock. This hands-on display encourages visitors to guide the ship through. The site also boasts an audio-visual presentation about the canal and the seaway, and exhibits portraying the history of St. Catharines and the Niagara Peninsula.

■ guided tours; study guides — elementary grades

Art Gallery of Hamilton 22a

123 King St. W.
Hamilton, ON L8P 4S8

☎ (905) 527-6610

Hamilton's modern art gallery houses a veritable treasure: more than 7000 paintings, graphics, photographs, and sculptures. Its permanent collection includes the complete, limited-edition works of Karel Appel. In addition to its permanent and special exhibitions, the Art Gallery of Hamilton presents a number of special programs and activities: art-film screenings, lectures, artists' talks, children's classes, and classes for the disabled. Make special note of *Wet Paint*, a series of performances incorporating music and theatre with audience participation.

■ guided tours; special programs; teaching materials

Canadian Football Hall of Fame and Museum 22b

58 Jackson St. W.
Hamilton, ON L8P 1L4

☎ (905) 528-7566

The game of football is as much a part of the Canadian autumn as woodsmoke and flying geese. The Canadian Football Hall of Fame and Museum enshrines the history of football in Canada for the past century. On display are the Canadian Football League "crown jewels," such as the Grey Cup and the Schenley Trophy. Learn about the many great Canadian players, watch a continuous video that shows replays of Grey Cup highlights, and shop for CFL souvenirs.

■ guided tours

Dundurn Castle 22c

York Blvd.
Hamilton, ON L8R 3H1

☎ (905) 522-5313

Dundurn Castle, built in 1835 by Sir Allan MacNab, Upper Canada's pre-Confederation prime minister, is an example of the Tuscan-villa style of architecture and typical of the lifestyle of Hamilton's well-to-do in the 19th century. In addition to his term as prime minister, MacNab helped bring the railway to Hamilton and quell the Rebellion of 1837 — a service for which he was knighted. The magnificent villa has been faithfully restored to the days when it was inhabited by the MacNab family. Dundurn Castle presents demonstrations of the domestic arts of the period. While visiting, be sure to see jams and other preserves being prepared, or bread and cookies being baked in the traditional manner. And keep your eyes open — rumour has it that Dundurn Castle has its very own ghost!

■ guided tours; special programs; materials

Hamilton Children's Museum 22d

1072 Main St. E.
Hamilton, ON L8M 1N6

☎ (905) 549-9285

One of the most exciting places in Hamilton for small and not-so-small fry is the Hamilton Children's Museum. The injunction here to kids ages 3–13 is "Do! Touch! Experience!" A variety of changing exhibits allows children to explore their environment and gain a better understanding of the world they live in. The series of ever-changing, creative, hands-on activities were designed especially for them. In recent years, shows have included such themes as fairy tales, animals, printing, and architecture. Children will delight in such innovative items and activities as a garden-hose telephone, a jack-in-the-box in which the child plays Jack (or Jacqueline), and paper helicopter making.

■ on-site; all grades

Hamilton Museum of Steam and Technology 22e

900 Woodward Ave.
Hamilton, ON L8H 7N2

☎ (905) 549-5225

In the 1850s, Hamilton was a growing industrial centre. Growth brought with it a pair of problems: the potential for fire, and the spread of cholera, an often fatal disease caused by bacteria in untreated water. To combat these problems, the city built a waterworks to force water from Lake Ontario into a reservoir above the city. The waterworks, which succeeded in virtually eliminating the twin threats, is now preserved as the Hamilton

Museum of Steam and Technology. Housing the only mid-19th-century waterworks pumping engines on original foundations in North America, the museum is uniquely suitable for portraying the life of the 1850s worker, discussing the urban issues of the 1850s and today, and demonstrating the principles of simple machines and energy.

■ on-site interactive; all grades and post-secondary; materials; videos; of particular interest to science and social sciences teachers

Royal Botanical Gardens 23

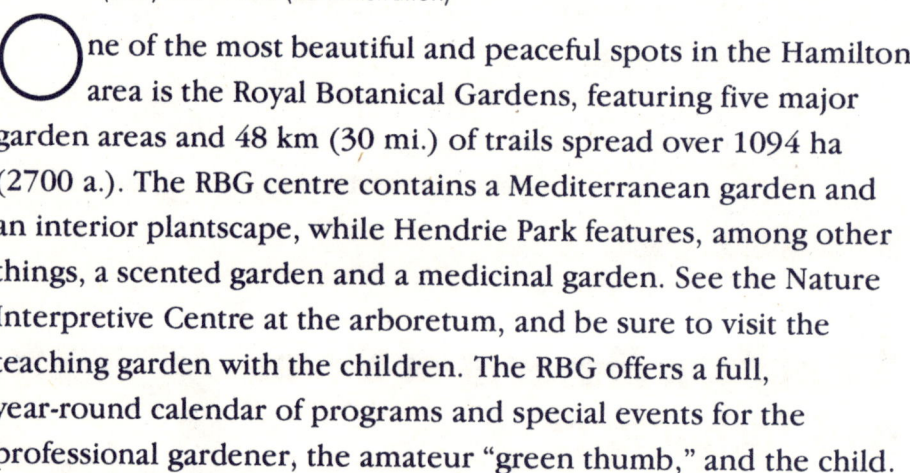

680 Plains Rd. W., Burlington

✉

P.O. Box 399
Hamilton, ON L8N 3H8

☎ Infoline: (905) 527-8938;
Toll Free Ontario/Quebec: (800) 668-9449;
(905) 527-1158 (administration)

One of the most beautiful and peaceful spots in the Hamilton area is the Royal Botanical Gardens, featuring five major garden areas and 48 km (30 mi.) of trails spread over 1094 ha (2700 a.). The RBG centre contains a Mediterranean garden and an interior plantscape, while Hendrie Park features, among other things, a scented garden and a medicinal garden. See the Nature Interpretive Centre at the arboretum, and be sure to visit the teaching garden with the children. The RBG offers a full, year-round calendar of programs and special events for the professional gardener, the amateur "green thumb," and the child.

■ on-site for adults and children; teacher workshops

Crawford Lake Conservation Area 24a

Steeles Ave. and Guelph Line, Milton

✉

Halton Region
Conservation Authority
2596 Britannia Road W.
R.R. 2, Milton, ON L9T 2X6

☎ (905) 336-1158 or (905) 854-0234 (weekends)

Crawford Lake has been described as a "time capsule" for some very good reasons. This unusual lake, which covers a relatively small surface area, is incredibly deep. For this reason, very little oxygen can penetrate to its lower levels, thereby preserving anything that might be there. Such a lake is called "meromictic." Scientists probing the lake's depths uncovered evidence of human habitation from as early as 1290. They established that a Native village had existed at Crawford Lake between then and 1610. This village has been reconstructed; it offers visitors an authentic look at life in a typical settlement of this type during the 1434-1459 period. It consists of a defensive stockade; two complete longhouses, which would have accommodated a number of families; and gardens suitable to the time and region, growing vegetables such as corn, beans, and squash, as well as tobacco for ceremonial occasions. Included in the village are displays of artifacts such as bows and arrows, pottery, and clothing.

■ on-site; all grades; teacher workshops; facilities and programs for the physically challenged

Ontario Agricultural Museum 24b

144 Tremaine Rd.

✉

P.O. Box 38
Milton, ON L9T 2Y3

☎ (905) 878-8151

A short distance west of Toronto near the town of Milton you'll find the Ontario Agricultural Museum, a sprawling complex of more than thirty buildings on 32 ha (79 a.) of land, which constitutes a traditional farming community. Here visitors are invited to explore and experience Ontario's rich agricultural history. As you wander through the buildings, chat with the costumed interpreters, who will happily demonstrate and explain traditional skills involved in farming and blacksmithing, crafts such as candle making, weaving and more. Stop in the tiny one-room schoolhouse and imagine what it would have been like to go to school in the last century. Note the museum's huge collection of antique farm equipment. And don't miss the farm animals that make the museum complex their home. The museum also hosts a number of special events throughout the year. Call ahead or write to find out what is planned.

▲ ■ on-site; all grades

Peel Heritage Complex 25

9 Wellington St. E.
Brampton, ON L6W 1Y1

☎ (905) 451-9051

Visit the Peel Heritage Complex and go directly to jail! This Peel Region museum is housed in the renovated 19th-century Peel County Jail and adjacent Registry Office. The displays cover aspects of local life from prehistory to the present. The jail itself was built in 1866 and is notable for three hangings that took place there between 1909 and 1946.

▲ limited service

Wildcare Wildlife Rehabilitation Centre 26

R.R. 2
Woodbridge, ON L4L 1A6

(905) 832-6957

Wildcare Wildlife Rehabilitation Centre provides a very important service to Ontario's wildlife. This non-profit organization is dedicated to the rescue, rehabilitation and release of injured, orphaned and displaced wild animals native to and resident in Ontario. The centre does not encourage the general public to visit the site because such visits raise the stress levels of the orphans and patients being cared for. However, the centre conducts an extensive program designed to foster awareness and concern for the wildlife in Ontario.

- school visits with slide show; opportunities to sponsor a selected species; newsletter

McMichael Canadian Art Collection 27a

10365 Islington Ave.
Kleinburg, ON L0J 1C0

(905) 893-1121

Tucked away in the picturesque village of Kleinburg, just north of Toronto, sits a wonderful building of hand-hewn logs, natural stone, and huge picture windows overlooking the Humber River Valley. This was the home of collectors Robert and Signe McMichael, which they donated along with 4 ha (10 a.) of land and 177 works of art to the province of Ontario in 1965. Since then, the McMichael Collection and its building have expanded to become a leader in Canadian cultural expression. Wander through the grand exhibition halls and intimate galleries; see how the log walls and the view of the surrounding area serve to enhance the art on display and to lend a uniquely Canadian flavour to the experience. Note that the permanent collection consists of over 5000 works, including a spectacular assemblage of work by

✍ Canada's Group of Seven. In addition to the permanent collection, the gallery features 12 special exhibitions each year. After viewing the displays, step outside to stroll along the trails. Look around you at the landscape to understand what has motivated and inspired Canadian artists. Complementary programs of lectures, tours, talks, storytelling, films, and music are available to enrich your visit.

▲ ■ on-site; all grades; teacher resource materials; teacher workshops

Kortright Centre for Conservation 27b

Pine Valley Dr., Kleinburg

✉

5 Shoreham Dr.
Downsview, ON M3N 1S4

☎ (905) 832-2289
or (905) 661-6600

To fully appreciate the natural beauty of the Kleinburg region, put a visit to Kortright Centre for Conservation on your agenda. The 324 ha (800 a.) in the Humber Valley include a variety of ecosystems. The 18 km (11 mi.) of trails lead to the marsh, through the river valley, to the spring peeper pond, and past energy exhibits and a bee house. Check ahead of time for any special programs. Depending on the time of year, you could take part in a maple syrup demonstration, a kite festival, an environmental festival, or a honey festival.

■ Over 40 curriculum-related programs; all grades including preschool

Puck's Farm 28

R.R. 3
Schomberg, ON L0G 1T0

☎ (416) 939-4632

Puck's Farm, near the pretty village of Schomberg, just north of Toronto, offers no end of exciting things to do and discover, especially for the younger set. Try your hand at milking Dainty Doris or her friends (Doris also makes school visits); pick your own raspberries, corn, apples, or whatever else is in season; meet Bartholomew, a rare four-horned Jacob ram, and his buddies, many of whom are retirees from the Moscow Circus and who have appeared in films; or go for a pony ride. Whatever the season, Puck's Farm offers an unique opportunity to experience some country living first-hand. And remember — where do pigs do their laundry? At the hogwash, of course!

▲ ■

Paramount Canada's Wonderland 29

Rutherford Rd., exit off Hwy. 400, Maple

✉
P.O. Box 624
Maple, ON L6A 1S6

☎ (905) 832-7000

For family fun and entertainment on a warm summer day, nothing can beat Paramount Canada's Wonderland. Whether you come for the thrill of zooming along on the gravity-defying rides, cooling off in the huge water playground, watching your favourite cartoon characters star in their own shows, or taking in a live concert featuring top names from the world of entertainment, you'll find plenty to do at Paramount Canada's Wonderland.

David Dunlap Observatory 30

Box 360, 123 Hillsview Dr.
Richmond Hill, ON L4C 4Y6

☎ (905) 884-9562

On a clear night, you can see forever — particularly at the University of Toronto's David Dunlap Observatory, the place to be for budding astronomers and astrophysicists. The main dome contains the largest optical telescope in Canada. The centre functions as a research centre, particularly in the structure and evolution of galaxies and star clusters, "black holes," the nature of stars, and the "interstellar medium out of which our sun and we ourselves were formed." For the best visit, come on a Saturday night. Watch a slide presentation and a demonstration of the operation of the telescope. If the night is clear, staff will open the dome so you can view an interesting celestial object.

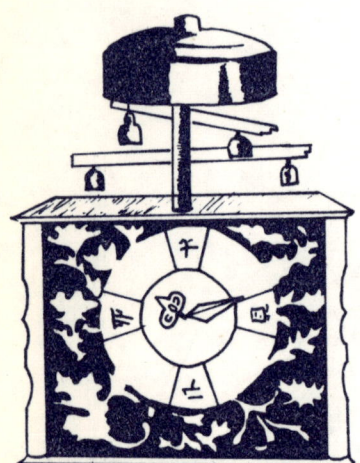

Thornhill Antique Clock Museum 31

447 Mullen Dr.
Thornhill, ON L4J 2N9

☎ (905) 731-1695

Hickory, dickory, dock! Where would we be without a clock? At the Thornhill Antique Clock Museum, you can explore the history of timekeepers from 1650 to 1940. On display are an original tower clock (c. 1850) in perfect working order, weight-driven clocks, and vintage neon clocks from the 1930s and 1940s, as well as Toronto's "Lipton" clock.

Addiction Research Foundation Museum 32a

33 Russell St.
Toronto, ON M5S 2S1

☎ (416) 595-5017

Next time you pop into a drugstore to pick up a remedy for that nagging cough or queasy tummy, stop to think about some of the cures of yesteryear. Fretting, teething babies were often treated with "Dr. Fahrney's Teething Syrup," which contained morphine and chloroform. At one time, a much-touted remedy for whooping cough was to "put a trout's mouth into the patient's." For a fascinating look at the development of pharmaceuticals in the treatment of disease, both prescription and the over-the-counter variety, as well as traditional homemade remedies, visit the Addiction Research Foundation Museum.

▲ ■ materials for all ages, on loan

Art Gallery of Ontario 32b

317 Dundas St. W.
Toronto, ON M5T 1G4

☎ (416) 977-0414

Surely one of the most dynamic centres of cultural expression, not only in Toronto but in the province, is the newly refurbished Art Gallery of Ontario. Works of art spanning 600 years are displayed in some 50 different galleries — and what you see is only a fraction of the gallery's permanent collection of 16 000 pieces. The curators organize each of the galleries or suites of galleries around specific themes or objectives, whose purpose is to reveal the "stories" embedded in the art and to allow the viewer to see relationships among them. Note that each gallery has been enhanced with architectural details and historically correct colours, innovative lighting techniques, informative panels, and audio-visual aids in order to provide as enriching an experience as possible for the visitor. Of special interest is the Henry Moore Sculpture Centre, which contains the world's largest public collection of Henry Moore's works. All visitors, especially the younger set, will enjoy "Off the Wall!," an interactive discovery program designed to make it possible for everyone to explore, enjoy, and learn about art.

▲ ■ courses; all grades

Bata Shoe Museum 32c

131 Bloor St. W.
The Colonnade, 2nd Floor
Toronto, ON M5S 1R1

☎ (416) 924-7463

The old lady who lived in the shoe truly would not have known what to do if she had had the opportunity to visit the Bata Shoe Museum, located in the Colonnade on Toronto's fashionable Bloor Street. With over 450 shoes and related artifacts to view, the museum allows the visitor a fascinating look at history through one of the body's most overlooked parts, the feet. Visitors can view everything from Native North American footwear to royalty and celebrity footwear; Egyptian sandals, c. 320 B.C.; moon-walking boots; and shoes worn by such notables as Elvis Presley, Pierre Trudeau, Elizabeth Taylor and baseball star Dave Winfield. The museum contains a 19th-century cobbler's shop, a theatre, and interactive displays. Visitors can learn the origin of expressions such as "well-heeled" and "sabotage," see special-purpose shoes worn in times past by a wide spectrum of people — from wooden clogs worn by smugglers to delicate little slippers for enhancing the tiny bound feet of Chinese ladies — and learn about the contribution of feet and shoes to literature and the arts.

■ guided tours

Black Creek Pioneer Village 32d

1000 Murray Ross Pkwy.
Toronto, ON M3J 2P3

☎ (416) 736-1733

The colourful poster from Black Creek Pioneer Village reads "Life in the Past Lane." This amazing complex of 40 buildings, representing a typical crossroads village of the 1860s, is designed for the visitor to experience just that. Stroll through the village to stop in the homes where costumed interpreters will chat with you while they spin or cook over an open hearth. Drop in to the artisan shops to see the traditional skills of blacksmithing, clock making, gunsmithing, broom making, barrel making, and others. Stop at Roblin's Mill to watch wheat ground exactly as it was 120 years ago. Be sure to visit the Pioneer Gardens, including the herb garden, the weaver's shop dye garden, the doctor's medicinal garden, and the Pennsylvania German square garden, as well as the vegetable garden and the all-important apple orchard. Take a special souvenir home with you. Freshly baked bread and various crafts produced in the buildings of the village are for sale.

▲ ■ on-site; all grades; themed programs; teachers' workshops; guided tours

Canada's Sports Hall of Fame 32e

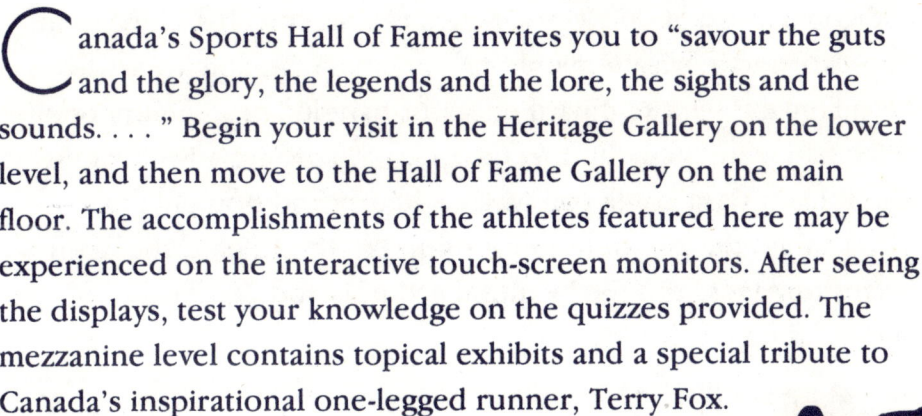

Exhibition Place
Toronto, ON M6K 3C3

☎ (416) 260-6789

Canada's Sports Hall of Fame invites you to "savour the guts and the glory, the legends and the lore, the sights and the sounds. . . . " Begin your visit in the Heritage Gallery on the lower level, and then move to the Hall of Fame Gallery on the main floor. The accomplishments of the athletes featured here may be experienced on the interactive touch-screen monitors. After seeing the displays, test your knowledge on the quizzes provided. The mezzanine level contains topical exhibits and a special tribute to Canada's inspirational one-legged runner, Terry Fox.

▲ ■ guided tours

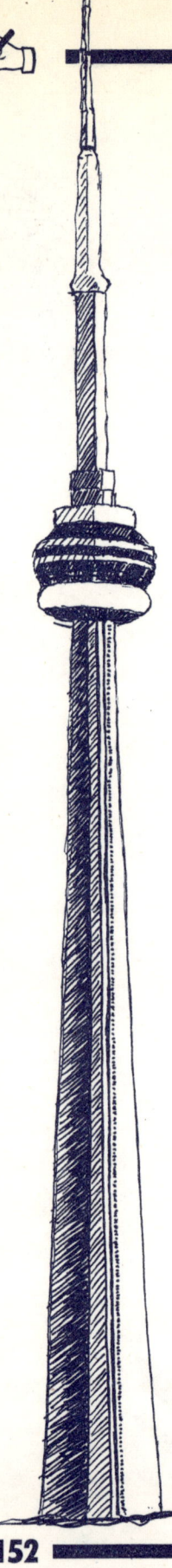

Casa Loma 32f

1 Austin Terrace
Toronto, ON M5R 1X8

☎ (416) 923-1172

In the heart of Toronto stands a wonderful medieval castle that looks like it might have been transported directly from a book of fairy tales. But Casa Loma (meaning "house on the hill") is no fantasy. Built in 1910 by Sir Henry Pellatt, a Toronto financier who amassed (and lost) a fabulous fortune, this amazing building was intended to replicate the wonderful castles Pellatt had seen in Europe. It has 98 rooms, including (unlike the ancient castles on which it is patterned) 15 bathrooms; and 5000 electric lights, the first electric elevator in Toronto, and a private telephone system. (When Sir Henry lived at Casa Loma, the switchboard operator handled more telephone calls than were made in the entire city of Toronto!) Everywhere you look in Casa Loma you will see luxury and opulence. And don't forget the 244-m (800-ft.) tunnel to the stables, the many secret passages, and the beautiful grounds and gardens surrounding the castle.

▲ ■ guided tours

CN Tower 32g

301 Front St. W.
Toronto, ON M5V 2T6

☎ (416) 360-8500

Soaring some 550 m (1800 ft.) into the air and dominating the Toronto skyline is the celebrated CN Tower, the tallest freestanding structure in the world. For many visitors, the 58-second ride in the tower's futuristic elevators and the chance to survey their surroundings from the observation areas provide enough thrills. But the tower has more to offer. Not to be missed is the thrilling "Space Race," rated one of the 10 best rides in North America by *OMNI* magazine. Produced by George Lucas' Industrial Light and Magic film company, Space Race is an intergalactic action ride on a 747 flight simulator. Or try a game of Q-Zar, a futuristic, live-action laser tag game, great fun for all ages. And if these space-age entertainments hold no appeal, enjoy 36 holes of golf at the Putt-Putt (miniature) Golf Course, shop for souvenirs, or have some refreshments after enjoying your bird's-eye view of Toronto.

▲ ■ including co-operative education placements

Colborne Lodge 32h

High Park, Toronto

✉

Toronto Historical Board
Marine Museum, Exhibition Place
Toronto, ON M6K 3C3

☎ (416) 392-6910

Built in 1837 in the beautiful area that is now High Park, Colborne Lodge was the home of John Howard, a celebrated Toronto architect. Declared a Provincial Historic Site in 1957, Colborne Lodge is a stellar example of an early North American Regency-style villa intended as a rural retreat for a middle-class family. Guides dressed in 1870s period costume relate the story of the Howards, their home, and the role played by John Howard in the development of Toronto. Note the wine cellar, the winter and summer kitchens, and one of Toronto's first indoor bathrooms. The house retains most of its original furnishings, and visitors may enjoy as well John Howard's own water-colour drawings of the Toronto of his day.

▲ ■ all grades, including special education classes; teacher workshops; guided tours

George Brown House 32i

50 Baldwin St.
Toronto, ON M5T 1LA

☎ (416) 324-6969

For any serious student of Canadian history, a visit to the George Brown House is a must. George Brown — Father of Confederation, entrepreneur, and founder of the newspaper that is now *The Globe and Mail* — lived in this gracious home, now a National Historic Site. Admire the morning and drawing rooms, furnished in the style of the late Victorian period, and the marvellous mahogany-panelled dining room before stopping in the library, which contains over 2000 books from George Brown's own library. Peruse an exhibit of artifacts unearthed during restoration of the building, and watch a video that presents a century of history.

▲ ■

Historic Fort York 32j

Garrison St.

✉

Toronto Historical Board
Marine Museum, Exhibition Place
Toronto, ON M6K 3C3

☎ (416) 392-6907

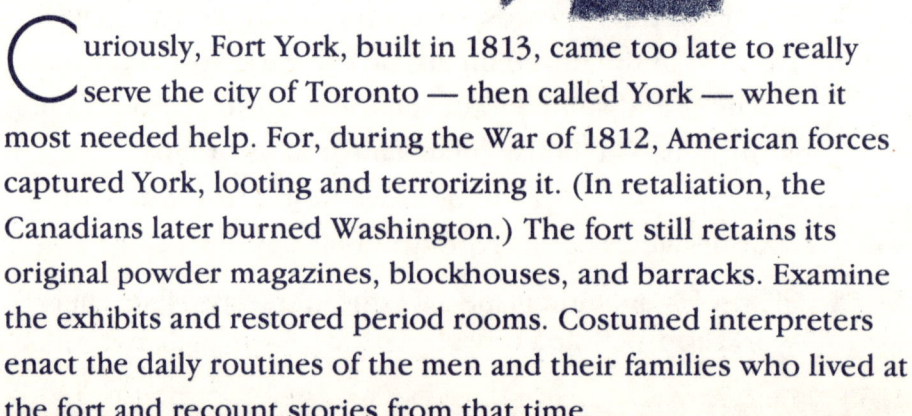

Curiously, Fort York, built in 1813, came too late to really serve the city of Toronto — then called York — when it most needed help. For, during the War of 1812, American forces captured York, looting and terrorizing it. (In retaliation, the Canadians later burned Washington.) The fort still retains its original powder magazines, blockhouses, and barracks. Examine the exhibits and restored period rooms. Costumed interpreters enact the daily routines of the men and their families who lived at the fort and recount stories from that time.

▲ ■ on-site; in-school; all grades

Hockey Hall of Fame 32k

BCE Place
30 Yonge St.
Toronto, ON M5E 1X8

☎ (416) 360-7735

You can relive all the wonderful, heart-stopping moments in Canada's national sport at the Hockey Hall of Fame. As you move into the hall, see and hear "Great Moments in Hockey" being played on a video screen more than 2m (8 ft.) high. Examine the History Zone, which presents the various eras of hockey in its bi-level displays. Indulge your curiosity about what goes on behind the scenes when you pause in the Dressing Room Zone. Thrill to "The Game," a video, complete with sound effects, shot from the players' perspective. Relive your favourite hockey moments in the TSN Broadcast Zone, test your skill and knowledge on the Trading Card Arena Zone's simulations, or enjoy the interactive games in the Coca-Cola Rink Zone. Learn about international hockey, the growth of hockey in North America, or pay homage to the hockey greats in the Bell Great Hall, home to the Honoured Hall of Fame Members, the Stanley Cup, and other prestigious trophies and awards.

▲ ■ currently being developed

Mackenzie House 32l

82 Bond St.
✉
Toronto Historical Board
Marine Museum, Exhibition Place
Toronto, ON M6K 3C3

☎ (416) 392-6915

William Lyon Mackenzie, newspaper publisher, Toronto's first mayor, politician, rebel, and volatile leader of the 1837 Upper Canada Rebellion, was given this Victorian townhouse by his friends in 1859 in recognition of his tireless efforts to reform an unpopular and ineffectual political system. Visit this fully restored house and let the costumed interpreters help you experience the lifestyle of the family. Enjoy the demonstrations in the kitchen and the 19th-century printshop. And keep this in mind: rumours persist that Mackenzie's ghost wanders through his former home!

▲ ■ on-site; all grades

Marine Museum 32m

Exhibition Place
Toronto, ON M6K 3C3

☎ (416) 392-6827

Toronto's Marine Museum brings to life the city's history as an inland port and the subsequent importance of Great Lakes traffic to its social and economic development. Exhibits, video presentations, and carefully designed activities invite you to explore the fur-trade era in Toronto, the naval aspect of the War of 1812, the history and operation of steam-powered vessels, the social history of Great Lakes sailors, and the history of Toronto Harbour. As an added bonus, during the months that span Victoria Day to Thanksgiving you may also visit the *Ned Hanlan*, a 1932 steam tug.

▲ ■ grades K–8; on-site and in-school

Norman Elder Museum 32n

140 Bedford Rd.
Toronto, ON M5R 2K2

☎ (416) 920-0120

A visit to the Norman Elder Museum is a journey into the fascinating, the unique, and the bizarre. Norman Elder is an explorer, and his house (the museum) is a monument and a tribute to his adventures and experiences. Here, visitors can learn to puff through a blow gun, hold a python, and taste honey made by killer bees. View the intriguing collection of primitive weapons, voodoo dolls, tribal weapons, and 50 living creatures, including the aforementioned python and a rooster who crows on command and does tricks. Touring the house is itself an adventure. With 13 staircases, several underground tunnels, and a basement tomb, it served as the location for a scene in David Cronenberg's film, *Naked Lunch*.

Note: visits by appointment only

■ guided tours

Ontario Place 32o

955 Lakeshore Blvd. W.
Toronto, ON M6K 3B9

☎ (416) 314-9811

Ontario Place, situated on the shores of Lake Ontario and open from May to September, has something special for everyone. Come to see a concert staged in the Forum. Children will enjoy attractions such as the Lego Creative Play Centre, Children's Village, Waterplay, and the flume ride, Wilderness Adventure. Other features include miniature golf, Ontario North Now (a ten-pavilion complex highlighting Ontario's North), HMCS *Haida*, a World War II Tribal Class Destroyer, bungy-jumping, parasailing, and the Nintendo Power Pod. Ontario Place also offers three theatres, including Cinesphere, the world's first permanent IMAX theatre, and 13 restaurants to cater to every taste.

▲ ■ on-site

Royal Ontario Museum 32p

100 Queen's Park
Toronto, ON M5S 2C6

☎ (416) 586-5549

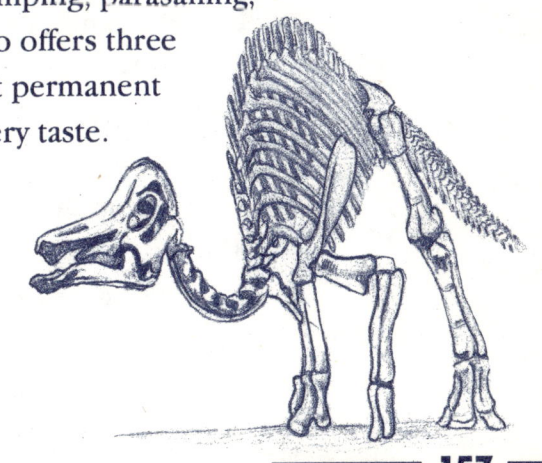

McLaughlin Planetarium

Step back in time to enter whatever era you wish at the Royal Ontario Museum (the ROM). The largest museum in Canada, the ROM encompasses four buildings in its complex: the main building, the McLaughlin Planetarium, the George R. Gardiner Museum of Ceramic Art, and the Sigmund Samuel Building (closed to the public). Travel to ancient Egypt to make the acquaintance of Djedmaatesankh, the ROM's resident mummy, or wander through a Ming tomb to gaze at the marvellous statuary. If you are a fan of the medieval world, then you'll enjoy the suits of armour included in the display of protective clothing (which includes modern hockey equipment). Marvel at the collection of dinosaur skeletons, and, if you dare, step into the creepy Bat Cave! If other worlds interest you, then drop in next door to the McLaughlin Planetarium. Lie back in your seat and watch the imaginative and informative projections on the circular dome overhead, or take advantage of the many interactive exhibits. Don't miss the George R. Gardiner Museum of Ceramic Art, across the road from the planetarium. This building displays 2000 pieces of ceramic art, reflecting a wide range of artistic styles and periods.

▲ ■ on-site; all grades

SkyDome 32q

1 Blue Jays Way
Toronto, ON M5X 1JT

☎ (416) 341-2770

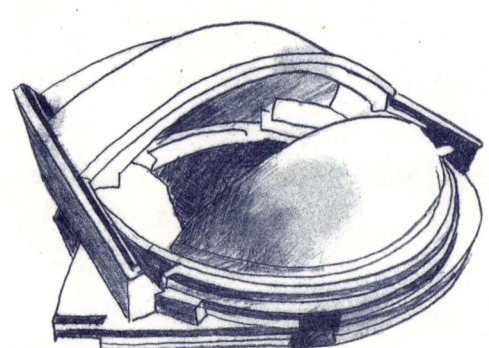

Blue Jays, Argos, Wrestlemania, or Rolling Stones! Whatever your fancy, chances are you can take it in live at SkyDome, Toronto's magnificent domed stadium. SkyDome is big enough to accommodate a 32-house subdivision; even with the roof *closed* there's enough height for a 31-storey building. While at SkyDome, stroll along the Walk of Fame, where the names of outstanding athletes and entertainers who have performed here are embedded in the floor, or examine the 1400 or so artifacts that were uncovered in excavations for SkyDome's foundations. These include a cannon from the War of 1812 and various household items used by Torontonians during the 19th century.

Spadina 32r

285 Spadina Rd.

✉

c/o Toronto Historical Board
Marine Museum, Exhibition Place
Toronto, ON M6K 3C3

☎ (416) 392-6910

Courtesy Toronto Historical Board

For a taste of the graciousness and elegance of a bygone era, little in Toronto can match Spadina. Built in 1818 by Dr. William Warren Baldwin, father of the Honourable Robert Baldwin, and later purchased by James Austin, a leading Toronto businessman, Spadina remains much as it was during that period. The room settings, which have been meticulously preserved, include a formal drawing room, reception areas, and a large billiard room. The art, furnishings, and gaslighting help the visitor to experience, however vicariously, the lifestyles of the four generations of Baldwins and Austins who lived there. A glimpse at the Edwardian kitchen and butler's pantry offer a rather striking contrast.

▲ ■ on-site; all grades

Toronto's First Post Office 32s

260 Adelaide St. E.
Toronto, ON M5A 1N1

☎ (416) 865-1833

Toronto's First Post Office began operation in 1833, serving at that time as the fourth post office in the town of York, and later, after the incorporation of the City of Toronto, as Toronto's first post office. Replicas of the original 204 post-office boxes are available for rent and all recent issues of postage stamps are for sale. Mail sent through the museum may bear the distinctive stamp — "York–Toronto 1833" or "City of Toronto, U.C." Visitors may view a slide presentation, see the exhibits, and shop for writing materials of the early 19th century — notepaper, seals, sealing wax, quill pens, and ink. The museum offers a number of special programs, such as lectures, tours, and workshops, on subjects such as quill cutting, calligraphy, and paper making. Families may enjoy the annual Valentine-making bee.

▲ ■ on-site with costumed interpreters; all grades; special education and ESL

The Toronto Stock Exchange 32t

The Exchange Tower
2 First Canadian Place
Toronto, ON M5X 1J2

☎ (416) 947-4700

Bulls and bears are loose in the city of Toronto — not animals from the zoo, but highs and lows on the Toronto Stock Exchange (TSE). The visitors centre, open weekdays, provides an opportunity for you to watch trading on the floor from the viewing gallery. Curious about the world of investment and high finance? The TSE offers free public presentations and a large assortment of informative material.

■ guided tours; teaching kit; game; video

Montgomery's Inn 33

4709 Dundas St. West
Etobicoke, ON M9A 1A8

☎ (416) 394-8113

The experience of staying in a hotel nowadays differs considerably from that of 1830 when Thomas Montgomery, an immigrant from Ireland, built Montgomery's Inn. The inn flourished for many years, not only as a stopping place for travellers, but also as a centre for business and community activities. Now a "living museum," the inn has been restored to the 1847-50 period. The worn floorboards by the bar attest to its popularity, and records left by Montgomery detail the types of drinks he served. As you move through the inn, note the difference between the relatively comfortable living quarters of the family and the more sparsely outfitted guest rooms. Unlike today, most guests registering at the inn did not rent a room or even a bed. Rather, they rented *space* in a bed, sharing it with two or three other people, often strangers. Before leaving the premises, be sure to taste the delicious scones and lemon cake, freshly baked over hot coals in the blackened open hearth.

▲ limited services

■ on-site; in-school; grades K–8

Ontario Science Centre 34a

770 Don Mills Rd.
Don Mills, ON M3C 1T3

☎ (416) 429-0193

The invitation from one of the most exciting places in Canada, the Ontario Science Centre, reads "Explore Space! Tickle Technology! Be a Sport! Call on Communications! Play in a Science Arcade!" In the exhibit halls, more than 650 interactive displays on themes such as communications, space, earth, food, environment, energy, Canadian resources, sports, and technology invite the visitor to touch, try and test. Imagine playing a musical instrument without touching it, or writing with a talking typewriter. Would you like to shake hands with a skeleton? Would you like to see a laser burn a hole in a brick? Perhaps you are more interested in exploring the Arecibo message sent into space in search of extra-terrestrial intelligence. Do you long for a career in the major leagues? At the science centre, you can check out the science of throwing a curve and have your own fastball measured for speed and accuracy. Plan on making several trips to this science centre — it is so big that you could never take in everything in the space of a day.

▲ ■ on-site; all grades and post-secondary; resource materials; student workshops; teacher workshops

Holocaust Education and Memorial Centre of Toronto 34b

4600 Bathurst St.
Willowdale, ON M2R 3V2

☎ (416) 635-2883 ext. 153

A visit to the Holocaust Education and Memorial Centre shows you the depths to which humankind can fall, as well as the heights of heroism ordinary people can achieve. The huge bronze doors designed by Canadian artist Andrew Poza depict a stylized letter of the Hebrew alphabet, *shin,* the first letter in three Hebrew words: *shesh* meaning six, as in the 6 million who died; *shoah* meaning holocaust; and *shalom* meaning peace. The doors swing open and the visitor enters a darkened passage lit on either side by panels of photographs showing Jewish life in Europe prior to the dark days of the Nazi reign of terror. Symbolically, the floor slopes downward as the days of normal life were taken over by the gathering storm clouds of war and annihilation. In the little theatre, you can see an audio-visual presentation narrated by the late Lorne Green and accompanied by the haunting musical score of Toronto composer Srul Irving Glick. In the tiny, round, pure white chapel, lit naturally from above by a skylight, survivors have lovingly placed memorials to family members who perished. The displays are sobering: a striped uniform such as concentration camp inmates were forced to wear; a used cannister of Zyklon B, the gas used for mass extermination; and pathetic postcards sent by victims to their relatives, intended to reassure them of their "resettlement." As you leave, silent and alone with your thoughts, note that the floor slants symbolically once again, this time upward in hope, as you pass testimonials to the many non-Jews who risked their own lives and that of their families to save Jewish lives. The Holocaust Education and Memorial Centre is not a fun place to visit. However, as you reflect on the images appearing almost daily in our news media of neo-Nazis in the streets, "ethnic cleansing" in some countries, and the obscenity of Holocaust-denial, reflect on the work done by this place and recognize that only by educating ourselves and our children can we hope to ensure that such a tragedy is never allowed to happen again, to anyone, anywhere.

■ guided tours; guest speakers; teacher workshops

Todmorden Mills Heritage Museum and Arts Centre 34c

67 Pottery Rd.

✉

East York Parks and Recreation Department
850 Coxwell Ave.
East York, ON M4C 5R1

☎ (416) 425-2250/778-2199

Nestled in the Don River valley is the tiny village of Todmorden Mills. It originated in the early part of the 18th century when Loyalists Isaiah and Aaron Skinner were granted land by Governor Simcoe to construct a sawmill. The sawmill prospered, and in time a grist mill, a brewery, and a paper mill were added. Many of the original buildings have been restored. Visitors are invited to step into the Parshall Terry House, which dates back to 1797; the Eastwood & Skinner Paper Mill, which serves as an art centre; the William Helliwell House, complete with period furnishings; the Don Train Station; and Helliwell Brewery, which houses a number of interesting displays relating to the site.

■ on-site; elementary grades

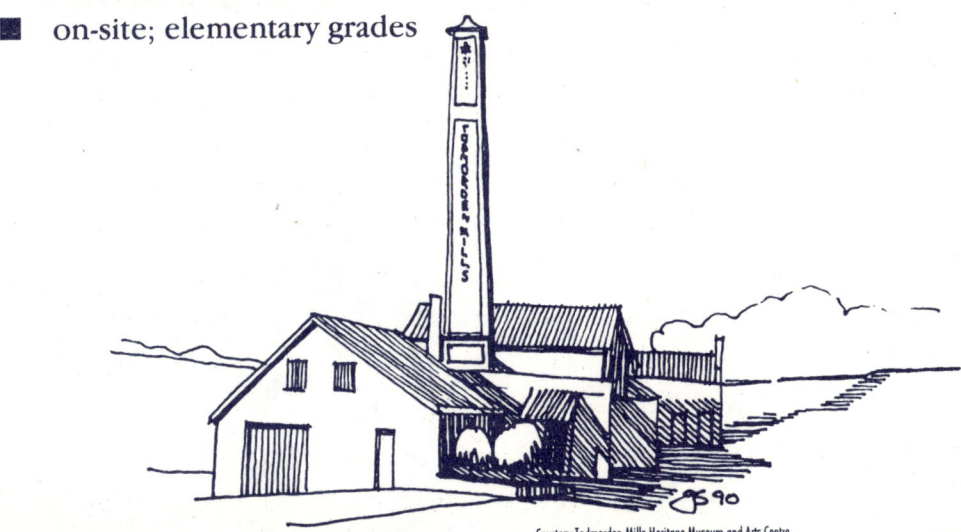

Courtesy Todmorden Mills Heritage Museum and Arts Centre

Metro Toronto Zoo 35

Meadowvale Rd.

P.O. Box 280
West Hill, ON M1E 4R5

☎ (416) 392-5900

No visit to Toronto would be complete without a day at Toronto's world-class zoo. Unlike traditional zoos, here you won't see rows of cages but rather rolling countryside and glass-roofed pavilions. The animals live in approximations of their natural habitats carefully constructed with trees, flowers, and vines native to them. If you've never visited the zoo before, start with the Round the World Tour. Then proceed to whatever takes your fancy — the Lion Trail, the Camel Trail, or perhaps the Grizzly Bear Trail. Tired of all the walking? Hop on the zoo's monorail or the zoomobile to enjoy the sights in comfort. Both conveyances stop at various places, so you can get off for a better look. Hungry or thirsty? Food outlets are available at various points on the site. Animal lovers will want to find out about the many special programs that the zoo offers throughout the year. Don't forget to pick up a souvenir at the gift shop on your way out!

▲ ■ including co-operative education opportunities

Cullen Gardens and Miniature Village 36

300 Taunton Rd. W.
Whitby, ON L1N 5R5

☎ (905) 668-6606 (Whitby);
(416) 294-7965 (Toronto)

Cullen Gardens features 10.5 ha (26 a.) of exquisite gardens and delightful miniature communities. The miniatures, built to 1/12 scale, represent a typical southern Ontario town, including a non-stop freight train and a VIA

train that stops at the Whitby station. Most visitors delight in the miniature country fair, whose rides are equipped with moving parts. More recently "Cottage Country" was added to the miniature displays. Modelled after the popular Muskoka region, Cottage Country even has a little ferry that docks on schedule. The on-site museum, the Lynde House, has been reconstructed and furnished to the 1850 period.

Darlington Generating Station 37

Box 1000
Bowmanville, ON L1C 3W2

☎ (800) 461-0034/(905) 623-7122

Situated on the shores of Lake Ontario is the Darlington Generating Station, which houses the CANDU system. Darlington produces a large percentage of the nuclear energy powering homes and industries in the province of Ontario. The facility welcomes visitors. Begin with a film in the comfortable theatre, and then examine the exciting exhibits on the history of the Darlington project and the development of electricity in Ontario. After touring the site, stop by the reference area to pick up more information on items such as nuclear power and the environment, fuel storage, and the economics of nuclear power.

▲ ■ on-site and in-school, for secondary grades

Lang Pioneer Village 38a

County Rd. 34

R.R. 3
Keene, ON K0L 2G0

☎ (705) 295-6694

Courtesy Lang Pioneer Village

Just north of the Serpent Mounds Provincial Park, look for Lang Pioneer Village. Described as a "living village museum," Lang Pioneer Village consists of 20 authentic (original and reconstructed) buildings. The village brings to life the Peterborough area of the mid-19th century. Of particular note is David Fife's log cabin. David Fife developed Red Fife Wheat, a hardy, high-yield strain that became immensely popular with Canadian and American farmers. Depending on the time of year, you can find much to see and do here at Lang. Interpreters go about the daily chores and routines of pioneer life: gardening, tending to the animals, housework, printing handbills and hammering horses' shoes. Enjoy a corn roast and a refreshing cup of apple cider from the village's own press. Watch the sheep shearing and participate in a traditional harvest thanksgiving.

▲ ■ on-site and classroom visits; all grades

Serpent Mounds Provincial Park 38b

R.R. 3
Keene, ON K0L 2G0
☎ (705) 295-6879

Situated in a secluded spot overlooking the tranquil waters of Rice Lake, the Serpent Mounds have a mystical, almost eerie beauty. Here lies an ancient Indian burial ground, estimated by archaeologists to have originated nearly 2000 years ago. It consists of nine burial mounds, one of which resembles a coiled snake. Similar mounds have been identified in Ohio in the United States. Drop into the park's visitor centre to look at displays and a video presentation about the mounds. Be sure to follow the self-guided tour around the site.

■ guided tours in spring and fall only; teachers' kit

Hutchison House 39

270 Brock St.
Peterborough, ON K9H 2P9

☎ (705) 743-9710

Hutchison House is both a museum and a tribute to John Hutchison, a Scottish physician who settled in Peterborough in the 19th century. His practice served not only the local citizenry but also the Natives of Curve and Rice Lakes. Another inhabitant of Hutchison House was a relative of Dr. Hutchison, Sir Sandford Fleming, the celebrated engineer. Fleming stayed with the Hutchison family for two years while he sought to establish himself. Visitors to Hutchison House are afforded an opportunity to see a typical doctor's study of the 1840s and a room equipped with Sir Sandford Fleming memorabilia, including one of his original maps. Hutchison House offers a number of special events throughout the year. Of particular interest are the daily Scottish teas, which are available through the summer months. Visitors may tour the house and then settle down for tea or lemonade, scones, oatcakes and other delicacies.

■

Fort Kente 40

✉
Kente Portage Heritage Conservation Society
R.R. 2, Carrying Place, ON K0K 1L0

☎ (613) 394-2313

Beyond a doubt, the best time to visit Fort Kente is the middle of July when it hosts the annual Kente Portage Festival. Fort Kente was built by the British in 1813 to protect the portage, a vital roadway from Wellers Bay to the Bay of Quinte, from attack by the Americans. The portage itself is the oldest road in Ontario. During the Kente Portage Festival, canoes take to the water and costumed interpreters re-enact life at Fort Kente as it was in the past.

▲ ■ instruction to school groups

The Loyalist Cultural Centre 41

✉ P.O. Box 112, R.R. 1
Bath, ON K0H 1G0

☎ (613) 373-2196

In 1784, with the uprising of the colonies along the American seaboard, many people still loyal to Britain fled to Canada. Known as United Empire Loyalists, many of these new arrivals settled in the Kingston area. The Loyalist Cultural Centre in picturesque Adolphustown on the shores of Lake Ontario marks the spot where, according to tradition, the first bateaux bearing the Loyalists landed on June 16, 1784. At the centre, staff clad in period costume will gladly tell you the story of the coming of the Loyalists and their contributions to life here. Enjoy the rich collection of Loyalist memorabilia, and then take a walk to admire the many historic sites, including the cairn that marks Sir John A. Macdonald's boyhood home.

Historic Babcock Mill 42

Bridge St.

✉ Township of Ernestown
263 Main St., Box 70
Odessa, ON K0H 2H0

☎ (613) 386-7351

Photo by Jack Chiang, courtesy Babcock Mill

A tisket, a tasket, Babcock makes better baskets! In 1856, Joshua Booth constructed the Babcock Mill, which was used in its early years for a variety of milling enterprises. In 1907, John Henry "Cap" Babcock purchased it, primarily as a source of baskets and truck bodies. The mill now operates during the summer months, manufacturing "Better Baskets by Babcock." Visitors can see the water-powered woodworking machinery and watch the entire process of basket making. You may purchase baskets produced by the mill, and other souvenirs.

Bellevue House National Historic Site 43a

35 Centre St.
Kingston, ON K7L 4E5

☎ (613) 545-8666

During the 1830s, Kingston offered untold opportunities for a man of ambition and ability. It is therefore not surprising that one John A. Macdonald, a young lawyer and member of the Legislative Assembly — and a rising star in the political realm — would live and practise law there. In August of 1848, he rented Bellevue House. Set at that time outside the town, surrounded by mature trees and just a stone's throw from the shores and breezes of Lake Ontario, Bellevue House had been constructed in the style of an Italian villa by a prosperous local grocer, Charles Hales. Renting Bellevue proved too costly, and Macdonald moved after only 13 months. But the association with Canada's first prime minister was set, so Bellevue House was designated a National Historic Site. The restoration is accurate in every detail to the 1840s when the Macdonalds occupied it. Of particular interest are the grounds surrounding the house. The grass looks a little ragged because the gardeners cut it with a scythe rather than a lawn mower. You won't find any vegetation around the foundations of the building either because this was the fashion of the time. All plants, flowers, fruit-bearing trees, and vegetable gardens are planted in the style of the 1840s as well. It is the wish of the interpretive staff that visitors get not only a sense of the site during the period when it was occupied by the Macdonalds, but an environmental message as well. Tours begin with an audio-visual presentation and an exhibit on the life of Sir John A. Macdonald. Interpreters (costumed during the summer) are on hand to assist and answer questions about the house and life of our first prime minister.

▲ ■

Canadian Forces Communications and Electronics Museum 43b

Vimy Barracks
CFB Kingston, ON K7K 3R0

☎ (613) 541-5395

Courtesy Department of National Defence

Visit the Canadian Communications and Electronics Museum to learn why communication is essential to success on the battlefield and how Canada has contributed to improving such communication. Your tour begins appropriately in a briefing room, where a staff member fills you in on the history behind the exhibits: the Signal Corps and the evolution of modern communications. The rooms of the museum and its 4000 artifacts highlight different themes, including World War I, a classroom at Camp Borden in the 1920s, World War II, Telecommunications, Modern Technology, the Northwest Territories and the Yukon (including the hunt for the "Mad Trapper of Rat River"), the German Room (displaying items captured in both world wars), and the United Nations Room. A theatre is available for viewing audio-visual presentations. And before leaving, pause to reflect for a moment at the Book of Remembrance, which commemorates signalmen who died in the line of duty.

▲

Fort Henry 43c

Box 213
Kingston, ON K7L 4V8

☎ (613) 542-7388

Overlooking the city of Kingston and commanding a magnificent view of Lake Ontario stands Fort Henry, permanently fixed in the year 1867. The fort was constructed in 1812 by the British to protect Kingston's dockyard from an American attack during the War of 1812, and was garrisoned until 1870. It was occupied briefly by troops en route to Saskatchewan to put down the Riel Rebellion in 1885-87, and later served as an internment centre for German prisoners of war during both world wars. In 1936, it was restored as part of a make-work project during the Depression, and in 1938 it was officially declared a Provincial Historic Site. Since that time, it has evolved into one of the most exciting and colourful "living museums" in the country. Visit the fort schoolroom to experience lessons as children of the soldiers would have done. Or "enlist" as a raw recruit, be issued a "uniform," and participate in a Military Muster Parade after being "whipped into shape" by one of the guard! During the summer months, enjoy the daily Pay Parade, when the members of the guard receive their wages; the Officer of the Day Parade; the famous Sunset Ceremony; or relax to the music of a fife and drum concert. Wander around the grounds and take in the historical exhibits, but be sure not to miss the daily appearance of David, one of Fort Henry's most popular attractions. A white Saanen goat, David is integral to the Fort Henry Guard. (*Never* call him a mascot!) Accompanied by his handler, the Goat Major, David meets with the fort's visitors to be photographed. Freshly groomed, horns gilded, and wearing his breast plate, he proudly leads the whole Fort Henry Guard in formal parade. Show proper respect for this goat — rumour has it that one of his predecessors broke the leg of a soldier from another regiment who teased him!

▲ ■ A variety of educational programs are available ranging from guided tours to overnight experiential activities.

MacLachlan Woodworking Museum 43d

Grass Creek Park

Township of Pittsburgh, Box 966
Kingston, ON K7L 4X8

☎ (613) 542-0543

For the pioneers arriving in our country so many years ago, shelter from the harsh winters was crucial. Wood was a major resource for building homes and tools. More than 5000 artifacts in two buildings illustrate and develop the MacLachlan Museum's theme of "Wood in the Service of Man." The original building, a two-storey house constructed in 1853 from hewn logs of white cedar, nestles in a meadow of wildflowers much like its original setting. It contains displays of traditional woodworking tools, reconstructions of the shops of traditional craftsmen (the cooper, wheelwright, blacksmith, and cabinet maker), and an exhibit of a pioneer farmer's tools in his working environment, along with his wife's period kitchen. The new building, opened in 1988, houses a gallery devoted to trees — their growth and their technical uses — as well as a display of wooden objects (toys, furniture, etc.) in the traditional home and workplace. Of particular note are a Paleolithic-era maul, an axe head, and an adze belonging to local Native people, circa 6000–8000 B.C. Temporary exhibits supplement the permanent collection.

▲ guided tours; experiential learning activities; resource materials

Marine Museum of the Great Lakes at Kingston 43e

55 Ontario St.
Kingston, ON K7L 2Y2

☎ (613) 542-2261

Have you ever stayed overnight in a museum? The largest artifact in the Marine Museum is the ship itself, the 3050 t (3000 ton) *Alexander Henry*, once a Canada Coast Guard icebreaker and now a bed and breakfast establishment during the summer months. Exhibits trace the development of shipping on the Great Lakes. Note the old dry dock, officially opened by Sir John A. Macdonald, Canada's first prime minister, which has been made a National Historic Site. Learn about shipping methods and manufacturing from ancient Native civilizations to the present. Ship ahoy!

▲ limited service ■

Kingston Mills Blockhouse 44

Kingston Mills Rd., Kingston Mills

✉

Rideau Canal,
Southern Area Office
Parks Canada, P.O. Box 10
Elgin, ON K0G 1E0

☎ (613) 359-5377

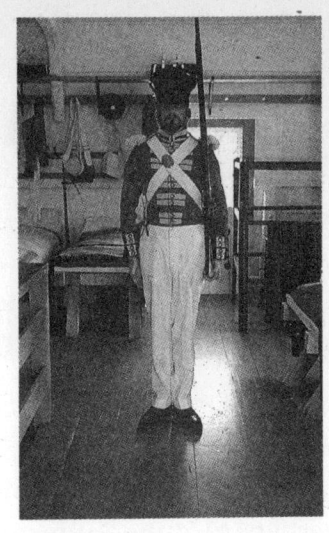

The scenic Rideau Canal in eastern Ontario, now a favourite route for pleasure boating and picnicking, was built to defend the area from attack by the Americans. Blockhouses were built at lockstations on the canal to protect the locks, which were vital to shipping. The Kingston Mills Blockhouse, built in 1833 and restored in 1979, is one of the oldest surviving buildings on the canal. It was intended not only to accommodate the lock attendant, but also to serve as a "secure arms depot in time of war for provisions, ammunition and small arms for the militia." When visiting the blockhouse, note the stone walls, which are over a metre (4 ft.) thick as protection against fire and bombs.

▲ ■

Old Stone Mill 45

Main Street, Delta

✉

Box 172
Delta, ON K0E 1G0

☎ (613) 928-2658

Built in 1810, the Old Stone Mill in Delta, a National Historic Site, is one of the earliest and finest mill buildings in Ontario. The mill was originally powered by a water wheel, but in 1860 it was replaced by a turbine that eventually generated electricity for the whole village.

■ guided tours

The Battle of the Windmill Historic Site
46a

Fort Wellington National Historic Site, 370 Vankoughnet St.

✉

P.O. Box 479
Prescott, ON K0E 1T0

☎ (613) 925-2896

Try to imagine the frustration of living in Upper Canada during the early part of the 19th century, when the region was governed by the "Family Compact," a clique of officials appointed by the British government. In 1837, settlers' frustrations about political, religious, economic, and social problems reached the boiling point and erupted into open rebellion. The Rebellion of 1837 was put down, but many of the leaders, including firebrand William Lyon Mackenzie, fled to the United States, where they continued to dream and plan for an independent, democratic, and republican Canada. In 1837, the rebels were ready for another battle. Their goal: to capture Fort Wellington! Things did not go as planned, and the rebels were challenged at Windmill Point, one mile below Prescott, by a British gunboat. The rebels took up positions in the stone windmill and remained there for four days until, recognizing the futility of further resistance, they surrendered unconditionally to the British. Their leaders were hanged. The stone windmill still stands, mute testimony to the tumultuous events of that era.

▲

Fort Wellington National Historic Site
46b

370 Vankoughnet St.

✉

P.O. Box 479
Prescott, ON K0E 1T0

☎ (613) 925-2896

In order to protect its crucial St. Lawrence–Great Lakes water route during the War of 1812, the British built a series of forts, including Fort Wellington. Constructed in 1813 at the head of a treacherous 80-km (50-mi.) stretch of rapids on the St. Lawrence River, it became an important transfer point for goods and troops moving between Montreal and Upper Canada (Ontario). Although Fort Wellington itself was never attacked, its garrison was instrumental in both the capture of the American fortifications at Ogdensburg, New York, and the Battle of Crysler's Farm. Visitors to the fort can see the original 1813 fortifications, the 1838-39 blockhouse, officer's quarters, and other features. The buildings have been refurnished to the 1846 period. During the third weekend in July, Fort Wellington hosts Canada's largest annual military pageant, which includes large-scale mock battles and demonstrations of 19th-century activities. You might want to time your visit to an evening in late August, when there is a just a hint of fall in the air; you will enter a time warp where ghosts of the past go about their business all around you!

▲ ■ on-site simulation activities; classroom speakers; grades 7–8; guided tours

Upper Canada Village 47

R.R. 1
Morrisburg, ON K0C 1X0

☎ (613) 543-3311

Upper Canada Village offers so much to see that you should plan on spending at least four hours here — and come equipped with a good pair of walking shoes. However, should your feet get tired, there are other conveyances: a bateau plying the St. Lawrence River, on whose shores the village is situated; the bright yellow stagecoach, which carries the mail (and visitors); and horse-drawn "carry-alls," all typical of the 1860s. Upper Canada Village is a meticulous reconstruction of a typical Ontario riverfront community of that time. Covering 27 ha (66 a.), it contains two farms, three mills, two churches, two hotels, and 25 other agricultural, domestic, and commercial buildings. Be sure to visit the Tenant and Louck farms, complete with livestock; the cheese factory; and the printing office, with its typical village newspaper. See the schoolhouse and watch the manufacture of blankets and yarn at the woollen mill. And, if after all this you feel tired and hungry, drop into one of the village's eateries, including Willard's Hotel, whose costumed staff serves full-course meals and teas with a historical flavour.

▲ ■ extensive; themed and live-in programs

Watson's Mill 48

Dickinson Square Conservation Area

Box 599
Manotick, ON K4M 1A5

☎ (613) 692-3571

Who knows what really draws visitors to Watson's Mill: that it's one of the best examples of mid-19th century grist mill architecture in Canada, or that it has a fabled resident ghost, Anne Currie. Thomas Langrell of Ottawa built the five-storey mill in 1860, using limestone cut from the riverbank. In 1972, financial assistance from both the provincial and federal governments allowed the Rideau Valley Conservation Authority to purchase the old mill and restore it to 1860s operating condition. Visitors may watch the process of milling wheat into flour, which they can then purchase. Take a bag of stone-ground flour home with you, dreaming all the way of freshly baked bread milled in the time-honoured way of our ancestors! As for the ghost, ask the guides at the site to tell you the story — and then watch the upper floors of the mill at dusk . . . .

▲

Bytown Museum 49a

P.O. Box 523, Stn. B
Ottawa, ON K1P 5P6

☎ (613) 234-4570

Visit the Bytown Museum tucked behind the Parliament Buildings on the shores of the Rideau Canal. While the focal points of the museum are the life of Colonel John By, the founder of Ottawa, and the history of the canal, a number of other exhibits are worth noting. Of particular interest to small fry is the turn-of-the-century toy store, which reflects the time when factory toy manufacture was growing. See model trains and dolls with porcelain heads imported from Europe.

▲ ■ guided tours with hands-on activities

The Canadian Museum of Caricature 49b

136 St. Patrick St.
Ottawa, ON K1N 5J8

☎ (613) 995-3145

Children love comics and cartoons, but few grown-ups outgrow an affinity for caricature, either. Why else does the editorial cartoon remain one of the most popular features in the country's newspapers? Caricature is an art form, a specialized comment on current political, social, and economic events. The mandate of the museum is to acquire, preserve, and make accessible to the public cartoons about Canada by Canadians. Its collection of approximately 30 000 pieces is supplemented by an optical digital disk system; new caricature exhibitions are presented every four months.

▲ ■ on-site; all grades and post secondary; school tours

The Bank of Canada's Currency Museum 49c

Bank of Canada Bldg.
245 Sparks St.
Ottawa, ON K1A 0G9

☎ (613) 782-8914

When you think of money, do pictures of pennies, quarters, and dollar bills float through your mind? The history of money spans as many centuries and cultures as make up the history of humanity. At various times and in various places, legal tender has consisted of whales' teeth, glass beads, cowrie shells, elephant hair, and copper bracelets. The six galleries of the museum tell the history of money through the ages, the history of Canada, and the technical process of minting coins and printing bank notes. Make a special point of seeing the National Currency Collection, a complete collection of Canadian notes and coins.

▲ ■ for children 5–15 years of age; self-directed

Canadian Museum of Nature 49d

Victoria Memorial Museum Bldg.
McLeod St. at Metcalfe, Ottawa

✉

P.O. Box 3443, Stn. D
Ottawa, ON K1P 6P4

☎ (613) 990-6273

This museum sets out to lead Canadians in the adventure of discovering and understanding the natural world and of learning how to live in balance with it. Through the museum's collections and programs, visitors are invited to journey back to a time before life existed on earth and to follow the evolution of life from the dinosaurs to the creatures who share our world today. Six permanent exhibition halls, supplemented by temporary exhibits, present visitors with dioramas, audio-visual shows, visitor-operated displays, maps, charts, and diagrams.

▲ ■

Canadian Ski Museum 49e

457A Sussex Dr.
Ottawa, ON K1N 6Z4

☎ (613) 233-5832

During the late fall, when the nights grow longer and a hint of frost hangs in the air, over 6 million Canadians start to "think snow" in anticipation of their favourite winter pastime, skiing. Whether downhill or cross-country fans, skiing enthusiasts will enjoy browsing through the displays at the Canadian Ski Museum. See the exhibit based on the life of the legendary "Chief Jackrabbit" Herman Smith Johanssen; examine the equipment used by Canada's distinguished honour roll of Olympic and World Cup champions; and learn about this popular Canadian sport in the museum's library and photographic archives.

Courtesy Canadian Ski Museum

▲

The Canadian War Museum 49f

330 Sussex Dr.
Ottawa, ON K1A 0M8

☎ (613) 996-1420

It is a sad emblem of human nature that never in the history of our species has there ever been a period when one nation was not in conflict with another. The Canadian War Museum has no desire to glorify war or the participation of Canadians in war, but rather to help us examine war as an undeniable part of our history and to remind us that the objective has always been peace. The displays range over the centuries. You may examine a grisly skull with healed fractures and an arrow embedded in a vertebra, dating from the sixteenth century; gaze at the impressive array of medals and decorations awarded to Canadians for valour; and examine the various posters produced and distributed during wartime exhorting Canadians to enlist or to do their part by

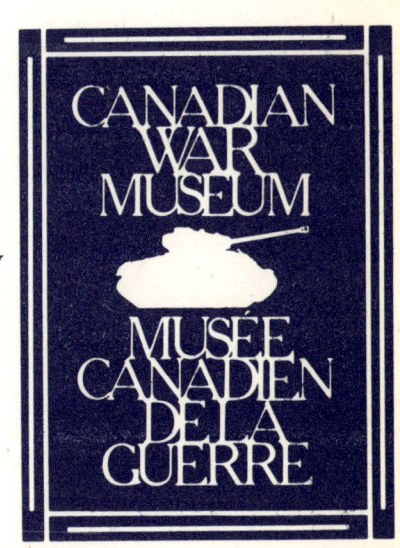

purchasing victory bonds. See the famous Sopwith Camel, one of the first military aircraft. On display as well are the medals of World War I flying ace Billy Bishop, a Mercedes limousine used frequently by Adolf Hitler, and various pieces of artwork depicting war and its heroes.

▲ ■ guided tours

Central Experimental Farm 49g

Sir John Carling Bldg.
Ottawa, ON K1A 0C5

☎ (613) 995-5222

Agriculture Canada suggests that you begin your visit to the Central Experimental Farm in the dairy barn, where a sign posted by the entrance invites you to "come on in and meet the girls." Stop by the nursery to see the little calves, and then browse through the agricultural museum to contrast farming now with methods of yesteryear. See the other animals, and then wander through the magnificent Tropical Plant Show and the beautifully groomed collection of trees and shrubs in the arboretum. Do not lose sight of the fact that this is a working farm and that significant developments in farming methods originate here. And if all the walking tires you out, continue your tour by jumping on board the Tally-Ho wagon, pulled by the farm's own Clydesdales.

▲ ■ guided tours

Laurier House National Historic Site 49h

335 Laurier Ave. E.
Ottawa, ON K1N 6R4

☎ (613) 692-2581

Laurier House holds a unique place among Canadian historical sites because of its intimate association with two Canadian prime ministers, Sir Wilfrid Laurier and the Right Honourable William Lyon Mackenzie King. Built in 1878 by Ottawa jeweller John Leslie, it was purchased by the Liberal Party of Canada in 1896 as a residence for their newly elected prime minister, Wilfrid Laurier, and his wife Zoe. In 1923 King took up residence, whereupon he named the building "Laurier House." Approximately 10 000 artifacts in the house help develop the themes of the site's interpretive program: the careers and accomplishments of Laurier and King as national political leaders, and the personal and domestic lives of the two men. The King period prevails, and visitors will delight in his collection of unusual souvenirs and gifts, including Sir Winston Churchill's cigars and King's now-notorious crystal ball.

▲

Museum of Canadian Scouting 49i

1345 Baseline Rd., Ottawa

✉

P.O. Box 5151, Stn. F
Ottawa, ON K2C 3G7

☎ (613) 224-5131

Of interest to anyone who was ever a Boy Scout, Girl Guide, Cub, Brownie, Spark or Beaver, the Museum of Canadian Scouting contains more than a dozen display cases, including memorabilia of the founding of the Scouting movement by Lord and Lady Baden-Powell. The various displays follow the life of Lord Baden-Powell, the beginning of Scouting, and the development of Scouting in Canada, from its early days, through World War II, and up to the present. The 21-m (68-ft.) totem pole, which was carved by the late Chief Mungo Martin and Henry Hunt, both of the Kwakiutl nation (Fort Rupert, B.C.), was presented by the Boy Scouts of British Columbia.

▲

National Aviation Museum 49j

Building 194, Aviation Pkwy.

✉

P.O. Box 9724, Ottawa Terminal
Ottawa, ON K1G 5A3

☎ (613) 993-4243

Up, up and away to the National Aviation Museum! Stroll along the "Walkway of Time," which tells the story of Canadian aviation through 50 aircraft presented in exhibits, interactive displays, and films. Admire the reproduction of Alexander Graham Bell's *Silver Dart*; examine the Sopwith Snipe, the plane used by World War I flying ace Billy Bishop; and see the reconstructed *La Vigilance*, Canada's first bush airplane, which was recovered from a lake in northern Ontario. Test yourself on the "Plane Trivia" game, and then design your ideal aircraft on the museum's computer.

▲ ■ interactive demonstrations; preschool and all grades; guided tours

National Gallery of Canada 49k

380 Sussex Dr.

✉

P.O. Box 427, Stn. A
Ottawa, ON K1N 9N4

☎ (613) 990-1985

The magnificent National Gallery of Canada resembles a crystal palace in the air. See Canada through the eyes of artists such as Cornelius Kreighoff, Clarence Gagnon, Jean-Paul Riopelle, and the renowned Group of Seven. Share the unique vision of Canada's Inuit artists. Admire the intricate sandstone sculptures dating from the third century A.D. in the Asian Gallery. Gaze at the masterpieces from the Middle Ages to the present on display in the European and American galleries. Wander through the Contemporary Gallery; take in the exhibits of prints, drawings, and photographs; and then, before you go, pause in the Garden and Water Courts to reflect on the beauty all around you.

▲ ■ on-site; all grades; post-secondary internships; guided tours

National Museum of Science and Technology 49l

1867 St. Laurent Blvd.
Ottawa, ON K1G 5A3

☎ (613) 991-3044

"Observing and learning about the impact of technology and science on everyday life" reads the mandate of this museum. With this in mind, enjoy the museum; it will provide you with endlessly fascinating experiences. Specially designed exhibits that come alive with sound and movement when you push buttons, pull levers, and turn dials introduce you to the main themes of the museum: science, transportation (land and marine), broadcasting, astronomy, communications, space, computer technology, agriculture, and graphic arts. Explore the model of a space shuttle flight deck, hold newborn chicks in your hand, forecast the weather from satellite images, and make your own paper — you will find no end of exciting and interesting projects in this museum.

▲ ■ on-site; all grades

Royal Canadian Mint 49m

320 Sussex Dr.
Ottawa, ON K1A 0G8

☎ (613) 993-0035

Courtesy Royal Canadian Mint

Do you have a jar full of pennies in your home? Then you've been engaged in numismatics, the practice of collecting coins. Whether numismatics is a hobby or an accident with you, The Royal Canadian Mint is *the* place to watch coin production! Since the beginning of recorded time, humanity has needed some form of legal tender. The first settlers to arrive in Canada bartered with beaver pelts. As immigration grew, coins began to appear, representing the homelands of the many different nationalities arriving on our shores. It soon became obvious that we required a standard form of money, and so, in 1858, the first Canadian coins were authorized and produced. Until 1907, all Canadian coins were produced in England. At that point, Canada's own mint began operation. As well as producing Canada's legal money, the Royal Canadian Mint also assays and refines gold, and designs and produces various medals and commemorative coins. Numismatic societies around the world value the mint's coins for their fine craftsmanship.

Parliament Hill 49n.

Ottawa, ON K1A 0A6

☎ (613) 992-4793

The heartbeat of the nation's capital is Parliament Hill, seat of Canada's government. Parliament Hill consists of three buildings: the Centre Block, which houses the Commons, the Senate, and the Prime Minister's Office; and the East and West Blocks, which contain the offices of the members of parliament, committee rooms, and administrative space. Watch history in the making! When Parliament is in session, visitors can watch the debates live from the public galleries of the House of Commons and the Senate. Guided tours, available all year long, will point out the ornately carved limestone walls and panelled, domed library. See the Memorial Chamber with its huge books of calfskin parchment that record the names of Canada's war dead. Take the elevator to the top of the Peace Tower to enjoy the panoramic view. Stroll past the bronze statues of seven former prime ministers and Queen Victoria, and don't forget to pause for a moment at the Centennial Flame.

▲ ■ teachers' kits; students' kits; guided tours

Storyland 50

Storyland Rd., R.R. 5
Renfrew, ON K7V 3Z8

☎ (613) 432-5275

Relive your childhood at Storyland! Wander through the extensive grounds to meet the characters from your favourite fairy tales. Play mini-golf, go pedal boating, or relax and watch a puppet show.

Courtesy Storyland

▲ ■ on-site; resource materials for teachers

Bonnechere Caves 51

✉
Box 495
Eganville, ON K0J 1T0

☎ (613) 628-2002

A descent into the Bonnechere Caves is an adventure in time travel — all the way back to the Ordovician period, an era that predates even fish! Five hundred million years ago, the caves were at the bottom of a tropical sea. Before entering the caves, pay careful attention to the guide, who will explain the fossils found on the site. Follow the strangely twisting passages through the rock, and take note of the eerie beauty of the stalactites, the coral, and the fossils still embedded in the rock. And don't forget to use your camera!

▲

Bon Echo Provincial Park 52

✉
R.R. 1
Cloyne, ON K0H 1K0

☎ (613) 336-2228

If you thought that Gibraltar existed only somewhere in the Mediterranean, think again. Bon Echo Provincial Park is home to majestic Mazinaw Rock, dubbed "the Canadian Gibraltar." An endless source of fascination to visitors, this rock is special primarily because of the pictographs, or rock paintings, on its surface. More than 200 pictographs — the largest visible collection in Ontario — bear witness to the tremendous religious significance of Mazinaw Rock in early Native cultures. Painted in red ochre, they consist of birds, animals, and humanlike figures. Beautiful, inspiring, baffling — it's hard to describe the impact of these ancient and mysterious rock paintings.

▲

Petroglyphs Provincial Park 53

✉

Box 500
Bancroft, ON K0L 1C0

☎ (613) 332-3940

From the moment you step inside the high-ceilinged glass structure built to protect the glyphs from careless visitors and further erosion by weather, you know you are in the presence of something immensely spiritual. Petroglyphs Provincial Park has the highest concentration of this type of aboriginal art in Canada. The drawings, representing boats, animals, humanlike figures, birds, and a large turtle — a fertility symbol to the ancient Algonkian peoples — all have religious significance. Archaeologists believe that the carvings were made between 900 and 1400 A.D. When visiting the park, be sure to walk along the Nanabush Trail. Nanabush, in Ojibwa lore, was a teacher sent by Kitchi Manitou, and so the Nanabush Trail is intended to be instructive. Watch for the stone cairns along the trail; they will introduce you to the culture and legends of the Algonkian peoples.

■ guided tours

"Kinomagewapkong," by David A. Johnson, Whetung Art Gallery, Curve Lake, Ontario; courtesy the artist

Algonquin Park 54

✉ P.O. Box 219
Whitney, ON K0J 2M0

☎ (613) 637-2828

Of Ontario's many provincial parks, Algonquin Park is the oldest, the largest, and the most venerated. Now 100 years old, the park offers a vast array of activities to the sports-minded and naturalist alike. A recent, extremely popular event now organized during the month of August is the Public Wolf Howl. Park naturalists attempt to locate a wolf pack. If they are successful, they organize a Howl. Park visitors accompany the staff to a specified location where a designated staff howler simulates a howl. If luck holds, members of the pack will howl in reply. Park naturalists preface the Howl with an informative and amusing slide show and lecture at the park's outdoor theatre. Another recent addition to the park is its new logging museum, which consists of a reception building with an introductory audio-visual presentation, a reconstructed camboose logging camp, and several exhibit pods that portray the history and development of the logging industry.

▲ ■ on-site; interpretive program

Atomic Energy of Canada Limited Research Laboratories 55a

Chalk River Laboratories
Chalk River, ON K0J 1J0

☎ (613) 584-3311

The friendly staff at AECL Research Laboratories in Chalk River near Ottawa make no bones about it: they *want* visitors at their facility! They aim to educate *everybody* about nuclear energy and the work in which they are engaged. Radiation has been instrumental in improving the quality of life for Canadians in many different ways, from breeding better seed corn to tracing water-pollution sources and treating cancer. More recently, AECL developed "Molly-99." Now used in hospitals worldwide, Molly-99 has been described as medicine's most versatile diagnostic instrument. A site tour often begins with a visit to the museum, where you will see the Zero Energy Experimental Pile (ZEEP), the original reactor built in 1947. ZEEP has been designated an Ontario Historic Site because of its contribution to nuclear development. In the visitors' centre, test your dexterity by manipulating the mechanical arms, and then use monitors to measure radiation levels in a chunk of uranium ore. See models of the research reactors and the CANDU power reactor displays. Watch a film explaining the work being done on the site, and enjoy the guided tour.

▲ ■ guided tours

Petawawa National Forestry Institute
55b

✉

Box 2000
Chalk River, ON K0J 1J0

☎ (613) 589-2880

In this environmentally conscious era, the Petawawa National Forestry Institute has an important role to play. Join the more than 20 000 people who visit this "living laboratory" each year. Find out just what is taking place in the field of tree breeding and genetics. Discover how computer technology contributes to managing forest fires. And enjoy the institute's hospitality: visitors can dine on such treats as spit-roasted pork and sand-baked beans. Or come in the early spring when the sap is flowing to enjoy a pancake breakfast with local maple syrup. After devouring all that wonderful food, walk it off on the many beautiful land and water trails, all with interpretation.

▲ ■

Samuel de Champlain Provincial Park
56

✉
P.O. Box 147
Mattawa, ON P0H 1V0

☎ (705) 744-2276

Samuel de Champlain Provincial Park celebrates an important and romantic era in Canada's history: the time of the voyageurs and the fur trade. Beginning in the 17th century and continuing for more than 200 years, the fur trade dominated North American commerce. Approximately 80 percent of the trade traversed the Mattawa River route, through the site of the present-day park. Visitors are encouraged to stop in at the Voyageur Heritage Centre, whose exhibits, indoor theatre, and audio-visual presentations interpret the fur-trade and voyageur era.

▲ ■ on-site

The Dionne Quints Museum 57

1375 Seymour St. N.

✉
P.O. Box 747
North Bay, ON P1B 8J8

☎ (705) 472-8480

The live birth of quintuplets, an unusual occasion these days, was even rarer in the 1930s. On May 28, 1934, in a little cabin in Corbeil, Ontario, near North Bay, Elzire and Oliva Dionne became the parents of quintuplets, five tiny baby girls. The sisters quickly became a subject for scientific study. And during the dismal days of the Depression, the quints became a major tourist attraction, infusing nearly $20 million into the strapped Ontario economy. As many as 6000 people a day would come to stare and gawk at the little girls, who were displayed four times a day to the tourists. This publicity robbed the quints of a normal childhood and caused deep tension within the Dionne family. The little house where the quints were born, the site of the present-day museum, still attracts the interested and the curious. On display are clothes, photographs, advertisements, and personal items, as well as other assorted Dionne memorabilia.

Cobalt's Northern Ontario Mining Museum 58

24 Silver St.

P.O. Box 215
Cobalt, ON P0J 1C0

Cobalt has long been recognized as a centre for the mining of silver. The Northern Ontario Mining Museum contains a unique collection of mining equipment and artifacts in seven rooms, but many people come to see what is probably Canada's finest collection of Native silver. To complement the museum is the Heritage Silver Trail, a self-guided drive to five principal sites, each chosen to illustrate a different aspect of Cobalt's mining industry and history. Silver is still mined in the area, and new mines are presently being developed.

■ on-site

Underground Gold Mine Tour 59

The Underground Treasures Shoppe
70 Cedar St. S.
Timmins, ON P4N 2G6

☎ (705) 268-9211

Gold! The very word conjures up images of luxury, war, and conquest. The yellow metal has played an important role in the history of civilization. The Underground Gold Mine Tour takes you below the surface at the Great Hollinger Mine. Your guides, retired hard-rock miners, will explain the process as it unfolds before you. Your tour begins in the parking lot, where you can see many different types of mining equipment. You will change into complete mining gear and watch an informative video before going underground. Here, one of the main attractions is a simulated drilling and blasting display. Other site attractions include a ride on an underground rail system, Hollinger House, and a prospector's trail and cabin. And if you find yourself bitten by gold fever, try your hand at panning for gold at "Prospectors Haven." Good luck!

▲

White Otter Castle 60

✉

Friends of White Otter Castle
P.O. Box 2096
Atikokan, ON P0T 1C0

☎ (807) 597-1377

"A man's home is his castle," goes the old saw, but in the case of Jim McQuat, a rather eccentric Scottish immigrant who came to Canada in 1893, this was no metaphor. Finding a spot on White Otter Lake to his liking, McQuat proceeded to construct a castle, two storeys high, complete with a four-storey tower, and all out of logs. It took 17 years to build, and McQuat enjoyed life in his castle for a scant four years. He drowned when he became entangled in his fishing nets after a fall into the water.

Amethyst Mine Panorama 61a

Mine: East Loon Rd.
Factory: 400 East Victoria Ave., Thunder Bay

✉
P.O. Box 832
Thunder Bay, ON P7C 4X7

☎ (807) 622-6413

The Amethyst Mine Panorama includes visits to both the Thunder Bay Amethyst Mine, approximately 56 km (35 mi.) east of Thunder Bay, and the factory in town. Tour the mine and try your hand at sifting the tailings. At the factory, you can watch the polishing of pieces of jewellery and other items set with amethyst. Amethyst, a semiprecious gemstone, was adopted as the official mineral of Ontario in 1975.

▲ limited service   ■ guided tours

Old Fort William 61b

✉
Vickers Heights P.O.
Thunder Bay, ON P0T 2Z0

☎ (807) 577-8461

Old Fort William enjoys the distinction of being the world's largest reconstructed fur-trade post. Step inside and find yourself in the early years of the 19th century, when the fur trade dominated. The site includes 42 historic buildings and covers 4 ha (10 a.). See a working farm, a wharf, and a canoe landing. Tour a Native encampment; wander into the fur stores where pelts are on display; and study primitive medical instruments in the apothecary. The site is staffed with interpreters in costume, who participate in dramatic presentations, work at the tasks and trades of the time, and will happily answer your questions.

■ on-site; elementary grades

Winnie-the-Pooh Statue 62

✉ The Corporation of the
Township of White River
Economic Development Office
P.O. Box 70
White River, ON P0M 3G0

☎ (807) 822-2478

Winnie-the-Pooh! How many generations of little children have delighted in the tales of this adorable little bear and his friends? The original Pooh stories were written by A.A. Milne, an Englishman whose young son, Christopher Robin Milne, was enchanted by the London Zoo's popular bear, Winnie. An orphaned cub, she had been found and kept by a kindly trapper in 1913. In August of 1914, during World War I, a veterinarian named Harry Colebourn, travelling with fellow recruits on a troop train, spotted the little bear and adopted her. He named her Winnipeg, after his home town. "Winnie" was popular with the whole regiment, and when the men were posted to England, she went with them. When Colebourn was called to the front lines in France, Winnie took up residence at the zoo. Colebourn continued to visit her there until she died in 1934. In Winnie's honour, a statue by British Columbia sculptor George Barone, based on a Walt Disney design, watches over White River and the annual Hometown Festival.

Courtesy Corporation of the Township of White River

Fort St. Joseph National Historic Site 63

✉ P.O. Box 220
Richards Landing, ON P0R 1G0

☎ (705) 246-2664 (May–October); (705) 942-6562 (November–April)

The British built Fort St. Joseph, one of several forts they constructed in Upper Canada in the latter part of the 18th century to safeguard their colonial interests. Fort St. Joseph had the questionable distinction of being the most westerly and most isolated of the British outposts; hence, desertion was a common occurrence. In 1974, archaeologists undertook a full-scale excavation of the fort. The stabilized ruins, now open to the public, tell an exciting tale of life at the fort. On display in the visitor centre are many of the artifacts recovered during the excavation period. Exhibits of tools, furs, and military uniforms help bring the fort to life. Films on archaeology and the fur trade are shown daily.

▲ ■ on-site; off-site

Science North 64

100 Ramsey Lake Rd.
Sudbury, ON P3E 5S9

☎ (705) 522-3701

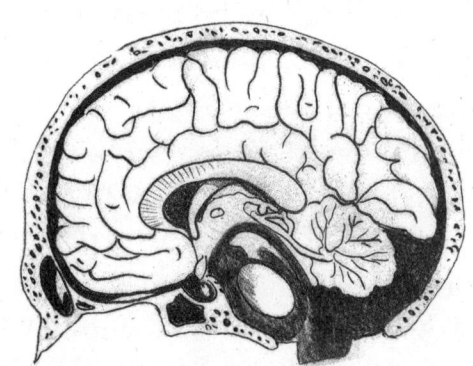

Science North is wonderful! From the moment you enter the two futuristic snowflake-shaped buildings overlooking Ramsey Lake until the time you leave, Science North is an action-packed, fun-filled experience in learning. Six themes are presented: biology, meteorology, geology, communications, astronomy, and human anatomy. The complex also contains five mini-theatres, with continuous short productions. Visit the Biosphere area to stroke a tame porcupine or play with a tarantula. In the Atmosphere display, have fun creating your own snowstorm or watch a tornado in a glass chamber. Move on to the Geosphere area to identify mineral samples or dig for a fossil. How healthy are you? In the Humanoshere you can take your blood pressure and test your reflexes. Or get introduced to a real brain: yours, in the humorous, participatory, audio-visual presentation, "Your Amazing Brain." Explore communications in the Infosphere by composing synthesized music, eavesdropping on ham-radio conversations or trying the many other hands-on activities. And have you ever wondered how East Indian swamis lie on a bed of nails? It's easier than you might imagine — in the Astrosphere try it and find out why it doesn't hurt. Part of the Science North Complex is the Big Nickle Mine. Here, visitors have an opportunity to learn about different mining methods, watch a simulated blast, mail a letter from Canada's only underground mailbox, and see an underground garden.

▲ ■ on-site; all grades

Bethune Memorial House 65

235 John St. N.
Gravenhurst, ON P1P 1S3

☎ (705) 687-4261

Courtesy Bethune Memorial House/Parks Canada

I wish to tell you of our doctor, our Doctor Bethune. He died on the night of many stars. He knew, we all knew, he would die. We wept . . . the heavens wept. He had healed our children. He had brought life to the wounded. He was our healer and our teacher." This tribute to Dr. Norman Bethune was penned by his friend, Lang Lin. Bethune, a revered hero to the Chinese, was virtually unknown in Canada until recently, because of his strong socialist views. In 1938, he went to China and joined Mao Zedong's army fighting the invading Japanese. He was the only doctor trained in Western medicine among 14 million people. He set up hospitals, trained doctors and nurses, translated medical texts into Chinese, and performed surgery where he could: in caves or Buddhist temples, usually with inadequate supplies. In 1939, he accidentally cut himself during surgery. The wound turned septic and he died the next day of blood poisoning. Bethune Memorial House is the home where he was born. It has been restored to recall the period of his birth and childhood. A modern exhibit tells of Bethune's career and the controversy of his politics. The visitor centre features a display of gifts from the People's Republic of China. Approximately 18 000 visitors from China visit the memorial each year.

▲ ■ all grades

Stephen Leacock Museum 66

Old Brewery Bay

✉

P.O. Box 625,
Orillia, ON L3V 6K5

☎ (705) 326-9357

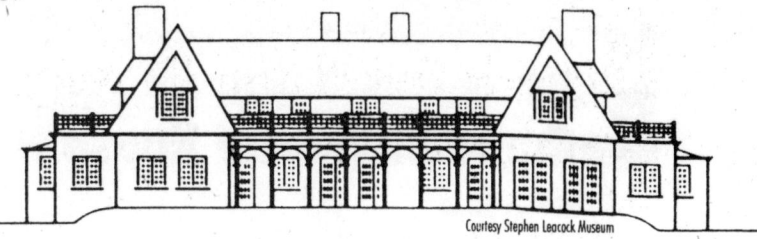
Courtesy Stephen Leacock Museum

Most people enjoy a good laugh! Foremost among Canada's humorists is Stephen Leacock, whose *Sunshine Sketches of a Little Town* made him *persona non grata* with his satirized neighbours in Orillia. Leacock was born in 1869 and died in 1944. He was a tireless writer who produced 34 volumes of humour. The museum is located in Leacock's home, which has been preserved as it was when he lived there.

■ all grades

Huronia Museum and Huron Indian Village 67

Little Lake Park

✉

P.O. Box 638
Midland, ON L4R 4P4

☎ (705) 526-2844/526-8757

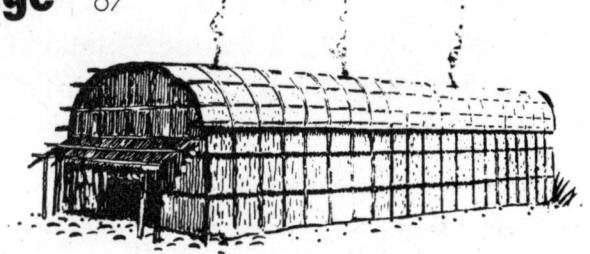

Visitors to the Huronia Museum and Huron Indian Village are invited to step into a typical Huron Indian community of 400 years ago, before the arrival of the Europeans. The palisades were intended to protect the village from attack. Inside the village, you will find a tobacco patch and garden. Tobacco's role was largely ceremonial and spiritual — it was burned as an invocation to the spirits. Step inside the longhouses where the villagers lived and note the wigwams, which provided shelter to visitors. The shaman had his own home. He was thought to receive his powers supernaturally through dreams or visions, and would treat various ailments with herbs and ointments. Among the other places of interest are the sweat bath and the burial rack. The museum contains some half-million artifacts, tracing the social and cultural development of Huronia from before the arrival of the Europeans.

■ on-site; grades 1–10; most subject areas

Historic Naval and Military Establishments 67b

Church St.

✉

Huronia Historical Parks
P.O. Box 160
Midland, ON L4R 4K8

☎ (705) 526-7838

Navigation on the Great Lakes has long been recognized as a key to political and economic advantage in Canada's history. This aspect of our past has been carefully explored and preserved at Penetanguishene's Historic and Naval Establishments. At the entrance are the keel and original hull timbers of the *Tecumseth*, a circa 1812 British ship. Other attractions include reconstructed buildings, such as the dockyard centre, the office of the clerk-in-charge, the sailors' barracks, and a working replica of the HMS *Bee*. The past comes to life through guided tours, dramatizations, drills, and special programs for children.

▲ ■

Sainte-Marie Among the Hurons 67c

✉

P.O. Box 160
Midland, ON L4R 4K8

☎ (705) 526-7838

Sainte-Marie was a remarkable village and Jesuit mission where two 17th-century peoples made contact: the European and the Wendat (the Huron). Meticulously reconstructed to reflect life in the 17th century, the village provides its visitors with a special experience. A visit begins with an audio-visual presentation; suddenly you find yourself in the middle of a bustling village overlooking the peaceful Wye River. Artisans in period costume go about their tasks, hewing logs and building canoes. In the longhouse, an Ojibwa explains Native customs and traditions to you. During the summer months, dramatizations, candle-lit tours, and canoe trips help to enhance the experience. An interpretive museum helps emphasize the two cultures and the events of that turbulent time. Visitors should also stop at the Martyr's Shrine, which honours the memory of fathers Jean de Brebeuf and Gabriel Lalement along with five other Jesuits, all of whom were tortured and killed by an invading band of Iroquois at Sainte-Marie in 1649. The shrine has the distinction of being the only Catholic shrine in North America outside of Mexico.

▲ ■ history, native studies, science; all grades; teacher workshops

Simcoe County Museum 68

R.R. 2
Minesing, ON L0L 1Y0

☎ (705) 728-3721

The Simcoe County Museum has an extensive collection of displays and artifacts documenting the history of the county. The museum galleries contain archaeology and Native displays, a 19th-century street of shops, a Victorian wing, and a gallery of changing exhibits. Visit the open-air exhibits, which include a variety of barns for different purposes, a train station, a sugar shack, a schoolhouse, a church and a smokehouse.

■ on-site and outreach; all grades

Nancy Island Historic Site 69

119 Mosley St.

✉

c/o Wasaga Beach Provincial Park
P.O. Box 183
Wasaga Beach, ON L0L 2P0

☎ (705) 429-2516

The architecture of the museum at the Nancy Island Historic Site is symbolic. Look hard and you will get the impression of sails straining against the winds of the Great Lakes. HMS *Nancy*, for whom the site is named, was built in 1789 for the fur trade. However, when the War of 1812 broke out, the British pressed her into service as a transport ship. In 1814, three American ships spotted HMS *Nancy* in Nottawasaga Bay and shelled the ship. It suffered a direct hit, burned to the water line, and sank. The wreck remained for 150 years. The remains of the *Nancy* created a blockage in the Nottawasaga River, causing sand and silt to accumulate until an island (Nancy Island) was created. The site museum interprets the HMS *Nancy*, the War of 1812, and water travel and trade on the Nottawasaga River in the 1800s. Note the large, fully-rigged model of the *Nancy* and the full-scale replica of the figurehead. Find the hull of the original *Nancy* in a climate-controlled enclosure. Various other exhibits extend the nautical theme of this Historic Site.

■ grades K–8

The Billy Bishop Museum 70

948 Third Ave. W.

✉

P.O. Box 535
Owen Sound, ON N4K 5R1

☎ (519) 371-0031

Courtesy Billy Bishop Museum

The childhood home of World War I flying ace Billy Bishop is the site of this museum. By the end of the war, Bishop's official "kill" tally was 72, but unofficially, it exceeded 100. His accomplishments earned him the Victoria Cross, the Distinguished Flying Cross and other honours. Volunteers recount the life and career of Billy Bishop to visitors. Much of the original furniture is in place, so you can easily visualize young Billy in some of his favourite spots. Don't be surprised that you don't find a huge display of military hardware — the purpose of the museum is to humanize the Bishop legend.

Fathom Five National Marine Park 71

P.O. Box 189
Tobermory, ON N0H 2R0
☎ (519) 596-2233

Fathom Five has the distinction of being Canada's first national marine park. Here, over the years, many ships have foundered and sunk in the treacherous waters off the Bruce Peninsula. Thus, the most interesting features of this unique park are the 21 known wrecks of sail and steam vessels that lie on the bottom of the lake within the bounds of Fathom Five. Visitors may explore these underwater relics, or view them from a boat in Big Tub Harbour (the waters of Lake Huron are unusually clear). Other interesting features include Flowerpot Island, whose fantastic rock pillars resemble flowerpots.

▲ ■ on-site

QUEBEC

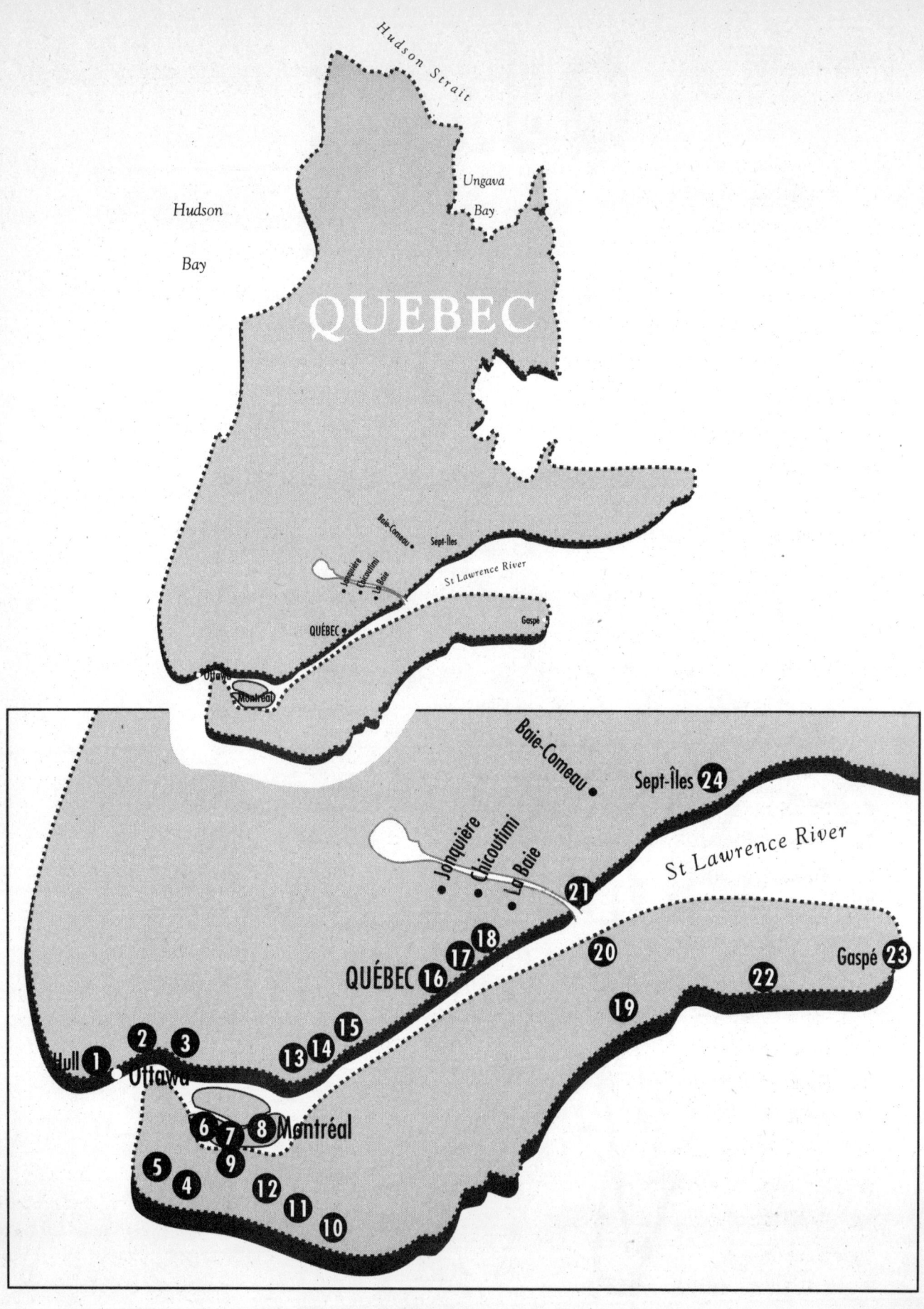

1	Canadian Museum of Civilization	12	J. Armand Bombardier Museum
2	Mackenzie King Estate	13	Sir Wilfrid Laurier National Historic Site
3	Manoir Louis-Joseph Papineau	14	Gilles Villeneuve Museum
4	Battle of the Chateauguay National Historic Site	15	The Forges of St-Maurice National Historic Site
5	Coteau-du-Lac National Historic Park	16a	Musée de l'Amérique française
6	The Fur Trade at Lachine National Historic Park	16b	Musée du Québec
7	Fleming Mill	16c	The Citadel of Quebec
8a	Montreal Botanical Garden	16d	Artillery Park National Historic Site
8b	Insectarium	16e	Fortifications of Quebec National Historic Site
8c	Montreal Museum of Fine Arts	16f	The Old Port of Quebec National Historic Site
8d	McCord Museum of Canadian History	16g	Grosse-Île National Historic Site
8e	Bank of Montreal Museum	16h	Cartier-Brébeuf National Historic Site
8f	Museum of Contemporary Art	16i	National Battlefields Park
8g	Cinémathèque Québécoise and Cinema Museum	16j	Hôtel-Dieu Museum
8h	Pointe-à-Callière Museum of Archaeology and History	16k	Fort No. 1 at Point Lévis National Historic Site
8i	Centre d'histoire de Montréal	17	Trait-Carré Historic Site
8j	Post House Museum	18	Bee Museum
8k	Museum of Decorative Arts	19	Fort Ingall
8l	David M. Stewart Museum: Museum of Discoveries	20	Excursion to l'Île-aux-Basques
8m	Sir George-Étienne Cartier House National Historic Site	21	Saguenay Marine Park
8n	National Circus School	22	Battle of the Restigouche National Historic Site
8o	Biodôme	23	Forillon National Park
8p	International Museum of Humour	24	Mingan Archipelago National Park Reserve
8q	Canadian Centre for Architecture	25	Fort Temiscamingue National Historic Site
8r	Montreal Holocaust Memorial Centre	26	Musée Amérindien de Pointe-Bleue
8s	Biscuit Puppet Theatre and Museum		
8t	Images of the Future		
8u	Montreal Planetarium		
9a	Fort Chambly National Historic Site		
9b	Fort Lennox National Historic Site		
10a	World's Longest Suspended Footbridge		
10b	Beaulne Museum		
11	Louis S. St-Laurent National Historic Site		

In the site descriptions, note that:

▲ indicates that second language services are available: English in Quebec and French elsewhere in Canada. Where "limited service" is given, it would be wise to call ahead for specifics

■ indicates that educational services are available

Canadian Museum of Civilization

100, rue Laurier
C.P. 3100, Succ. B
Hull, PQ J8X 4H2

☎ (819) 776-7000

From the moment you arrive at the Canadian Museum of Civilization, you feel you stand in the presence of something unique. The curves and angles of the building at first look simply pleasing: then you notice that the area around the main entrance looks like a West Coast

Native mask. The museum's architecture symbolizes what the museum is all about: " . . . this continent, its forms sculpted by the winds, the rivers, the glaciers. It [speaks] of the emergence of man from the melting glaciers; of man and woman living in harmony with the forces of nature and evolving with them. It [shows] the way in which man first learned to cope with the environment, then mastered it and shaped it to the need of his own goals and aspirations." The inside of the museum is no less spectacular. The history of humanity is presented in a way that encourages participation and interaction. Marvel as you wander past the world's largest colour photograph, the world's best collection of totem poles and six Pacific Coast Indian house facades joined by a shoreline and boardwalk, all in the Grand Hall. The History Hall includes a Children's Museum, where children up to the age of 14 can enjoy a unique opportunity to broaden their cultural experiences and learn about the world. Phone or write to find out about temporary exhibits and special events of all sorts, and to see what's playing at the IMAX/OMNIMAX theatre.

▲ ■ extensive; workshops for students and teachers; all grades; post-secondary placements in education and museology

Mackenzie King Estate

rue Barnes, Gatineau Park, PQ

✉ 161 Laurier Ave. W.
Ottawa, ON K1P 1J6

☎ (819) 239-5000/827-2020

Kingswood, the magnificent estate of former prime minister William Lyon Mackenzie King, was in many ways the realization of a dream. Visitors may stroll all through Kingswood, which has been restored to recall the period of King's terms in office (1921-1930 and 1934-1948). It is helpful to start with a video that provides a look at King's life and his political career. Of particular interest are the grounds of the estate. Mackenzie was an eccentric, and one of the things he did to beautify the grounds was to place "ruins" here and there on the property. He felt that these would create a more distinguished ambience. Walk along the same pathways where King strolled with his little dog, Pat. Informative guides and interpretive panels help to enrich your visit.

▲ ■ all grades

Manoir Louis-Joseph Papineau

392, rue Notre-Dame
Montebello, PQ J0V 1L0

☎ (819) 423-6341

Born in 1786, Louis-Joseph Papineau was the fiery leader of the Rebellion of 1837 in Lower Canada (Quebec). He was born and raised in Montreal, trained as a lawyer, and enjoyed a distinguished career in politics. He was unhappy with the proposed Act of Union, which was to unite

Upper and Lower Canada (Ontario and Quebec), and cost the French Canadians their language rights. The rebellion he led fizzled, and Papineau fled to the United States. He returned to Quebec in 1844 and resumed his career. Manoir Louis-Joseph Papineau, now a museum, stands on the grounds of a hotel on the Ottawa River. The land was granted to the Papineau family under Quebec's old seigneurial system. The *manoir* was built between 1846 and 1850; 20 rooms, restored and furnished in the style of the period, are open to viewing.

▲ ■ guided tours

Battle of the Châteauguay National Historic Site 4

Allan's Corner

✉

R.R. 4
Ormstown, PQ J0S 1K0

☎ (514) 829-2003 or 763-5631

Step inside the interpretation centre, which invites you to experience the historic battle that took place on this site on October 26, 1813, during the War of 1812. American forces attacked Quebec City, but were soundly defeated by the Canadians under the leadership of Commander Charles-Michel de Salaberry. An audio-visual presentation will place you right on the battlefield next to de Salaberry. Climb the site's lookout tower to scan the actual battleground. See a scale model of the battlefield and discuss military strategy with the guide-interpreter. Also, learn about the difficult conditions under which soldiers lived during that period.

▲ ■ elementary grades

Coteau-du-Lac National Historic Park 5

C.P. 550, ch. du Fleuve
Coteau-du-Lac, PQ J0P 1B0

☎ (514) 763-5631

Built by the British in 1779–80, Coteau-du-Lac was the first lock canal in North America, and the forerunner of the St. Lawrence Seaway. At this site, visitors can also see the remnants of the original Rigolet canal, which was built by the French around 1750, and an  octagonal blockhouse as well. Waterways were crucial for transporting goods and troops, and this was a strategic spot for the British during the 18th and 19th centuries. Here they defended ships laden with military supplies and bound for the Great Lakes. A scale model and interpretive staff tell the story of Coteau-du-Lac.

▲ ■ guided tours

The Fur Trade at Lachine National Historic Park 6

1255, boule. St. Joseph
Lachine, PQ H8S 2M2

☎ (514) 637-7433

The fur trade is central to much of Canada's history. The demand for furs in Europe pushed explorers ever farther into the interior; ultimately, their quest would result in the creation of a new nation. For more than 200 years, Montreal was a key player in the fur trade. Because of the city's strategic position on the St. Lawrence River, trade goods from Europe went to Montreal before being shipped out to Native trappers inland in exchange for furs. In turn, the furs were processed and baled in Montreal for shipment to Europe. The old stone warehouse at Lachine recreates those exciting days. See bales of fur awaiting shipment, and trade goods stocked on shelves. Learn the origin of the phrase, "mad as a hatter." Exhibits and interactive technology are supplemented by costumed animators, who play the roles of

Natives, French Canadian *coureurs des bois*, and Scottish merchants.

▲ ■ on-site; all grades

Fleming Mill

9675, boule. LaSalle, LaSalle

✉

c/o 1080, ave. Dollard
Lasalle, PQ H8N 2T9

☎ (514) 367-6439

Born in Scotland in 1786, William Fleming came to Lower Canada (Quebec) around 1814 to realize his dream of being a miller in his own mill. Grinding wheat was a privilege reserved for the Sulpicians of the Seminary of Montreal, so, at first, his wooden mill ground only barley and rice — for making beer. Not content with that, Fleming took matters into his own hands and began, illegally, to mill wheat as well. A long court case ensued, with no real resolution. So, Fleming continued to grind the wheat, replacing his wooden mill with a stone one in 1827. The mill has been completely restored to Fleming's time. It is the only mill of Anglo-Saxon design in Quebec. Be sure to note the mechanism for turning the sails windward. A modern interpretive centre presents visitors with interesting historical and socio-economic highlights of the early 19th century; Fleming's life, his mill, and the grains processed there. Costumed guides, in the roles of Fleming himself, his daughter Jane, Annie the archaeologist, and Judge Reid, welcome school groups.

▲ ■ on-site; teaching materials

Montreal Botanical Garden 8a

4101, rue Sherbrooke E.
Montréal, PQ H1X 2B2

☎ (514) 872-1400

Mary, Mary, quite contrary, how does your garden grow? At the Montreal Botanical Garden, the question is *which* garden? This oasis of beauty and serenity in the middle of a busy metropolis contains within its greenhouses and outdoor gardens a collection of over 26 000 species and varieties of plants. It covers an area of 73 ha (180 a.) and comprises 10 exhibition conservatories and 30 outdoor gardens. Allow plenty of time for your visit. The Rose Garden (seasonal) contains 200 types of roses and 7000 rose bushes. The Chinese Garden, prefabricated in Shanghai and shipped to Montreal, is the largest of its kind outside China. The Japanese Garden has a museum and gallery with lacquer screens, a peacock kimono, and feudal Japanese warriors in armour. Here you can see bonsai trees and participate in the tea ceremony. Sit and meditate quietly in the Zen Garden. On sunny days, seek refuge in the Shady Garden, or sit beside the Flowery Brook. Perhaps the most intriguing gardens of all are the Poisonous and Medicinal Plant gardens. Here you may see plants used by the pharmaceutical industry, plants associated traditionally with folk medicine, and plants that cause skin irritations, poisoning, or activate allergies, if touched or their pollens inhaled. Guided tours, interpretation paths, and a host of other services make a visit to the Botanical Garden a learning experience.

▲ ■ on-site

Insectarium 8b

4581, rue Sherbrooke E.
Montréal, PQ H1X 2B2

☎ (514) 872-8753

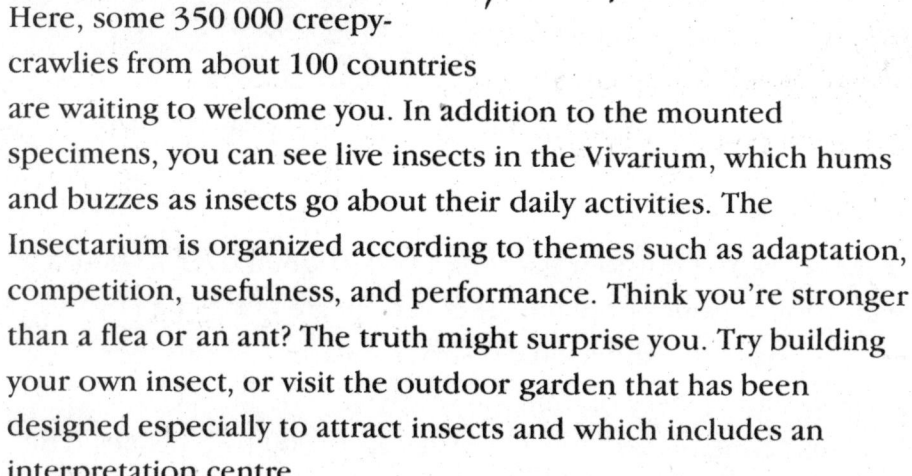

At Montreal's Insectarium, you can find out what's bugging you. Here, some 350 000 creepy-crawlies from about 100 countries are waiting to welcome you. In addition to the mounted specimens, you can see live insects in the Vivarium, which hums and buzzes as insects go about their daily activities. The Insectarium is organized according to themes such as adaptation, competition, usefulness, and performance. Think you're stronger than a flea or an ant? The truth might surprise you. Try building your own insect, or visit the outdoor garden that has been designed especially to attract insects and which includes an interpretation centre.

▲ ■ on-site

Montreal Museum of Fine Arts 8c

1380, rue Sherbrooke O.
C.P. 3000, Succ. H
Montréal, PQ H3G 2T9

☎ (514) 285-1600

Since its inception more than 130 years ago, the Montreal Museum of Fine Arts has assembled one of the finest and most comprehensive collections in North America, exceeding some 25 000 pieces. The recent addition of the new wing, itself a work of art designed by the renowned architect Moshe Safdie, has allowed the museum to display a large part of its collection on a permanent basis. The museum is justifiably proud of its Canadian art collection, which traces the history of Canada from its beginnings as New France, a struggling 17th-century colony, to the present. Media and genres in the Canadian collection include decorative arts; sculpture and painting; contemporary art; and Inuit and Amerindian art. As well, the museum displays works assembled around such areas as medieval art; the ancient world; the Renaissance; baroque, the 18th century; the 19th century; modern European art; and contemporary American and European art.

▲ ■ on-site; workshops; tours

McCord Museum of Canadian History 8d

690, rue Sherbrooke O.
Montréal, PQ H3A 1E9

☎ (514) 398-7100

The McCord Museum of Canadian History is the fulfilment of a dream. David Ross McCord, a prominent Montreal lawyer who died in 1930, donated his valuable collection of Canadian objects to McGill University, hoping that it would form the basis for a museum of Canadian history. The McCord Museum opened in 1971 and, in 1992, moved into its current establishment. The collections, which include over 80 000 objects and 700 000 photographs, have been organized in seven groups: ethnology and archaeology; costume and textiles; the Notman Photographic Archives; decorative arts; the archives; paintings, prints and drawings; and the library. The permanent displays cover mainly the time period from the 18th century to the present and the focus is on Montreal, Quebec, and Canada. This museum presents visitors with an exciting way to become better acquainted with our history.

▲ ■ curriculum-related

Bank of Montreal Museum 8e

129, rue St-Jacques, Place d'Armes
Montréal, PQ H2Y 3S8

☎ (514) 877-6892

The Bank of Montreal Museum will satisfy the curiosity of anyone who wonders about the roots of banking. The history of this bank is a long and honourable one. Established in 1817, the Bank of Montreal has been involved in the financing of some of Canada's greatest enterprises, including the Canadian Pacific Railway, canals, and telegraphs. In the museum you will see a replica of the bank's first office; displays of bank notes, gold, and coins; a collection of rare mechanical savings banks; and other bank memorabilia.

▲ ■ guided tours

Museum of Contemporary Art 8f

185, rue Ste-Catherine O.
Montréal, PQ H2X 1Z8

☎ (514) 847-6226

Montreal's Museum of Contemporary Art enjoys the distinction of being the only contemporary art museum in Canada. The museum's collections begin with the year 1939, at a point when art in Canada took a new direction. It was initiated by John Lyman, a teacher, painter, and art critic who had studied under Matisse in Paris and who was unhappy with the attitude of Canada's Group of Seven. Members of the Group of Seven believed that Canadian artists should reflect Canadian subjects. This Lyman called "souvenir painting." The museum's collection consists of over 4600 works, representing every major art movement of the last 60 years. The museum exhibits pieces of abstract expressionism, geometric abstraction, post-pictorial abstraction, Pop art, minimalism, conceptual art, photography, and video art. Artists represented include Warhol, Picasso, Mapplethorpe, and Lichtenstein.

▲ ■ workshops; films and videos; meetings with artists; tours

Cinémathèque Québécoise and Cinema Museum 8g

335, boul. de Maisonneuve E.
Montréal, PQ H2X 1K1

☎ (514) 842-9763

**CINÉMATHÈQUE QUÉBÉCOISE
Musée du cinéma**

Courtesy Cinémathèque Québécoise

There can be no question but that the invention of film as a medium transformed the performing arts. Montreal's Cinémathèque Québécoise aims to promote cinema, particularly Quebec film; to preserve film prints and film-related documentation; and to organize screenings and exhibitions. Its collection exceeds 28 000 films, in addition to thousands of posters, photographs, scripts, and press clippings. You can attend screenings most days. The museum houses a unique collection of film projectors, cameras, sets, costumes, and props. Attached to the museum and cinema is a specialized library, which you may use for research purposes.

▲

Pointe-à-Callière Museum of Archaeology and History 8h

350, Place Royale
Montréal, PQ H2Y 3Y5

☎ (514) 872-9150

Courtesy Pointe-à-Callière Museum

The Pointe-a-Callière Museum of Archaeology and History — one very exciting place — offers the visitor six centuries of history. Appropriately, it sits on the spot where the city of Montreal was founded. The museum is divided into three sections: the Eperon building, a modern structure erected on the ruins of older buildings; a crypt in the basement; and the renovated Ancienne Douane (formerly the Customs House of Montreal). See a stunning multimedia presentation on the history of Montreal; proceed to the basement, which contains Montreal's first Catholic cemetery; walk through a stone conduit, once the bed of the Little St-Pierre River, to enter the crypt where the archaeological remnants of different eras are on display. Interactive technology helps bring the city's colourful past to life.

▲ ■ on-site; all grades; workshops; guided tours

Centre d'histoire de Montréal 8i

335, place d'Youville
Montréal, PQ H2Y 3T1

☎ (514) 872-3207

Montreal is a living museum and the Centre d'histoire de Montréal will prove it to you. Here you can journey back through time to the founding of Ville Marie, where you can learn all about the people who have shaped this wonderful and exciting city. Begin your trip in the year 1642. Meet the Native peoples who lived here, and then the first Europeans to settle on the site. Proceed to the first floor to find yourself inside a fortified city; see buildings and public squares built by the two founding nations, the French and the English. Next you will see how Montreal, both as a port and as the hub of a railway network, has been the entry point to Canada for hundreds of thousands of immigrants. Learn how Montreal developed as a major industrial centre, a position it continues to enjoy. Step inside the living room of a typical Montreal duplex to get a feel for the lifestyle of a Montrealer. Be sure to see the interpretation centre. The exhibits are supplemented by interactive and audio-visual technology.

▲ ■ on-site; teaching materials

Post House Museum 8j

1035, rue St-Jacques
Montréal, PQ H3C 1H0

☎ (514) 846-5400

For anyone who has ever had a stamp collection, the Post House Museum has a lot to offer. The museum presents a number of exhibits that illustrate the development of mail delivery through history, particularly in England and France. As well, there are displays on such topics of interest as stamp collecting, stamp-printing techniques, mechanized mail processing, postal codes, and letter carriers' uniforms. Stamp collectors may wish to consult the material available in the specialized library. Various items related to the world of mail and stamp collecting are available; the staff will happily share their knowledge and expertise.

▲ ■ guided tours

Museum of Decorative Arts 8k

rue Sherbrooke and boule. Pie IX

✉
C.P. 12 000
Montréal, PQ H3C 3P3
☎ (514) 259-2575

Founded in 1979 by David M. Stewart and located in the Château Dufresne, which was built in 1918, the Museum of Decorative Arts presents a stunning collection of international design and decorative arts from 1935 to the present, a period generally considered to be one of the most innovative and diversified in the history of decorative arts and industrial design. The exhibits focus on designers as well as specific objects of design. See furniture, glass, textiles, ceramics, and graphic design.

▲ ■ on-site

David M. Stewart Museum: Museum of Discoveries 8l

The Old Fort–Île Ste-Hélène

✉

C.P. 1024, Succ. A
Montréal, PQ H3C 2W9

☎ (514) 861-6701

Located in the Old Fort on St. Helen's Island, the David M. Stewart Museum, truly a museum of discoveries, invites you to explore. By means of its displays and interactive technology, discover the New World of the 17th, 18th, and 19th centuries. The museum's permanent collection presents the major historical events of Canada, and the important developments in science, technology, and art during that same time period. See such diverse items as kitchen utensils, firearms, old maps, scientific instruments, navigational aids, and documents. Be sure not to miss the museum's new history gallery, which has been laid out in a linear plan that corresponds to the architecture of the fort. Visitors advance in time and space through the length of the fort's first floor, at the same time following the chronology of Canadian history from the discovery of North America to the rebellions of 1837-38. In the fort's courtyard, the 18th Fraser Highlanders and the Compagnie Franche de la Marine, dressed just like their forerunners who garrisoned France's New World outposts from 1683 to 1760, perform authentic 18th-century military manoeuvres.

▲ ■ on-site

Sir George-Étienne Cartier House National Historic Site 8m

458, rue Notre-Dame E.
Montréal, PQ H2Y 1C8

Sir George-Étienne Cartier, one of the Fathers of Confederation, was also a major participant in the construction of the transcontinental railway system. His home, consisting of two adjoining houses where Cartier and his family lived from 1848 to 1871, has been declared a National Historic Site. The career and accomplishments of Cartier are highlighted in the "East" house, where the displays and furnishings transport the visitor back to those decisive years for Canada in the 19th century. The "West" house represents an elegant Victorian residence. Walk through the bedrooms, living room, and the dining room, which has been set as if for a fine banquet. Animation offers an insight into the career and personality of this important figure in Canadian history.

▲ ■ on-site

National Circus School 8n

417, rue Berri
Montréal, PQ H2Y 3E1

☎ (514) 982-0859

Anyone who's ever had a desire to run away and join the circus will be fascinated by the National Circus School, the only one of its kind in North America. Students from both Canada and abroad come here to learn how to perform in a circus. The school teaches acrobatics, aerial techniques, balance techniques, manipulation techniques, circus acting, makeup, and costuming. The school's award-winning graduates perform in a variety of areas. They may be trapeze artists, acrobats, jugglers, clowns, ringmasters, and many other things as well. The school also offers a full high-school and junior-college program of studies. It is located in the former Dalhousie Train Station, which has its own story to tell. Built by the Canadian Pacific Company, it was the point from which the first transcontinental train bound for Vancouver departed in June 1886.

▲

Biodôme 8o

4777, ave. Pierre-de-Coubertin
Montréal, PQ H1V 1B3

☎ (514) 868-3000

BIODÔME DE MONTRÉAL

Courtesy Biodôme

Neither zoo nor aquarium nor botanical garden, Montreal's Biodôme is unique: a spectacular example of a living museum of natural and environmental sciences. Here the visitor can see live collections of plants and animals. No fewer than four ecosystems have been recreated in a space covering 10 000 m^2 (2 1/2 a.): the Tropical Forest; the Laurentian Forest; the St. Lawrence Marine Ecosystem; and the Polar Shield. "Ecotransits" between ecosystems highlight man's role in the natural world. The Biodôme also warns of the dangers threatening the global environment. Venture into Discovery Room, where you can explore how living things adapt to their environment. Animation, guides along the pathways, and interactive technology make this learning experience truly enjoyable.

▲ ■ on-site; teacher and student workshops

International Museum of Humour 8p

2101, boule. St-Laurent
Montréal, PQ H2X 2T5

☎ (514) 845-4000

Tickle your funny bone at the International Museum of Humour! Celebrate humour in all its forms, from all over the world and for all ages. Caricature, motion picture cartoons, film, literature, advertising — it's all showcased here. The museum, housed in a former brewery, contains an exhibition area, a documentation centre, a hall of fame, and a production centre. Visit the International Museum of Humour . . . just for laughs!

Canadian Centre for Architecture 8q

1920, rue Baile
Montréal, PQ H3H 2S6

☎ (514) 939-7000

For people who appreciate beauty in design, the Canadian Centre for Architecture offers many hours of pleasure and learning. This architectural museum offers the only collection of its kind in the world. It explores and interprets the world of architecture, including urban planning and landscape design. The museum mounts six to eight exhibitions each year, all developed around five broad themes: Aspects of Modernism; the Building of Canada; Photography and Architecture; Contemporary Theory and Practice; and the Historical Foundations of Architectural Discourse. Browse as well through the garden, veritably an outdoor museum. The centre also hosts a number of temporary exhibitions each year. The younger set will definitely enjoy the annual exhibit on toys, which occurs during the holiday season. To accompany this popular exhibit, the centre offers special play sessions for children. Beyond its service as an interesting and educational place to visit, the centre provides important resources for architects and architectural students.

▲ ■ guided tours

Montreal Holocaust Memorial Centre 8r

5151, ch. Côte-Ste-Catherine
Montréal, PQ H3W 1M6

☎ (514) 345-2605

Founded in 1979 by the Association of Survivors of Nazi Oppression, the Montreal Holocaust Memorial Centre collects documents and preserves personal memorabilia and testimonies about Jewish life from the early years of the 20th century through the years of the Nazi terror and the aftermath. You won't soon forget the centre's permanent exhibit, entitled, "Splendour and Destruction: Jewish Life That Was, 1919-1945." Trained guides will take you through, and at the end, a Holocaust survivor gives a brief testimonial and answers questions. You will leave the centre with a very clear sense of the need for tolerance and understanding in our world.

▲ ■

Biscuit Puppet Theatre and Museum 8s

221, rue St-Paul O.
Montréal, PQ H2Y 2A2

☎ (514) 845-7306

What can be more magical than a puppet show? Montreal's Theatre Biscuit blends music, marionettes, actors, colourful costumes and lighting, and wonderful stories to touch the hearts of people of all ages and all cultures. Puppetry is an art with a long and variegated history, and Theatre Biscuit, using primarily music and sound effects, reaches across language barriers to delight one and all. Most performances take place in the 55-seat theatre on St. Paul St., although, on occasion, performances are staged in the Old Port area of the city. The theatre also contains a small puppet museum.

■ on-site and outreach performances

Images of the Future 8t

15, rue de la Commune O.
Montréal, PQ H2Y 2C6

☎ (514) 849-1612

Take an opportunity to experience the stunning effects created when technology is applied to art

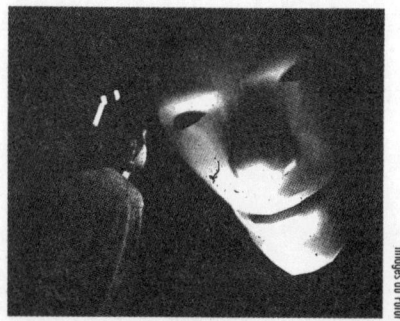

installation by Catherine Ikam and Jean-Louis Fléri, courtesy Images du Futur

and communication. See laser images, holographic pictures, light sculptures, interactive sculptures, computer-drawn pictures, videos, computer animation and virtual reality. Experience multimedia shows and electronic music. Come and touch the future!

▲ ■ on-site

Montreal Planetarium 8u

1000, rue St-Jacques O.
Montréal, PQ H3C 1G7

☎ (514) 872-4530

Fly to the moon and play among the stars at the Montreal Planetarium! The focal point is the Zeiss projector. This sophisticated device reproduces a star-studded sky as seen by the naked eye from any place on earth. Sometimes described as a time machine, it can duplicate the appearance of the sky at any time: past, present, or future. Special effects projectors are used to show the constellations, to indicate celestial co-ordinates, and to recreate current astronomical events such as a meteor shower, *aurora borealis* (the northern lights), and the slow passage of a comet. Visit the gallery, which holds exhibits on a variety of relevant topics. The planetarium invites you to explore the fascinating world of astronomy and discover the architecure of the universe through paintings, showcases, exhibitions, and interactive technology.

▲ ■ on-site

Fort Chambly National Historic Site 9a

2, rue Richelieu
Chambly, PQ J3L 2B9

☎ (514) 658-1585

The modern city of Chambly, located only 28 km (17 mi.) from Montreal, has its origins in Fort Chambly. The original wooden fortress was built in 1665 next to the Richelieu River rapids by Captain Jacques de Chambly. In 1709, struggling with the English for dominance in the New World, the Compagnies Franches de la Marine replaced the wooden fortifications with stone walls. In 1760, the fort fell to the British; for a brief time it was even occupied by Americans. The fort, restored in 1983, now welcomes visitors. It interprets the period of the British occupation from 1775 to 1871.

▲ ■ on-site; teaching materials

Fort Lennox National Historic Site

1369, rue Bourgogne
Chambly, PQ J3L 1Y4

☎ (514) 291-5700

Situated on Île-aux-Noix (Nut Island), near the American border, Fort Lennox has a long and checkered history. In 1759, the French began to build fortifications on the island to protect it from attack by the British. Unfortunately, the French, who were garrisoning the fortification in 1760, were ill-prepared for the attack when it came. They surrendered, after which the British destroyed the original French fort. The next occupants of the island were the Americans during the American Revolution, who used it as a base from which to launch an attack on Montreal. Following the American withdrawal, the British felt it necessary to fortify the island, and so, in 1779, a few blockhouses were built on the site of the original French fort. Later, between 1819 and 1829, these fortifications were enlarged and strengthened. The new fort was named after Charles Lennox, Duke of Richmond and former governor general, who had died in 1819 (after a bite from a rabid fox). The fort, which has been restored to the 19th century, illustrates the life of the soldiers who garrisoned it at that time.

Be sure to note the stoves; because the fort was built to defend against attacks launched by boat, it contained stoves with which to heat cannon balls. Red-hot cannon balls posed a serious threat to wooden vessels.

▲ ■ on-site

World's Longest Suspended Footbridge

Parc de la Gorge de Coaticook
135 Michaud
Coaticook, PQ J1A 1A9

☎ (819) 849-2331 or 849-6669

"I made it across the world's longest suspension footbridge," reads the certificate you will receive after crossing this incredible bridge. The bridge, which is 169 m (554 ft.) long, is suspended 58 m (192 ft.) high over the Gorge of Coaticook and the Coaticook River. Drop in to the visitor centre before crossing the bridge for an orientation to the park and its many attractions, for the park itself is very beautiful. Take in the towering rocky cliffs and walk nearly 3 km (2 mi.) of trails. The Couillard Tower offers a panoramic view of the entire site. Visit the cave and the remnants of an old dam.

▲ ■ on-site

Beaulne Museum

96 Union St.
Coaticook, PQ J1A 1Y9

☎ (819) 849-6560

Situated in the former home of a prominent industrialist, A.O. Norton, the Beaulne Museum offers a fine representation of the late Victorian period, 1885-1915. The salon contains fine period mahogany furniture. The elegant dining room features oak woodwork and furniture. Windowed cabinets with interior lighting show off the beautiful silver and china. See an exhibit of particular interest: a collection of dolls dressed in nuns' habits and other religious dress, which was the customary style at that time. The theme of clothing pervades the whole building, in keeping with the mandate of the museum: to research and present exhibits of clothing and textiles. The museum also hosts temporary and travelling exhibitions.

▲ ■ guided tours

Louis S. St-Laurent National Historic Site 11

6, rue Principale Sud
Compton, PQ J0B 1L0

☎ (819) 835-5448

Open to view is the home where Louis St-Laurent, prime minister of Canada from 1948 to 1957, was born and grew up. More than 2000 items that belonged to the family reveal something of the life and career of this remarkable leader. Once you have toured the house, move on to the general store. Here, an animator representing Louis's father, general merchant Jean-Baptiste Moise St-Laurent, will welcome you. Inside, you can listen in on the conversation of the villagers gathered around the coal stove. The store has retained its original counters and shelves, which the staff have stocked with reproductions of the type of merchandise that was sold here during Louis's boyhood. Next to the store, in an old warehouse, a sound-and-light show tells the story of Louis St-Laurent.

▲ ■ on-site; grades 4–6; teaching materials

J. Armand Bombardier Museum 12

1001, ave. J. A. Bombardier
Valcourt, PQ J0E 2L0

☎ (514) 532-2258

Winter in Canada brings with it many sports and pastimes,  some age-old and some modern — like snowmobiling. The snowmobile is a uniquely Canadian invention, and its uses are many (it is the vehicle of choice in northern communities). This museum documents the life and career, from 1960 to the present, of J. Armand Bombardier, inventor of the snowmobile. The museum documents the development of the snowmobile and introduces the visitor to some of the other products Bombardier has had a hand in.

Sir Wilfrid Laurier National Historic Site 13

250, 12e ave. Laurier

✉

P.O. Box 70
Ville-des-Laurentides, PQ J0R 1C0

☎ (514) 439-3702

Born in 1854 in the village of St-Lin-des-Laurentides, Wilfrid Laurier became Canada's first French-Canadian prime minister, a post he held from 1896 to 1911. The house in which he grew up welcomes visitors and offers a portrait of the man, his life and the lifestyle of the period. The interpretive centre contains an exhibit presenting Laurier's distinguished career as a lawyer, journalist, and politician. The house has been furnished and maintained as it was in Laurier's lifetime: a typical rural home of the mid-19th century. Of note is the old-fashioned kitchen complete with wood stove and antique furniture. Take time to walk around the grounds to enjoy the trees, flowers, and vegetable garden. Guides in period costume interpret the house and activities of the period.

▲ ■ on-site

Gilles Villeneuve Museum 14

510, rue de Frontenac
Berthierville, PQ J0K 1A0

☎ (514) 836-2714

Gilles Villeneuve, a legendary racing-car driver on the international circuit, died when the car he was driving crashed on the track. His home in Berthierville has been converted into a museum to which visitors are welcome. See the thematic exhibits, souvenirs from the Grand Prix, photographs and films, all of which tell about the life and accomplishments of Gilles Villeneuve. You might also want to peek at the racing cars on the site.

▲

The Forges of St-Maurice National Historic Site 15

10 000, blvd des Forges
Trois-Rivières, PQ G9C 1B1

☎ (819) 378-5116

Founded in 1730, the Forges of St-Maurice, complete with blast furnace and two forges, is the site of Canada's first heavy industry. Considered the "most technically advanced ironworks in America" for nearly 100 years, the forges produced stoves, agricultural and domestic implements, and, in later years, wheels for railway cars. The ironworks also experimented with steel making and cannon founding for a time. The forges ceased production in 1883, but an interpretation centre and archaeological remains bring this flagship of Canadian industry to life for the visitor.

▲

Musée de l'Amérique française
(Museum of French America) 16a

9, rue de l'Université

✉

C.P. 460
Haute-Ville, Québec, PQ G1R 4R7

☎ (418) 692-2843

Housed in the Séminaire de Québec for 300 years, this museum has built up an impressive collection of artifacts to preserve and explain Quebec's history, heritage, and culture, and tell the story of the French presence in North America. The collection, which consists of over 110 000 items, is divided into seven main groups: art, science, stamps, ethnology, rare and old books, and historical archives. Be sure to see the maps and plans, which date from 1500. Various aspects of the Quebec heritage are highlighted through temporary exhibitions.

▲ ■ guided tours

Musée du Québec 16b

1, ave. Montcalm, Battlefields Park
Québec, PQ G1R 5H3

☎ (418) 643-2150

Situated in historic Battlefields Park, the Musée du Québec strives to promote and preserve the art of Quebec. The museum's collection numbers around 18 000 pieces, most of which form and represent Quebec's cultural heritage from the late 18th century to the present. The collection reflects the various stages of artistic development in Quebec and provides a complete overview of all media: painting, sculpture, drawing, print making, goldsmithing, and the production of decorative works. In addition to the museum's permanent collection, you can also view temporary exhibitions organized by the Musée and other Canadian or foreign museums. Visitors are invited to relax in the Artist's Garden. Every year in the spring, a different artist creates a work that will remain on display until the following year.

▲ ■ on-site; outreach; all grades

The Citadel of Quebec 16c

Côte de la Citadelle, Haute-Ville

✉
C.P. 6020
Québec, PQ G1R 4V7

☎ (418) 648-3563

Quebec City enjoys the distinction of being the oldest walled city in North America, and no visit to Quebec would be complete without seeing the citadel. Built on top of Cap Diamant, with a view of the battlefields, the citadel is part of fortifications built by the British in 1820. It took 30 years to complete the project. A number of interesting historic buildings can be explored inside the citadel. The King's Bastion and the Cap Diamant Redoubt can both be traced back to 1693. The powder magazine was built in 1750 and, along with the old prison, has been transformed into a museum for Canada's Royal 22nd Regiment, the famous "Vandoos." The regiment has been stationed at the citadel since 1872, and the museum displays mementos that tell its proud military history. Examine the documents, guns, small arms, medals, uniforms, and diorama portraying life during the French regime. The regimental band is a favourite with Quebeckers. During the summer months, the ceremonial changing of the guard — which includes the participation of Batisse, the regimental goat — attracts an appreciative audience.

▲ ■ on-site

Artillery Park National Historic Site 16d

2, rue d'Auteuil

✉

C.P. 2474
Québec, PQ G1K 7R3

☎ (418) 648-4205

As the name suggests, Artillery Park has its roots in its strategic importance to the defence of Quebec under both the French and the British. It overlooks a plateau to the left and a river to the right and provides a vantage point for early warning of attack by land or water. It was garrisoned by the French until Quebec fell to the British, who garrisoned it in turn until 1879, when the Canadian government converted it into an armaments manufacturing facility. The munitions foundry now functions as the reception and interpretation centre. Here you can see on display an original early 19th-century scale model of Quebec, with over 1000 houses. See the officers' quarters in the park, and then proceed to the Dauphine Redoubt. Life was not easy for the soldiers. Small rooms housed up to 25 soldiers each. Each bed had only one cover; six soldiers were expected to share one plate; and soldiers worked and slept always wearing the same uniform. Certainly not a picnic!

▲ ■ guided tours

Fortifications of Quebec National Historic Site 16e

100, rue St-Louis

✉

C.P. 2474
Québec, PQ G1K 7R3

☎ (418) 648-7016

The Fortifications of Quebec National Historic Site provides visitors with a pristine example, over a distance of 4.6 km (nearly 3 mi.), of 300 years of military engineering. The first fortifications, primarily earthworks with a stockade and redoubts, were built when Britain and France first went to war against one another on North American soil, in 1690. The earthworks were later replaced by masonry. These fortifications have been well preserved, and visitors are invited to walk among the ramparts, bastions, and powder magazines. Walk along the top of the walls like the sentries of old, or along the Great Battery. The visitor reception centre, located at the Esplanade powder magazine by the St. Louis Gate, contains a display of the various stages in the development of Quebec's fortifications.

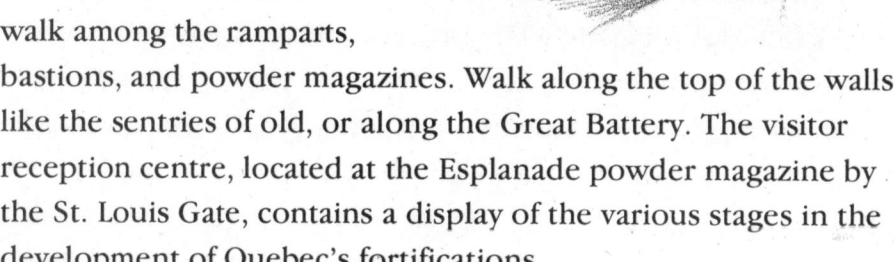

▲ ■ guided tours

The Old Port of Quebec National Historic Site 16f

100, rue St-André

✉
C.P. 2474
Québec, PQ G1K 7R3

☎ (418) 648-3300

Since its founding, the Port of Quebec has played a leading role in the economy of the surrounding region and the country as a whole. In the early part of the 18th century, the fur trade dominated, but as the century drew to a close, the fur trade was replaced by lumber and shipbuilding. The British demanded massive amounts of oak and pine for manufacture. Timber was floated downriver to Quebec, where it was received and loaded onto ships bound for England. Furthermore, a law passed in 1786 decreed that all cargo entering or leaving England had to be transported by ships built in British territory; nearly 2000 of the many ships needed to service the huge British Empire during the 19th century were built in Quebec. This was when The Old Port of Quebec was at its zenith of importance, and the National Historic Site highlights this era. Visit the interpretation centre, where you will step into a typical quay. As you proceed, exhibits will show you how shipbuilders produced their masterpieces. Audio-visual presentations dramatize the shipyards and workshops of the time. Mannequins dressed in period costume illustrate artisans and workers at their trades. Of interest is a diorama that introduces the viewer to Christopher Columbus, Jacques Cartier, and Jean Talon. Before leaving the centre, be sure to step out to the glassed-in terrace to observe the modern Port of Quebec.

▲ ■ guided tours

Grosse-Île National Historic Site 16g

✉

C.P. 2474
Québec, PQ G1K 7R3

☎ (418) 563-4009 or 648-4168

Grosse-Île stands as a reminder — not always a happy one — of the hopes and aspirations of immigrants to Canada, and the misery that not only spurred their immigration but, all too often, followed them. Between 1815 and 1941, more than 4 million immigrants arrived in Canada. Because Europe was beset with typhus and cholera epidemics between 1830 and 1860,

Grosse-Île was set up as a quarantine station where the travellers would be kept until they could be given a clean bill of health. The authorities considered the island ideal for this purpose because of its relatively isolated position in the St. Lawrence, approximately 50 km (31 mi.) from Quebec City. Unfortunately for many — particularly the Irish fleeing the ravages of the deadly potato famine of 1845–1848 — Grosse-Île proved the destruction rather than the realization of their dreams of a better life. Perhaps as many as 15 000 Irish immigrants died in the fever sheds on the island; they were buried there in mass graves. Staff will greet you on the pier and show you the site, which is divided into three sectors: the hotel sector, the village sector, and the hospital sector. Step into the bakery and the first-class hotel. See also the little churches on the island and the cemeteries. See a landmark of particular interest: the tall Celtic cross, erected in 1909 by the Ancient Order of Hibernians in memory of the Irish dead.

▲ ■ guided tours

Cartier–Brébeuf National Historic Site 16h

175, rue de l'Espinay

✉

C.P. 2474
Québec, PQ G1K 7R3

☎ (418) 648-4038

The Cartier–Brébeuf National Historic Site invites you to go back in time to the winter of 1535-1536, a particularly harsh winter by all accounts, when the French explorer, Jacques Cartier, stayed at this site with his crew. Although Viking and Irish explorers at various times had made their way to the Atlantic coast of North America, Cartier is generally regarded as the first European to penetrate the continent. The King of France had sent Cartier to search for a shorter sea route to Asia. He didn't find it, but his arrival marked the beginning of settlement in the New World by Europeans. The site also commemorates Jean de

Brébeuf, a member of the first Jesuit mission established here in 1626. Of particular interest is an exact replica of the *Grande Hermine*, Cartier's flagship. The replica, commissioned by the Canadian government, was constructed in 1966 as a display at Expo '67 (Montreal). Also on the site, see a Native longhouse and a reception centre. Here, visitors can learn about Jacques Cartier, the origins of Canada, Cartier's relations with the Native peoples, and the role played by the Jesuits. While you are there, have a taste of annedda, a brew made by boiling cedar branches. Provided to Cartier's men by the Natives of the area, this vitamin-rich infusion probably saved many of Cartier's men from succumbing to scurvy during that long, cold winter.

▲ ■ on-site; workshops

National Battlefields Park 16i

National Battlefields Commission
390, rue de Bernières
Québec, PQ G1R 2L7

☎ (418) 648-4071

National Battlefields Park covers more than 107 ha (250 a.) of land, and encompasses the Plains of Abraham, where the French and the English fought the decisive battle for Quebec in 1759, under their leaders, Montcalm and Wolfe. The 20 points of interest in the park include the Price Collection of historic guns; the Wolfe Monument, erected on the spot where Wolfe died from injuries sustained during the battle; the Montcalm Monument; and three Martello Towers built by the British as part of their defence network against the eventuality of an attack by the Americans during the War of 1812. Visit the visitor reception and interpretation centre. The park contains some 22 commemorative plaques and over 20 interpretation panels.

▲ ■ guided tours

Hôtel-Dieu Museum 16j

32, rue Charlevoix
Québec, PQ G1R 5C4

☎ (418) 692-2492

The Hôtel-Dieu was the first hospital to be built in North America. Its museum presents visitors with an overview of medical practices and the medical implements used during the last few centuries. See syringes made of silver, gold, and glass. Note the anesthesia mask made from a pig's bladder. See the wooden shoes that surgeons wore to protect their feet in case they dropped a scalpel. Of particular interest are the red gowns worn by surgeons; the colour red was chosen to camouflage the blood stains.

▲ ■ guided tours

Fort No. 1 at Point Lévis National Historic Site 16k

41, ch. du Gouvernement, Lévis

✉

C.P. 2474
Lévis, PQ G1K 7R3

☎ (418) 835-5182

In 1865, the British decided that they needed a stronger military presence at Quebec. They feared American reprisals against Canada for British policies held during the American Civil War. Furthermore, the Irish Fenians had begun to attack British colonies, in the hope that the British would be forced to deploy more troops there, leaving Ireland unguarded and the way clear for independence. A series of three forts was constructed, of which only one (Fort No. 1 at Point Lévis) still stands, directly across the St. Lawrence River from Quebec City. The three forts were never given names. The site of Fort No. 1 is higher than the Quebec City site, giving it a panoramic view of the entire region. The structure is that of a pentagon (five points) surrounded by a dry moat, an excellent example of military engineering of the time. See the caponiers (covered passages across the fort's ditches), casemates (vaulted chambers in the fort's walls), and powder magazines. Be sure to see the Armstrong rifle breech loader.

▲ ■ guided tours

Trait-Carré Historic Site 17

Charlesbourg, PQ

☎ (418) 624-7740

Trait-Carré, a historical zone, was designed by the Jesuits and constructed in 1665 by Intendant Jean Talon. It consists of six important buildings: the water mill, which dates from 1740; the municipal library and Bon-Pasteur Couvent, both of which were constructed in 1883; the socio-cultural centre; and the Bédard and Léfèbvre houses. Guided tours help to place this historical zone into the context of the history of the region and of Quebec.

▲ ■ guided tours

Bee Museum 18

8862, boule. Ste-Anne
Château-Richer, PQ G0A 1N0

☎ (418) 824-4411

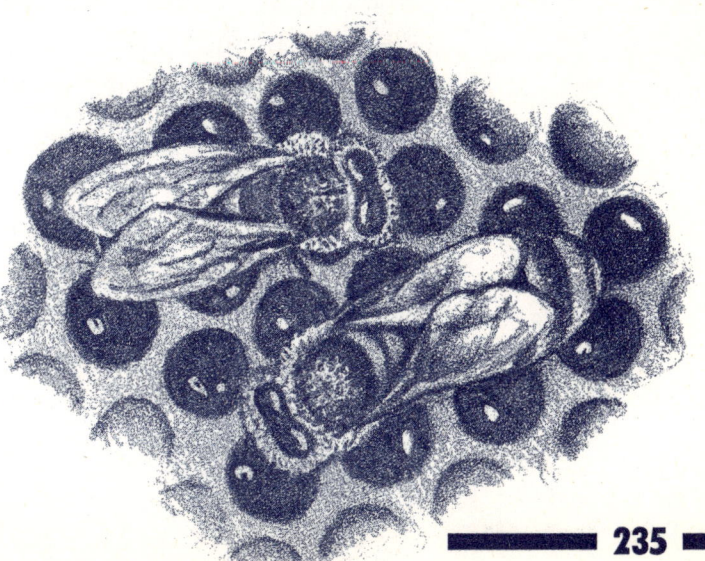

"How doth the busy little bee improve each shining hour?" By making honey! At the Bee Museum, you can learn all about the production of one of humanity's earliest and still most popular foods. Photographs, drawings, and videos all illustrate life in the hive: different types of bees, their anatomy, the queen, the drone, bee reproduction, the worker bees' duties, harvesting honey and pollen, the bee dance, and much more. Windows allow visitors to look directly into giant observation hives to observe first-hand the life of the hive. From a protected distance, watch the beekeepers perform their tasks. In the winery, learn about the production of mead (honey wine), the drink which has figured in Norse mythology and ancient history. Come to the Bee Museum and get buzzed!

▲ ■ on-site

Fort Ingall 19

81, ch. Caldwell
Cabano, PQ G0L 1E0

☎ (418) 854-2375

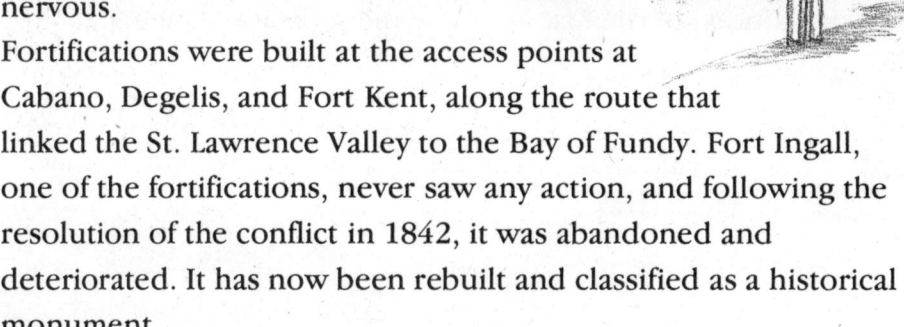

In 1839, a border dispute between Canada and the United States made the Canadians very nervous. Fortifications were built at the access points at Cabano, Degelis, and Fort Kent, along the route that linked the St. Lawrence Valley to the Bay of Fundy. Fort Ingall, one of the fortifications, never saw any action, and following the resolution of the conflict in 1842, it was abandoned and deteriorated. It has now been rebuilt and classified as a historical monument.

▲

Île-aux-Basques Excursion 20

c/o Tourist Service
5, ave. Notre-Dame E., C.P. 550
Trois-Pistoles, PQ G0L 4K0

☎ (418) 851-4649

In the 15th and 16th centuries, Basque whalers sailed into the St. Lawrence River in search of the huge water mammals. The whales were hunted primarily for their blubber, a source of oil. The oil was used in Europe as fuel for light and heat. The whalers established a station on Île-aux-Basques. You can still see the remains of three ovens used between the years 1525 and 1630 to render the blubber into oil. The island also holds a bird sanctuary and nature interpretation trails.

▲

Saguenay Marine Park 21

182, rue de l'Église
Tadoussac, PQ G0T 2A0

☎ (418) 235-4703
or 1-800-463-6769

The Saguenay Marine Park preserves, studies, and presents to visitors an ecosystem unique in the world. Here, at the confluence of the St. Lawrence and Saguenay rivers, very cold, briny water mixes with warmer fresh water to create an environment able to support a variety of species of marine life rarely found this far south. Three species of seal make this area their home, as do four types of whale: the beluga, the minke, the fin, and the blue. You can find traces of human history here as well. Basque whalers used the site several hundred years earlier to render whale blubber into oil, and Native tribes met here to trade and barter.

▲

Battle of the Restigouche National Historic Site 22

Route 132, C.P. 359
Pointe-à-la-Croix, PQ G0C 1L0

☎ (418) 788-5676

In the second half of the 18th century, England and France were battling for supremacy in the New World. In July of 1760, at the mouth of the Restigouche River, British ships commanded by John Byron defeated a French relief force led by François-Gabriel d'Angeac. You can visit an interpretation centre at the site, and trace the route taken by the small supply fleet sent to relieve New France. A film highlights the event. See the artifacts salvaged from the French frigate, *Le Machault*.

Courtesy Parks Canada

Forillon National Park 23

District of Gaspé, C.P. 1220
Gaspé, PQ G0C 1R0

☎ (418) 368-5505

Courtesy Parks Canada

Forillon National Park has, it seems, something of everything. To discover Forillon, take advantage of the extensive interpretation activities offered to visitors. These programs include the Underwater World at Grande-Grave (Grande-Grave is a beach); Life in the Tide Pools; Penouille, a World of Its Own (Penouille is an area of the park); the Secrets of Forillon's Rock; and a variety of hikes and lectures. Not all programs are offered in English. The park includes replicas of

early buildings and historic sites such as the Logan Monument to
Sir William Edmond Logan, considered to be the father of modern
geology; a monument to French explorer Jacques Cartier; and the
Lighthouse of Pointe-au-Père. As well, there are exhibits of the
wreck of *The Empress of Ireland*, a ship that sank in the St.
Lawrence in 1914 with a loss of over 1000 lives.

▲ ■ on-site

Mingan Archipelago National Park Reserve 24

1303, rue de la Digue

✉

C.P. 1180
Havre-St-Pierre, PQ G0G 1P0

☎ (418) 538-3331

Located in the Gulf of the St. Lawrence River, the Mingan Archipelago National Park Reserve offers you an opportunity to observe nature. Here you can discover puffins and other sea birds nesting. Look closely at the offshore waters; you may see porpoises, seals, or whales playing and feeding. You will certainly want your camera handy to capture the eerie shapes sculpted out of limestone by centuries of wind action. The park offers a variety of interpretation activities for visitors.

▲ limited service

Fort Temiscamingue National Historic Site 25

834, ch. Vieux Fort, C.P. 636
Ville-Marie, PQ J0Z 3W0

☎ (819) 629-3222

Located along Quebec's northeast border with Ontario, Fort Temiscamingue adds yet another piece to the mosaic of the

history of Canada's fur trade. In the 17th century, a fortified trading post was constructed near the present-day site of Fort Temiscamingue, but it was soon abandoned. In 1720, a merchant from Montreal decided to reconstruct it as a trading post. In 1795 it became the property of first the North West Company, then the Hudson's Bay Company, until it was closed in 1901. At the reconstructed fort, interpreters in period costume recreate the daily activities of French and English traders and Native peoples. Visitors are invited to participate in interpretation activities, such as exploring the "treasure chest of discoveries," trying on a beaver hat, feeling the texture of the furs, and sniffing the odour of castoreum — a substance obtained from beavers and used for different things, such as making perfume.

▲ ■ guided tours

Musée Amérindien de Pointe-Bleue 26

407, rue Amishk
Pointe-Bleue, PQ G0W 2H0

☎ (418) 275-4842

This museum, operated by the Montagnais nation, is committed to preserving and presenting this people's history and heritage. Get acquainted with the lifestyle and traditions of the first inhabitants of Quebec's Saguenay–Lac St-Jean region. The museum presents temporary and permanent exhibitions, films, slide shows, and guided tours. Learn about ancient Native civilizations. See contemporary Native art exhibits, traditional costumes, artifacts, and archaeological finds.

NEW BRUNSWICK

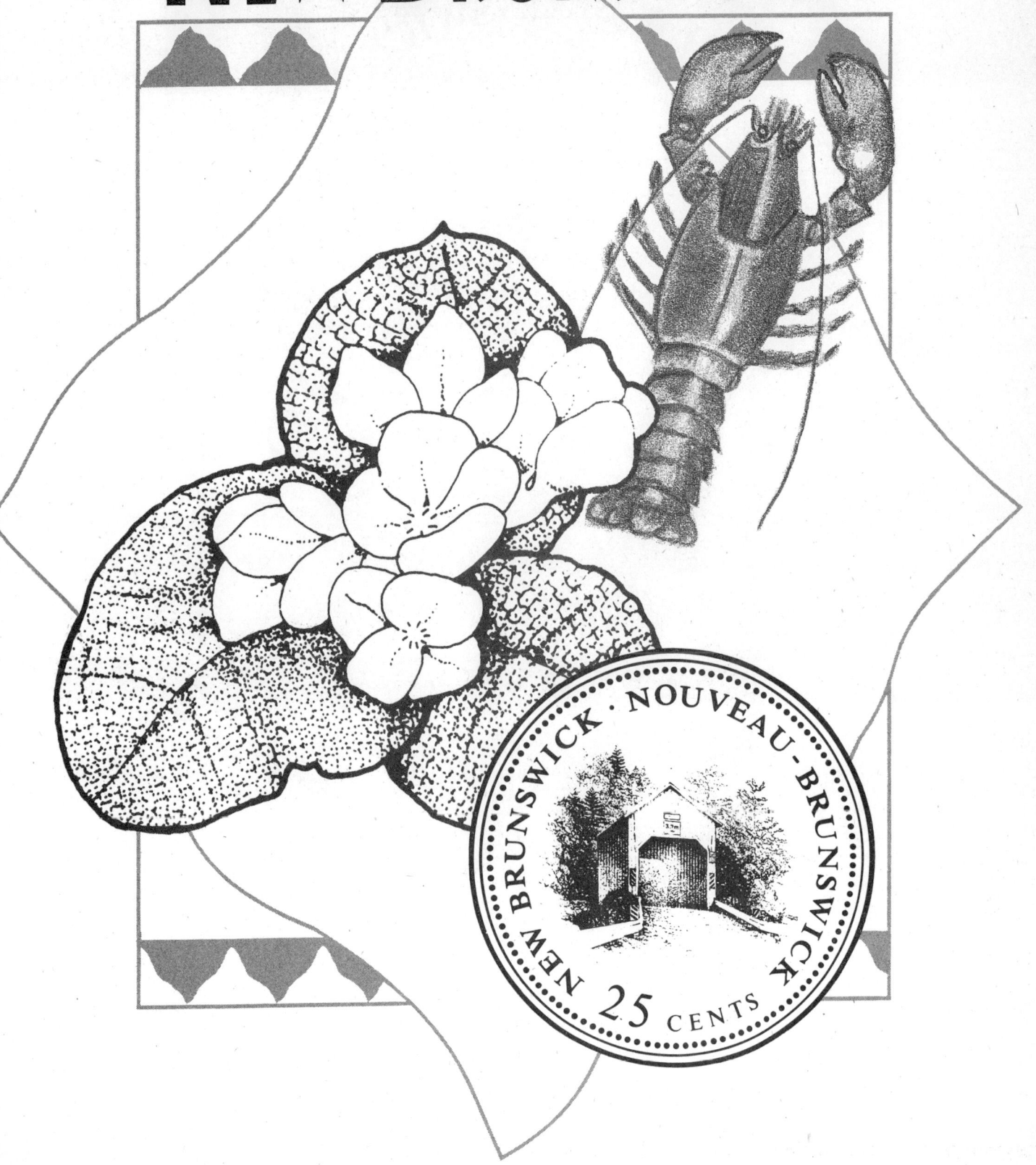

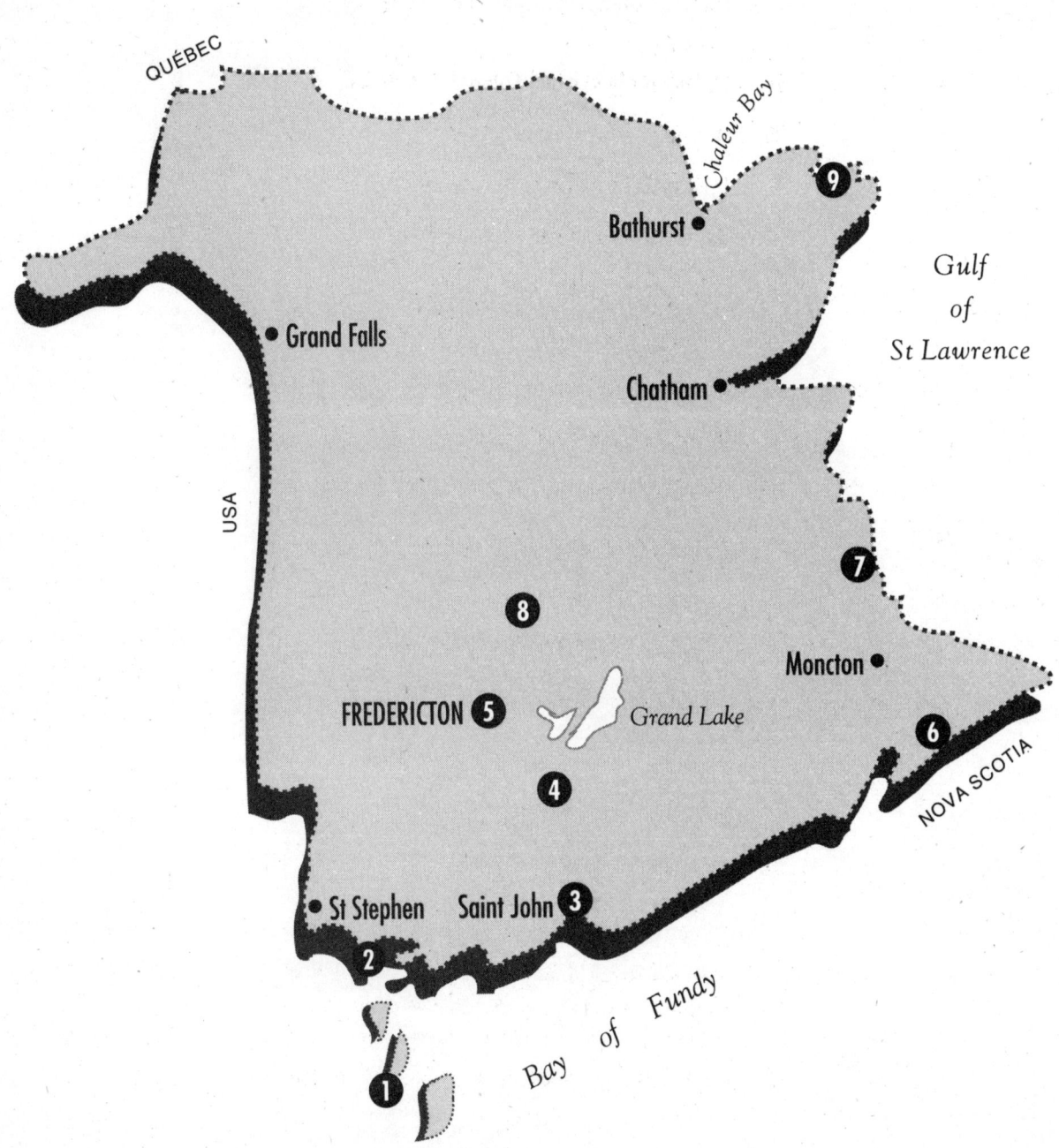

1   Roosevelt Campobello International Park and Natural Area
2a St. Andrews Blockhouse National Historic Site
2b Huntsman Marine Science Centre
3a Carleton Martello Tower National Historic Site
3b Bay of Fundy Tides and Reversing Falls
3c Partridge Island National Historic Site
4   Tilley House Museum
5a Beaverbrook Art Gallery
5b Kings Landing Historical Settlement
6a The Survival of the Acadians National Historic Site
6b Fort Beauséjour National Historic Site
7   Le Pays de la Sagouine
8   Central New Brunswick Woodmen's Museum
9   Historic Acadian Village

In the site descriptions, note that:
▲ indicates that second language services are available: English in Quebec and French elsewhere in Canada. Where "limited service" is given, it would be wise to call ahead for specifics
■ indicates that educational services are available

Roosevelt Campobello International Park and Natural Area

Campobello Island

c/o Executive Secretary
P.O. Box 9
Welshpool, NB E0G 3H0

(506) 752-2922

In 1883, James Roosevelt, father of former president of the United States Franklin D. Roosevelt, purchased property on Campobello Island as a summer home for his family. Young Franklin began summering here when he was just one year old, and he developed a deep and abiding love for it. Both the island, now an international park, and Roosevelt Cottage are open to the public. A visit to Campobello should begin in the visitor centre where you can see the film, *Beloved Island*. Walk to the Roosevelt Cottage and see the room used by the president as an office during his 1933 visit and the room in which Franklin D. Roosevelt, Jr., was born. Most of the furnishings are those used by the Roosevelt family. Of special interest are the chair used to carry the president after he was crippled by polio, the family telescope, a collection of canes, and a megaphone used for hailing boats off-shore. Don't forget to take a stroll down the interpretive nature trails as well.

▲

St. Andrews Blockhouse National Historic Site 2a

St. Andrews

c/o Historic Sites/New Brunswick
P.O. Box 3946, Stn. B
Saint John, NB E2M 5E6

☎ (506) 529-4270 or 636-4957

The War of 1812 made everyone in Canada nervous about the prospect of an attack by the Americans. In New Brunswick, a series of 12 blockhouses was built in 1813 along the coast to guard against an invasion from the sea. The St. Andrews Blockhouse is the only one still in existence. The blockhouses were garrisoned throughout the war, and again during the so-called Aroostook War (1838-1842), when lumbermen from New Brunswick and Maine clashed over their mutual, undefined border, and during the Fenian Raids (1866), part of an attempt by Irish-American nationalists to secure independence for Ireland. Visitors may tour the blockhouse, which has been restored, and the shore battery of three 18-pounders (guns) on reconstructed carriages and traversing platforms.

▲ ■ guided tours

Huntsman Marine Science Centre 2b

Brandy Cove
St. Andrews, NB E0G 2X0

☎ (506) 529-8895

The Huntsman Marine Science Centre is one exciting place. Twenty universities in Eastern Canada, along with the federal Department of Fisheries and Oceans, established the centre for conducting field research in marine biology and oceanography. The centre, open to the public, is well worth a visit. Here you will see displays along five interpretive themes: the St. Andrews scientific community, the physical environment of the Passamaquoddy region, plants and animals of the Passamaquoddy region, communities of the Passamaquoddy region, and humankind's interaction with the environment of the Passamaquoddy region (featuring aquaculture). The aquarium exhibits include invertebrates (animals without backbones) and fishes of the region, a beautiful seaweed exhibit, photographic exhibits, a deep-sea display of life-size models, and murals showing 50 different animal species. One of the two most popular attractions is the Touch Pool, containing many different kinds of creatures found in New Brunswick's coastal waters. Dip your hand in and touch! The other is a family of harbour seals that delights its audience with clownish antics, particularly when feeding time draws near.

▲ ■ on-site; outreach; all grades; teaching materials; teacher workshops; post-secondary summer field studies

Carleton Martello Tower National Historic Site 3a

Charlotte St. Extension

✉

P.O. Box 3946, Stn. B
Saint John, NB E2M 5E6

☎ (506) 636-4957

The Carleton Martello Tower is just one of many such towers that dotted the landscape of British North America, part of its defences during the War of 1812. Martello towers originated in the Mediterranean, where they served as watchtowers. The Carleton Martello Tower was completed in 1815, after the war had ended. Its design is typical of this type of fortification. The entrance is through a doorway in the second floor, where the barracks were located. The ground floor contained storage space and a powder magazine. The roof is flat to accommodate two 24-pounder guns and two 24-pounder carronades (short guns), and is surrounded by a parapet. In the centre stands a brick pillar that supports the brick walls and brick ceiling; this design allows the building to absorb artillery fire. The tower was garrisoned in 1866 in response to the threat of raids by the Fenians (Irish-Americans who sought independence for Ireland by attacking British North America). During World War I it served briefly as a detention centre for deserters. See the exhibits on the site and an audio-visual presentation.

▲ ■ guided tours

Bay of Fundy Tides & Reversing Falls 3b

The Falls View Park, Route 100
Reversing Falls Bridge

✉

c/o Saint John Visitor
and Convention Bureau
P.O. Box 1971
Saint John, NB E2L 4L1

☎ (506) 658-2990

The Bay of Fundy has the highest tides in the world; they can rise and fall as much as 15 m (50 ft.) a day. In turn, the action of the tides causes a natural phenomenon to occur at the point where the Saint John River empties into the bay: the Reversing Falls. At low tide, the water in the bay drops 4.4 m (14 1/2 ft.) below the level of the water in the Saint John River, causing the water in the river to crash forcefully through a narrow gorge into the harbour. Conversely, at high tide, the rising waters in the bay force the water in the river to change direction and flow upstream. See the interpretive film presented in the Reversing Falls Tourist Information Centre. Check the local newspaper for tide times.

▲

Partridge Island National Historic Site 3c

P.O. Box 6326
Saint John, NB E2L 4R7

☎ (506) 693-2598

Partridge Island does not evoke happy thoughts. Among other things, from 1785 until 1938 it was used as a quarantine station for hapless immigrants seeking a new home in Canada. Immigration seemed to arrive in waves, spurred on by events such as the Irish Potato Famine. However, the year that will live long and sadly in memory is 1847. From May 2 until November 1, 16 251 immigrants landed in New Brunswick; 14 881 were Irish. By the end of this period of time, 2115 had died, most from a typhus epidemic that swept over Partridge Island. The dead were buried in a mass grave. In May of 1854, the quarantine station on Partridge Island released immigrants who were infected with cholera into Saint John, resulting in the deaths of approximately 1000 people. The island contains a number of interesting sites for visitors to see. These include a disinfecting plant where all immigrants received a lice-killing shower, usually of kerosene; a general hospital and a smallpox hospital; a celtic cross memorial to the Irish who perished; gun positions from both world wars; a 20th-century graveyard divided into three sections: Protestant, Jewish, and Roman Catholic; and staff dwellings. Mercifully, we now have more humane facilities for welcoming immigrants to Canada.

▲

Tilley House Museum 4

Front St.
Gagetown, NB E0G 1V0

☎ (506) 488-2926

Samuel Leonard Tilley, born in this house on May 8, 1818, won himself a place in history as one of the Fathers of Confederation. He served as a member of the province's legislative assembly, and was premier of New Brunswick from 1861 to 1865. His career included two different cabinet posts in the new country of Canada and two terms as lieutenant-governor of New Brunswick. In 1879, he was knighted by Queen Victoria. The house has been restored and furnished much as it was when the Tilleys lived in it. It is staffed by interpreters in period costume. Visitors may see the room where Tilley was born. The upstairs rooms contain a number of interesting artifacts, including an afternoon dress worn by Lady Tilley to an 1879 garden party in England attended by Queen Victoria. Many of the items on display recount as well the history of Queens County.

■ guided tours

Beaverbrook Art Gallery 5a

703 Queen St.
Fredericton, NB E3B 1C4

☎ (506) 458-8545

The Beaverbrook Art Gallery is a gem. It was donated by the newspaper magnate and philanthropist Lord Beaverbrook in 1959, along with 300 works of art and an endowment fund. The gallery contains more than 2000 works of art, including paintings, drawings, sculptures, tapestries, and decorative arts. You can see a number of notable pieces on display. Of particular interest are the Cornelius Krieghoff collection and the magnificent 4 by 3 m (13 by 10 ft.) painting "Santiago El Grande" by Salvador Dali. See the Gobelin tapestries and British porcelain; and, on the lawn outside the gallery, poised to leap upon its prey, there is "The Leopard," a bronze sculpture by the British artist Jonathan Kenworthy.

▲ ■ on-site

Kings Landing Historical Settlement

✉
P.O. Box 522
Fredericton, NB E3B 5A6

☎ (506) 363-5090

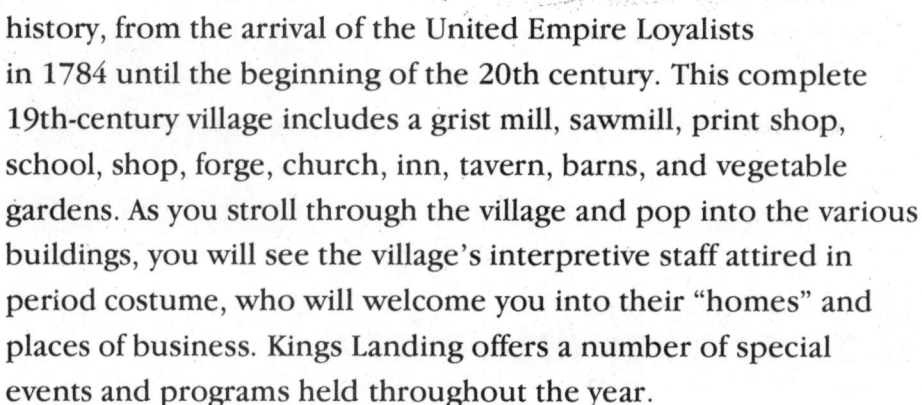

Described as a "living, breathing, outdoor museum," Kings Landing Historical Settlement offers everyone an opportunity to celebrate and explore New Brunswick's history, from the arrival of the United Empire Loyalists in 1784 until the beginning of the 20th century. This complete 19th-century village includes a grist mill, sawmill, print shop, school, shop, forge, church, inn, tavern, barns, and vegetable gardens. As you stroll through the village and pop into the various buildings, you will see the village's interpretive staff attired in period costume, who will welcome you into their "homes" and places of business. Kings Landing offers a number of special events and programs held throughout the year.

▲ ■ extensive on-site; K–9

The Survival of the Acadians National Historic Site 6a

St-Joseph de Memramcook

✉

c/o Parks Canada
Fort Beausejour
Aulac, NB E0A 3C0

☎ (506) 758-9783/536-0720

In the early part of the eighteenth century, a hundred or so families emigrated from France and settled around the Bay of Fundy, a region they called Acadie. Isolated from France and from other settlements, they developed their own distinct culture and identity. In 1755, Britain seized control of exploration and the fur trade in the New World and, over a period of six years, forcibly expelled 8000 Acadians; most of them were sent to British colonies in New England. In 1764, the British government relented and allowed the Acadians to return on condition that they not congregate in large numbers. The Acadians settled in remote areas and made their living by fishing and subsistence farming. Through all of this, their culture and spirit survived. At the Survival of the Acadians National Historic Site, the history and culture of this tenacious and spirited community are presented through various themes: religion, material culture, traditions, oral and written literature, music, drama, and the visual arts. See the Acadian newspapers, audio-visual programs, and displays featuring the work of contemporary Acadian artists and craftspeople. Interpretive staff will provide information and answer your questions.

▲   English and French   ■

Fort Beauséjour National Historic Site 6b

Aulac, NB E0A 3C0

☎ (506) 536-0720

The French built Fort Beauséjour in the 1750s to guard against territorial expansion by the British, who were already in Nova Scotia. The fort was attacked and fell after a 14-day siege in 1755. The British promptly renamed it Fort Cumberland. It was attacked again during the American Revolution in 1776 by American sympathizers, but this time withstood the assault. In the years prior to the War of 1812, Fort Beauséjour/ Cumberland was fully garrisoned; British soldiers were there until 1835, after which the fort was abandoned. It has since been restored, so visitors may tour the site. The visitor centre provides an overview of the fort and the surrounding area and has a comprehensive display of artifacts that were unearthed during archaeological excavations.

▲   ■   guided tours

Le Pays de la Sagouine 7

✉ P.O. Box 757
Bouctouche, NB E0A 1G0

☎ (506) 743-1400

When renowned New Brunswick author Antonine Maillet created the memorable character and one-woman play *La Sagouine*, she had no idea that the poor Acadian washerwoman with her pithy sayings would become a cultural icon for French-speaking Canadians. In recognition of *La Sagouine*, a little theme park reflecting her world has been constructed at l'Île aux Puces (Flea Island), near Bouctouche. See La Sagouine's own house, complete with quilt covered beds, a wood stove, and bottles of Evangeline soda pop. See the fishing shed of Gapi, La Sagouine's husband; the prudish La Sainte's little house; the shack and lookout belonging to the sea captain, Sullivan; a smokehouse; and a peculiar device called a mud dredger, used to bring up seabottom fertilizer for the fields. And don't forget La Sagouine herself, played by an actress. Visitors may gather around to hear La Sagouine tell her stories.

▲ English and French ■

Central New Brunswick Woodmen's Museum 8

✉ P.O. Box 7
Boiestown, NB E0H 1A0

☎ (506) 369-7214

New Brunswick is a maritime province of towering trees, so it is not surprising that fishing and logging have traditionally been its main industries. The Central New Brunswick Woodmen's Museum celebrates the history and contribution of logging and forestry. As you enter this unusual museum of 17 exhibition buildings on 6 ha (15 a.), stop at the wooden statues of "Mute & Still" to read the legends they tell. Take a ride on the

"Whooper." This little train will transport you through the woods and museum grounds. A traditional logging camp has been reconstructed here with displays of tools, trees, and explanations of the ways of the loggers. Of interest are the Maple Syrup Corner, with its display of equipment used for tapping trees, and the Craft Corner — here you'll see objects the loggers whittled to pass the time when inclement weather or other factors prevented them from working. Other buildings include a barber shop, a school, a church, early pioneer homes, a farm, a general store, a clothing store, and a sawmill, a bunkhouse where the loggers slept, and a cookhouse where their meals were prepared.

▲ ■ on-site

Historic Acadian Village (Village historique Acadien)

P.O. Box 820
Caraquet, NB E0B 1K0

☎ (506) 727-3467

Be sure to allow plenty of time for your visit to the Historic Acadian Village because you'll find so much to see and do here. No effort was spared in constructing an authentic Acadian village that would bring to life the history, culture, and traditional way of life of New Brunswick's Acadian people from 1780 to 1890. The site, consisting of 44 buildings, is staffed by interpreters dressed in period costume and engaged in traditional activities and crafts. Stop and chat with them; they will happily explain what they are doing and answer your questions. See the farm with its animals and outdoor root cellar; the general store; the printing press where the *Moniteur Acadien*, Shediac's first newspaper, was printed; the adjoining blacksmith's and wheelwright's shops; and the grist mill grinding grain into flour. See the Poirier Tavern and its jovial innkeeper. Children will delight in visiting the school, where a teacher holds a class for costumed students.

▲ English and French

■ on-site; audio-visual; seasonal programs and activities

NOVA SCOTIA

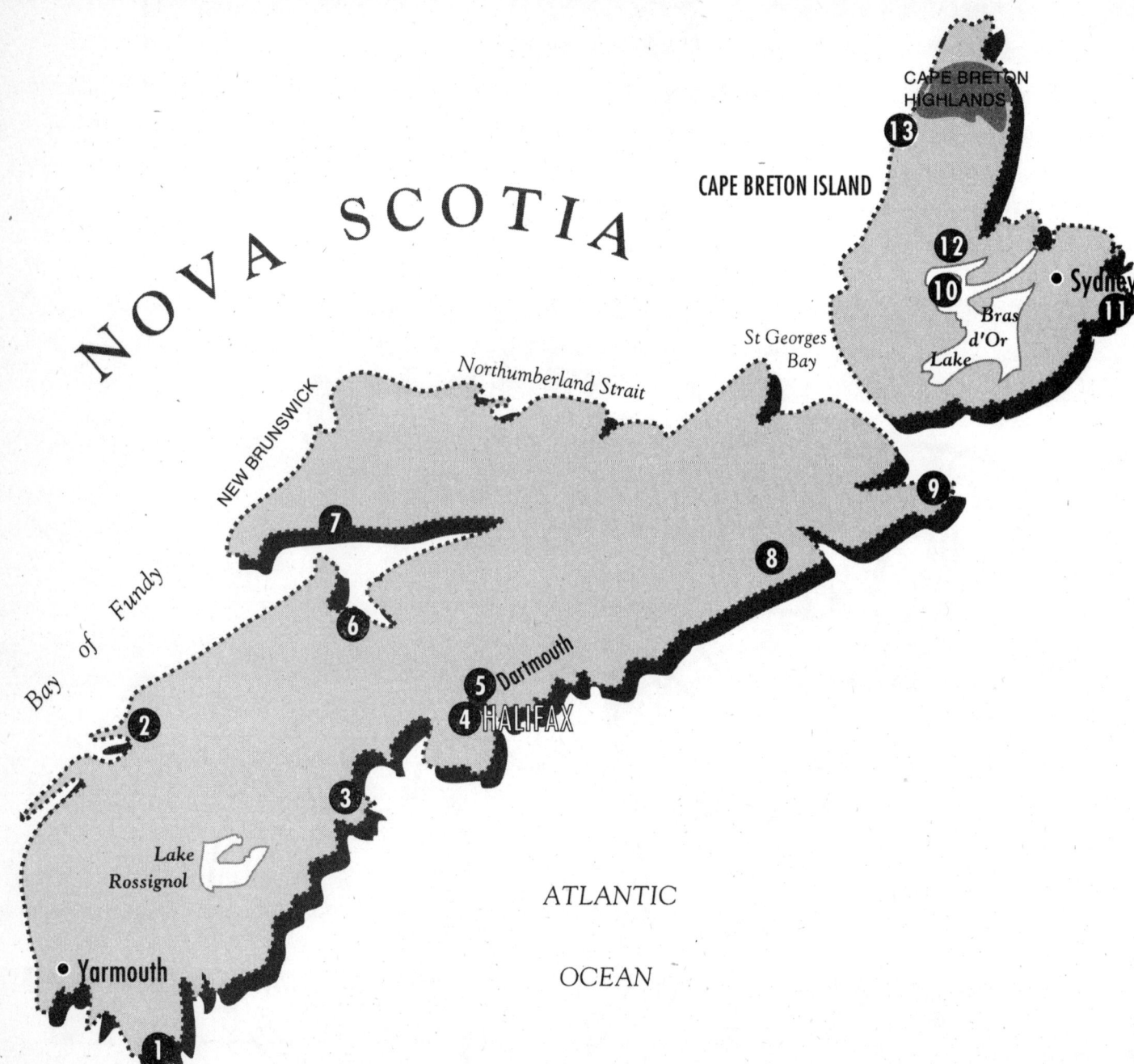

1   Archelaus Smith Museum
2a Fort Anne National Historic Site
2b Port Royal Habitation National Historic Site
3   Fisheries Museum of the Atlantic
4a Maritime Command Museum
4b Halifax Citadel National Historic Site
5a Maritime Museum of the Atlantic
5b McNab's Island
5c Black Cultural Centre for Nova Scotia
6a Grand-Pré National Historic Site
6b Fort Edward National Historic Site
7   Fundy Geological Museum
8   Sherbrooke Village
9   Grassy Island National Historic Park
10 Nova Scotia Highland Village
11 Fortress of Louisbourg
12 Alexander Graham Bell National Historic Park
13 Elizabeth Lefort Gallery

In the site descriptions, note that:
▲   indicates that second language services are available: English in Quebec and French elsewhere in Canada. Where "limited service" is given, it would be wise to call ahead for specifics
■   indicates that educational services are available

Archelaus Smith Museum

P.O. Box 190
Clark's Harbour, NS B0W 1P0

☎ (902) 745-2411

The Archelaus Smith Museum chronicles the history of Nova Scotia's Sable Island, renowned for its herds of wild horses. The museum building, built in 1896, has a variegated history, housing the local Temperance Society at one time and then serving as a community hall for a while. The museum's exhibits cover two floors and include a large model of an original Cape Island boat. See other marine artifacts, such as different kinds of boats, lobster traps, wooden buoys, sextants, quadrants, and items related to the fishing industry. A number of articles on display were salvaged from shipwrecks off the shores of Sable Island, a frequent occurrence in olden times.

Fort Anne National Historic Site

P.O. Box 9
Annapolis Royal, NS B0S 1A0

☎ (902) 532-2321

Declared a National Historic Site in 1917, Fort Anne has the distinction of being the first place to be so designated. It has a long history. Between 1610 and 1636 the area was the rope in a tug-of-war between the French and the British. After that there were several attacks from the New England colonies to the south, so in 1702, construction began on a fort. The fort withstood two attacks, but in 1710 the British gained control, renaming it Annapolis Royal. Visitors to Fort Anne may see many of the original features of the 1702 construction, including the storehouse in the northwest bastion, the powder magazine in the southwest bastion, and the earthworks. The officers' quarters, originally built in 1797, were restored as a visitor reception centre. See one of the most popular attractions: the Fort Anne Heritage Tapestry. The tapestry, still being created, is a visual representation of the history of the fort; it's quite spectacular.

▲ ■ on-site

Port Royal Habitation National Historic Site 2b

Port Royal
✉
c/o Historic Parks and Services
Southwestern Nova Scotia
P.O. Box 9
Annapolis Royal, NS B0S 1A0

☎ (902) 532-2898

Port Royal dates back to 1605, when a settlement was established by Sieur de Monts and a group of French colonists, accompanied by the famous explorer Samuel de Champlain. They had come to the new world in pursuit of furs. Port Royal was one of the first European settlements in North America. It has been reconstructed to the 17th-century era. Costumed interpreters conduct guided tours and demonstrate period activities for visitors.

▲ ■ on-site

Fisheries Museum of the Atlantic 3

✉
P.O. Box 1363
Lunenberg, NS B0J 2C0

☎ (902) 634-4794

Appropriately, this museum is housed in a former fish-processing plant. It presents a number of exhibits

related to the sea and fishing, which is the traditional industry of Lunenberg. Included in the museum's displays are two deep-sea fishing vessels, the schooner *Theresa E. Connor*, the side trawler *Cape Sable*, and the digby scalloper *Royal Wave*. The exhibits cover three floors. The first floor has an aquarium containing several varieties of fish and shellfish native to the Atlantic coast. Go to the Fish Demonstration Room to see demonstrations of fish splitting and filleting. The Hall of Inshore Fisheries presents different types of inshore fishing boats. Move on to the Wharf to see the marine engine display, and an informative display on whaling and whales. Up on the third floor, recall the exciting and romantic prohibition era when fishermen were engaged in dangerous but lucrative rum-running (smuggling liquor). The Ice House Theatre presents films on the fishing industry, and visitors are invited to try their hand at the traditional fishermen's skills of net mending, knotting, rope splicing, and working with canvas.

Maritime Command Museum 4a

Admiralty House, CFB
Halifax, NS B3K 2X0

☎ (902) 427-8250

Come to explore Canada's rich naval tradition at the Maritime Command Museum. Here you will see displays of the corvette HMCS *Sackville*, which has been restored; the HMCS *Niobe*, the Royal Canadian navy's second ship, which served both as a training vessel and then as a depot ship during World War I; and the HMCS *Rainbow*. Also exhibited are the official badges of ships that were lost in action, photographs, artifacts such as ship's bells, and medals and awards.

Halifax Citadel National Historic Site 4b

P.O. Box 9080
Stn. A
Halifax, NS B3K 5M7

☎ (902) 426-5080

Built between 1828 and 1856, the Halifax Citadel now looks down from a hill to the modern city of Halifax as if it were still standing guard against enemy incursions by land. It is the fourth such fortification to be built on this site — the first was constructed in 1749, when Britain was at war with France. Although it was garrisoned by the British until 1906 and then by the Canadian Armed Forces until after World War II, nobody ever attacked it. You'll find the design to be quite unusual: it has the shape of a star and with its tunnels and ditches it's altogether difficult to breach. Now recognized as a National Historic Site, it draws many visitors to Halifax. Be sure to time your visit so that you'll be there at noon when the gun is fired. Visit during the summer months, when students dressed in 1869 vintage uniforms garrison the citadel and the 78th Highland Regiment of Foot performs intricate infantry and artillery drills. See the informative audio-visual presentation, a restored nineteenth-century army schoolroom, a library, barrack rooms, a powder magazine, and a defence casement. Especially interesting features include the musketry gallery, the restored ramparts, and an army museum with its collection of Canadian military memorabilia.

▲ ■

Maritime Museum of the Atlantic 5a

1675 Lower Water St.
Halifax, NS B3J 1S3

☎ (902) 424-7490

The Atlantic Ocean has played a major role in the history and heritage of Nova Scotians. This is recognized especially at the Maritime Museum of the Atlantic. The museum, strategically located on the waterfront, treats visitors to a stunning panoramic view of Halifax Harbour from the exhibit and display centre. Then you can step inside a restored and well-stocked 19th-century chandler's shop, or see the collection of ships' figureheads and shipbuilding tools in the Days of Sail Gallery. Learn about the history of the Royal Canadian Navy. See equipment used in shipwreck rescue efforts, a boat collection, and an exhibit recounting the impact of steam-powered vessels. A popular attraction is the retired Canadian Hydrographic Survey ship *Acadia*, a National Historic Site berthed in the museum's wharves.

▲ ■ on-site; all grades; teaching materials

McNab's Island 5b

Halifax Harbour

✉

c/o Parks Canada
Atlantic Region, Historic Properties
Upper Water St.
Halifax, NS B3J 1S9

☎ (902) 426-3436

Courtesy McNab's Island

Named for the Scottish immigrant Peter McNab, who purchased the island in 1782, McNab's Island has a long and interesting history. Before the arrival of the Europeans, it was a seasonal home for Micmac Indians; later it was a French fishing station. McNab, his descendants, and their tenants cleared the island and transformed it into a farming community. In the late 19th century, the island was fortified by a martello tower and two forts. Fort Hugonin, which still stands, belongs to the Department of National Defence, but the remains of Fort McNab, a National Historic Site, is open to the public. These fortifications were designed in such a way as to present many hazards to would-be attackers. Today, they threaten unwary tourists, so exercise caution when visiting the sites. Between 1783 and 1809, the bodies of executed mutineers and deserters were tarred and chained to gibbets as a deterrent to others contemplating similar actions. These grim penalties provided Canadian writer Thomas Raddall with material for his novel *Hangman's Beach*.

Black Cultural Centre for Nova Scotia 5c

✉

P.O. Box 2128
East Dartmouth, NS B2W 3Y2

☎ (902) 434-6223

Much has been written of the history of Canada and the contributions of the Europeans, particularly the English and the French. However, there have been blacks in Canada as long as there have been whites, who have their place in the history of our country and have contributed much to our heritage and tradition. Prior to 1738, there were 1232 slaves in Nova Scotia. Then 3000 black United Empire Loyalists arrived after the American colonies declared their independence from Britain. Later groups of blacks came from Jamaica in 1796, followed by slaves fleeing the southern United States. Life in Nova Scotia was hard. These immigrants were segregated from the white population and given the poorest land to farm. Many left Nova Scotia to settle in Africa in Sierra Leone, but many more stayed and persevered. The Black Cultural Centre for Nova Scotia is a tribute and a commemoration of their history and achievements. The centre contains a museum, amphitheatre, library, and educational centre. See the artifacts on display, which depict the history, culture, and achievements of the blacks of Nova Scotia and the world. Cultural performances and lectures are presented in the ampitheatre.

■ on-site; outreach

Grand-Pré National Historic Site

P.O. Box 150
Grand-Pré, NS B0P 1M0

☎ (902) 542-3631

Grand-Pré National Historic Site commemorates a dark and shameful event in Canadian history: the expulsion of the Acadians in 1755. This area was the site of one of three major French settlements in the 17th century. In 1713, the Treaty of Utrecht ceded Acadia (Nova Scotia) to the British. Although the Acadians were politically nonaligned, they were a source of worry to the British who were competing with France, both in Europe and in North America. Accordingly, in 1755, Governor Charles Lawrence and his council required the Acadians to swear an oath of allegiance; those who refused would be expelled. Acadian deputies refused, and so, in 1755, some 6000 Acadians were deported; many more followed. Many Acadians eluded deportation and others managed to return to Nova Scotia. Grand-Pré National Historic Site presents the themes of the evolution of the Acadian community in the Minas Basin area, 1682–1755, and their subsequent expulsion. You may know of Longfellow's famous poem about the expulsion, *Evangeline*; a statue of Evangeline stands in the park. The focal point of the site is the church, whose exhibit chronicles the expulsion and which is itself a memorial. It was in this church that Acadians were held prisoner until they could be placed upon the ships waiting to deport them.

▲ ■ on-site; all grades; teaching materials

Fort Edward National Historic Site 6b

Windsor, Nova Scotia

✉ c/o Parks Canada
Grand Pré, NS B0P 1M0

☎ (902) 542-3631

Built in 1750, Fort Edward was intended to protect the overland route from Halifax to the Bay of Fundy. Its chief and still surviving feature is its blockhouse, built of squared timbers prepared in Halifax by Acadian workmen. The British garrisoned the fort until early in the 19th century, and then abandoned it as it no longer had any strategic importance. The fort has since disappeared, but the blockhouse remains, the oldest example of this type of fortification in Canada.

▲

Fundy Geological Museum 7

✉ P.O. Box 640
Parrsboro, NS B0M 1S0

☎ (902) 254-3814

Rock hounds and fossil hunters should put a visit to Parrsboro on their agendas. Many of the exhibits on display at the new Fundy Geological Museum were found locally — the area is rich in fossils and minerals. The museum's permanent gallery has 48 themes representing prehistoric landscape and life; the museum also has a temporary gallery, an audio-visual theatre, and an on-site laboratory. See the displays of local dinosaur finds, including the Otozoum, a sort of long-legged crocodile, and a tiny dinosaur whose tracks are no larger than a robin's. View the semi-precious stones, such as amethyst and agate. Enthusiasts should attend the Rock Hound Round-up every summer.

▲ limited service ■

Sherbrooke Village 8

✉ Box 295
Sherbrooke, NS B0J 3C0

☎ (902) 522-2400

Sherbrooke Village invites you to do a little time-travelling to a 19th-century lumbering and gold-mining community. The original town experienced a boom from about 1861, when gold was discovered, to 1881, and has now been restored to that period. You can visit approximately 30 buildings. Staff interpret many of the traditional activities. See earthenware produced in the local pottery shop or have your picture taken in an old-fashioned photographer's studio. See hand-operated presses in the village print shop; a water-powered sawmill; a working blacksmith's shop; a weaver busy at his craft; and, of course, the jail — a necessary place in a community of any size. Stop by the drugstore to view its supply of pills and medicine-making equipment. Mail a letter from the post office, which has been operating since 1860. Before leaving, drop into the emporium to buy a souvenir made by village craftspeople.

▲ limited services ■

Grassy Island National Historic Park 9

✉ c/o General Delivery
Canso, NS

☎ (902) 366-3136

The history of Grassy Island begins around 1600, when the first French arrivals discovered that it lay in excellent fishing waters rich with cod stocks. However, the ensuing struggle between France and Britain for dominance in North America left Grassy

Island — coveted by both the French and the English for the fish
— vulnerable to attack. Nonetheless, Canso and Grassy Island
built a thriving fishing industry that provided dried and salted fish
to Europe, the Caribbean, and North America in exchange for a
variety of goods. In 1744, the settlement was attacked and burned
in a French incursion from Louisbourg. It never fully recovered.
The settlement has not been reconstructed, but visitors to the site
may follow a trail that takes them through the ruins and explains
the different locations. See faintly visible terraces, cellar pits, and
scattered rubble mounds, which are the only remains of the
houses, storage sheds, and workshops that were destroyed in
1744. A number of artifacts that give clues to the nature of life at
the settlement have been discovered by archaeologists.

▲ ■ guided tours

Nova Scotia Highland Village 10

Hectors Point

✉

P.O. Box 58
Iona, NS B0A 1L0

☎ (902) 725-2272

Nova Scotia in Latin means "New Scotland,"
and the Nova Scotia Highland Village is a
tip of the hat to the Highland Scots who settled
the area. The village consists of ten historic
buildings: a Hebridean Black House, a log house,
three frame houses, a barn, a store, a forge, a
carding mill and a schoolhouse. The buildings
are staffed by costumed interpreters who demonstrate traditional
crafts and activities. Take a good look at the Highland cattle on the
site — this breed is 1500 years old. The village offers a number of
programs. People who wish to trace their ancestry may do so
through a program called "Highland Roots." The village also
provides instruction in the Gaelic language and local folklore.

■ on-site

Fortress of Louisbourg

P.O. Box 160
Louisbourg, NS B0A 1M0

☎ (902) 733-2280

The Fortress of Louisbourg is an astonishing historical site, one of the stellar attractions in all of Canada! Being a fortress rather than a fort, this is not a strictly military establishment, but a walled town. Louisbourg was built by the French in the 18th century to protect France's possessions in the New World against their traditional rivals and enemies, the British, and to function as a trading centre. It has been restored to the 1744 period, with 50 restored or reconstructed buildings and interpretive staff dressed in period costume going about the traditional activities of the time. The fortress sits on a promontory overlooking the Atlantic Ocean. If you have good weather on the day of your visit, then the view will be breathtaking. If it is overcast, then you'll get a true sense of the feelings of loneliness and desolation experienced by many of the French soldiers posted here. As you approach the fortress, peek inside the fisherman's cottage, where fish are drying. Be careful at the gates. In keeping with the tension of the times they portray, armed sentries standing guard will challenge

you in French. Anyone who speaks English is suspect! Once inside, you'll find no end of things to see and do. Stroll along the busy streets and wander into the buildings. Admire the furnishings and chat with the interpreters, who will happily explain the characters they represent, give a little history of the spot, and answer your questions. Learn about the traditional crafts of stone cutting and lace making by watching demonstrations. Admire the artifacts that archaeological excavations have unearthed. If you get tired of walking, relax in the theme lounges, where you can read an article or two about Louisbourg or watch a film. And if you get hungry or thirsty, step into one of the many eateries offering 18th-century French fare. Not all of the fortress has been reconstructed. Outside the ramparts, visitors may follow paths to the ruins. Special diving tours to explore the wrecks in Louisbourg's harbour may also be arranged.

▲ ■ on-site; teaching materials

Alexander Graham Bell National Historic Park 12

✉

P.O. Box 159
Baddeck, NS B0E 1B0

☎ (902) 295-2069

Photo by E. Joan Abeles

For anyone who celebrates creativity, the quest for knowledge, or the ability of an unconventional spirit and mind to achieve greatness, the Alexander Graham Bell National Historic Park is the place to come. Alexander Graham Bell, who emigrated to Canada from Scotland in 1870, is best known for his work with the deaf, and his subsequent invention of the hearing and speaking device, the telephone. But Bell did much more. He built his estate Beinn Breagh (Gaelic for "beautiful mountain") here at Baddeck, on the shores of the scenic Bras d'Or Lakes, and it was here at Beinn Breagh that much of his work was done. The exhibit area is divided into three thematic halls. Begin in the Teacher and Inventor Hall, where you can see displays featuring Bell's family and his youth, his work as a teacher of the deaf, and his invention of the telephone. Move on to the Experimenter's Hall to learn about Bell's experiments with such devices as rocket-powered propellers, X rays, a breathing device, and a solar telephone; and processes such as sheep-breeding, water purification, and powered flight. In the third hall, the Hydrofoil Hall, see displays of "winged" speedboats equipped with airplane engines. Beinn Breagh stands nearby, still in the possession of the Bell family. The estate and grounds, where Bell and his wife Mabel are buried, are not open to the public.

▲ ■

Elizabeth Lefort Gallery 13

✉

c/o Les Trois Pignons
P.O. Box 430
Chéticamp, NS B0E 1H0

☎ (902) 224-2612/224-2642

Dr. Elizabeth Lefort-Hansford, one of Canada's most talented and well-known artists, works wool produced by Cape Breton sheep into magnificent and enduring tapestries and rugs. She has hooked portraits of many notables, to whom she has presented her work. These include Queen Elizabeth II, former American presidents Eisenhower and Johnson, popes Pius XII and John XXIII, Jacqueline Kennedy Onassis, former prime minister John Diefenbaker, Lord Beaverbrook, television personality Arthur Godfrey, and Prince Charles. One of her most outstanding accomplishments is a tapestry featuring the presidents of the United States and important events that occurred during their White House tenures. Many of the beautiful tapestries of this unusual and talented Cape Breton artist can be seen on permanent display at a gallery in Trois Pignons, a museum and cultural centre committed to preserving and presenting the heritage of the Cape Breton Acadians.

▲

Prince Edward Island

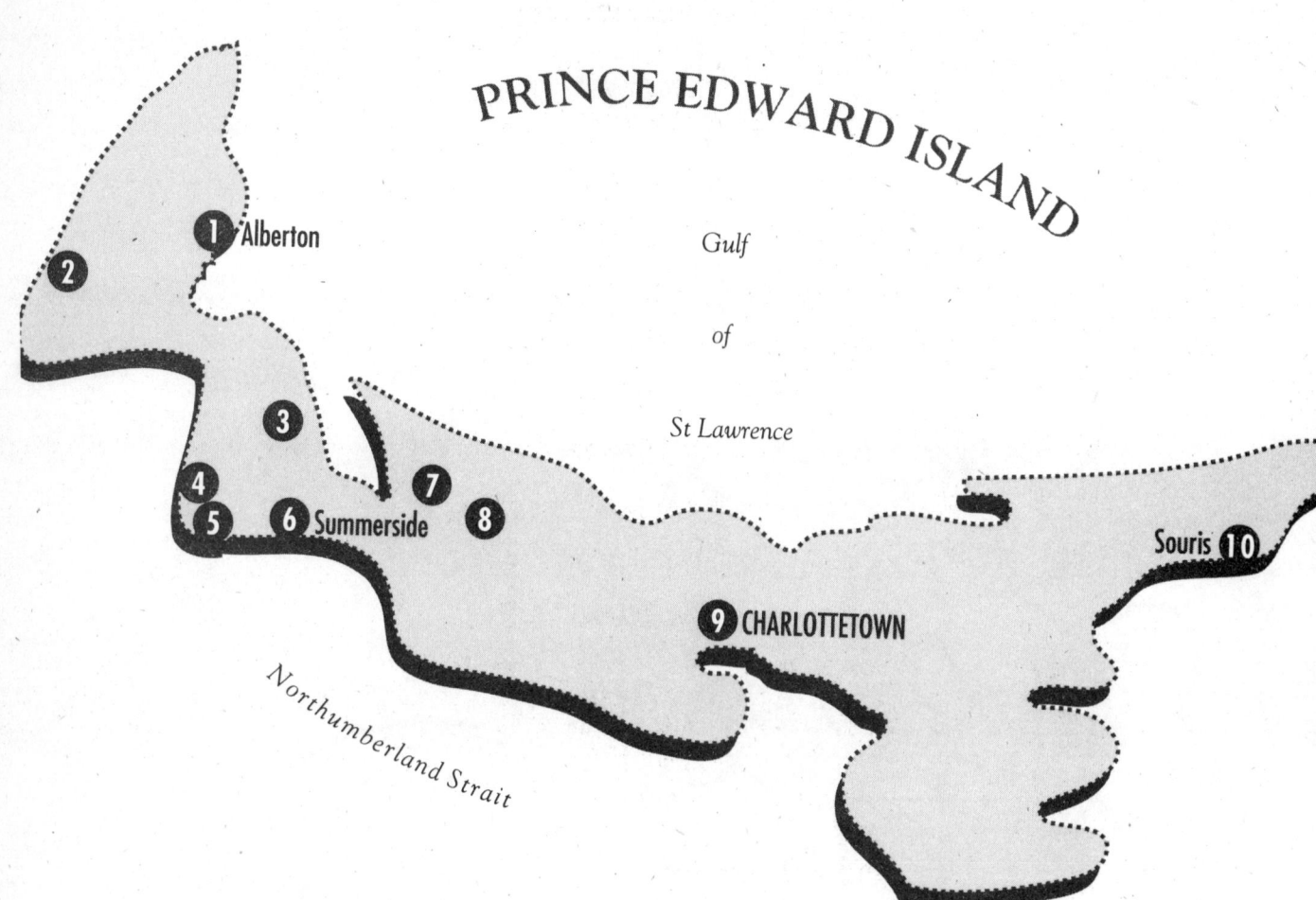

1   Prince Edward Island Miniature Railway
2   West Point Lighthouse
3   Green Park Shipbuilding Museum
4   The Bottle Houses
5   Le Village Mont-Carmel
6   Acadian Museum
7   Anne of Green Gables Museum at Silver Bush
8   The L. M. Montgomery Birthplace
9a   Province House National Historic Site
9b   Fort Amherst/Port La Joye National Historic Site
9c   Ardgowan National Historic Park
9d   Prince Edward Island Marine Aquarium
9e   Green Gables House
10   Basin Head Fisheries Museum

In the site descriptions, note that:
▲   indicates that second language services are available: English in Quebec and French elsewhere in Canada. Where "limited service" is given, it would be wise to call ahead for specifics
■   indicates that educational services are available

Prince Edward Island Miniature Railway 1

✉ Alberton R.R. 2
PE C0B 1B0

☎ (902) 853-3478

"A nature trail on wheels" is how passengers like to describe a ride on the Prince Edward Island Miniature Railway. The railway is built to one-eighth scale, 61m (200 ft.) long and 4 m (13 ft.) high at the highest point. It crosses a brook running into a salt water inlet and in among a wide variety of trees planted by the P.E.I. Forestry Department.

West Point Lighthouse 2

✉ O'Leary R.R. 2
PE C0B 1V0

☎ (902) 859-3605/859-3117

Rising 21 m (69 ft.) into the air, its distinctive black and white stripes visible in the distance, the historic West Point Lighthouse watches over the Northumberland Strait. Built in 1875 and manned until 1963 when the last keeper retired, the lighthouse is one of the Island's tallest. The lighthouse and the attached keeper's dwelling have been completely restored. Visitors may see artifacts, documents, photographs, and displays, all recounting the lighthouse's history. You can climb the 72 steps to the top for a stunning view of the Atlantic Ocean and a red sandy beach that goes on forever. Stay in one of the guest rooms at the site or dig in to a delicious chowder and lobster dinner served up by the lighthouse kitchen.

Green Park Shipbuilding Museum 3

✉
R.R. 1
Tyne Valley, PE C0B 2C0

☎ (902) 831-2206

For people who live on an island, shipbuilding is an industry that comes naturally. The Green Park Shipbuilding Museum is divided into three parts: a modern interpretive centre; the mansion of James Yeo, Jr., a wealthy Island shipbuilder, restored and furnished to the 1865 period; and a recreated shipyard. Begin your visit in the interpretive centre. Here a display of tools, graphs, and interpretive panels will give you some background information for the rest of your visit. The Yeo mansion is staffed by guides in period costume who provide tours, answer questions, and demonstrate crafts such as baking over an open fire (scones are a favourite with visitors), spinning, quilting, rug hooking, and soap making. Walk over to the shipyard. Here, you will see a blacksmith shop, a carpentry shop, and displays relating to the craft of shipbuilding.

■ on-site; June and September only

The Bottle Houses 4

Cape Egmont

✉
Box 72
Richmond, PE C0B 1Y0

☎ (902) 854-2987

In this day and age of environmental consciousness, what does one do with 25 000 empty bottles? If you are Edouard Arsenault, a retired Island fisherman (and there isn't a recycling program on your island), then you use them to build houses. Arsenault, who died in 1984, collected the bottles: wine bottles, liquor bottles, soft-drink bottles, water bottles, vinegar bottles, all sorts of bottles! He built three structures as a retirement project. The first building is a house that holds just a dozen people at one time. The second bottle house is a bar, complete with bottles on the counter, and the third building is a church. Unfortunately, Arsenault died before completing it. The church looks just like it did when he died, with pews and altar unfinished. Beautiful gardens, a goldfish pond, and a gift shop complete the site.

▲

Le Village Mont-Carmel 5

✉

Wellington R.R.
PE C0B 2E0

☎ (902) 854-2227

Le Village Mont-Carmel, a complex of log cabins, portrays the unique history and heritage of the Island Acadians. The historical village recalls the history of the Acadian community in the early part of the 19th century. A restaurant on the site specializes in Acadian cuisine, as does the Supper Theatre, which also stages a dramatic production. Visit the shop to purchase crafts made by local residents, and attend a workshop on traditional Acadian experiences such as cooking, handicrafts, lobster-fishing, history, and music.

▲ French and English   ■ on-site

Acadian Museum 6

✉

P.O. Box 159
Miscouche, PE C0B 1T0

☎ (902) 436-6237

The first Acadians arrived in Prince Edward Island in 1720, and their history was a turbulent one. When the British wrested Fortress Louisbourg away from the French in 1758, they shipped 3500 Acadians from P.E.I. back to France. But for some reason the

British neglected to provide transportation for the 30 families that lived in the tiny settlement at Malpeque. These families remained to form the nucleus of the Island's Acadian community. The museum preserves the heritage of the Island Acadians from 1720 to the present. It contains some 1700 artifacts, many of which have been donated by Island residents. These include a fine collection of wooden farm implements from the 19th century, and art.

▲ French and English ■

Anne of Green Gables Museum at Silver Bush 7

Box 491
Kensington, PE C0B 1M0

☎ (902) 436-7329

This museum contains the largest collection of artifacts associated with L. M. Montgomery, author of the beloved Anne stories. The house was Montgomery's home at different times, and it was here that she was married. The house, built in 1872, belonged to Montgomery's aunt, Annie Laura MacNeill, and her husband John Campbell. Next to the house is "the Lake of Shining Waters" found in *Anne of Green Gables*. In the house, visitors may see the bookcase described in *Anne*, the organ that provided the wedding march for Montgomery's wedding in 1911, the room in which Montgomery frequently stayed, the patchwork quilt she loved, a lap desk that was a gift to Montgomery from a cousin, autographed first editions of her books, letters she wrote and much more.

The L. M. Montgomery Birthplace 8

Clifton Corner
New London, PE

This house is where L. M. Montgomery was born on November 30, 1874. The house has been completely restored. The house has a number of points of interest. The room where Montgomery was born is on display. See Montgomery's wedding dress, thoughtfully arranged on a mannequin; *The Story Girl*, which Montgomery described as her favourite book; and scrapbooks and albums of her early writings.

Province House National Historic Site

2 Palmers Lane
Charlottetown, PE C1A 5V6

☎ (902) 566-7626

Courtesy Province House National Historic Site/Parks Canada

Come to where it all began! Province House was the site of the Charlottetown Conference in September 1864. This conference was attended by delegates from Prince Edward Island, Nova Scotia, and New Brunswick to discuss a union of the three maritime colonies. They were joined by representatives from Canada West and Canada East (Ontario and Quebec), led by John A. Macdonald and George-Étienne Cartier. By the time the conference ended five days later, the groundwork had been laid for Confederation and the new country of Canada. (Ironically, Prince Edward Island didn't join Confederation until 1873. In fact, the people of Charlottetown were far more interested in the circus that had come to town than they were in the historic conference taking place at the same time.) The building has been fully restored. Officials' offices, set up as they were in the 19th century, include that of the commissioner of Crown lands, the lieutenant-governor , the registrar of deeds and the colonial secretary. You may also view the room of Frances Preedy, the housekeeper who doubled as a receptionist. The Assembly Chamber still functions as the seat of the government of Prince Edward Island. The most important room of all is the Confederation Chamber. In this room the delegates met in 1864 to set Canada on the road to Confederation.

▲ ■ on-site

Fort Amherst / Port La Joye National Historic Site 9b

✉ c/o Parks Canada
P.O. Box 487
Charlottetown, PE C1A 7L1

☎ (902) 675-2220 or 566-7362

Travel back in time to 1720 when 300 French and Acadians sailed into what is now Charlottetown Harbour. Here they established Port La Joye, the first permanent settlement on what they called Île St-Jean. It was hoped that the settlers would farm the land and supply food to the Fortress of Louisbourg across the water. Life was hard for the settlers. They were plagued by famine and by mounting tensions between the French and the English. In 1758, after the fall of Louisbourg, the British sailed into Port La Joye and the Acadians surrendered. Île St-Jean forthwith became St. John's Island, and the British rounded up 3500 Acadians and shipped them to France. The British quickly built Fort Amherst. However, French supremacy in North America was at an end, and the British ceased to garrison the fort in 1768. Today, visitors to the site can see the earthworks that remain. A visitor centre with displays and an audio-visual presentation tell the story of Prince Edward Island's first settlement.

▲ ■ video

Courtesy Fort Amherst/Port La Joye National Historic Park/Parks Canada

Ardgowan National Historic Park

2 Palmers Lane, Parkdale

✉ c/o Parks Canada
P.O. Box 487
Charlottetown, PE C1A 7L1

☎ (902) 566-7050

Ardgowan was the home of William Henry Pope, one of Prince Edward Island's Fathers of Confederation. Pope was born in 1825. As a lawyer and land agent for some British absentee owners of Island estates, he was active in public life. Elected to the colonial legislature in 1859, he also edited Charlottetown's newspaper, the *Islander*. He was a firm advocate of Confederation until his death in 1879. The Popes were a prominent Island family, and their status is reflected in their home. There was room for servants and a governess for the children, a good library, and a horse and carriage in the stables. During the Charlottetown Conference, Pope hosted a gala luncheon at Ardgowan where guests dined on oysters and lobsters, accompanied by champagne. Ardgowan is a *cottage ornée* (picturesque cottage), a popular architectural style at the time. The building is occupied by the district office of Parks Canada, but the grounds and gardens have been restored to Pope's time. Trees, flowering shrubs, and beds of flowers create a beautiful environment. Note the small croquet lawn; the mixed orchards of apples, plums, and pears; and the kitchen garden complete with gooseberry and currant bushes to provide fruit for pies and preserves. An interpretive exhibit explains the site to visitors.

Courtesy Ardgowan National Historic Park/Parks Canada

Prince Edward Island Marine Aquarium

9d

68 Queen St., Stanley Bridge

P.O. Box 424
Charlottetown, PE C1A 7K7

☎ (902) 892-2203

There's more than fish to see at the Prince Edward Island Marine Aquarium. Of course, you'll see plenty of tanks containing fish and sea creatures indigenous to the area. But be sure to note the display of mounted butterflies, the exhibit of oyster cultivation, and the stuffed exotic birds and small animals. The most popular attraction is the pond with the live seals. These delightful creatures bob and swim and generally romp for visitors.

Green Gables House 9e

Prince Edward Island National Park

c/o Parks and People Association
P.O. Box 1506
Charlottetown, PE C1A 7N3

☎ (902) 894-4246

For all "kindred spirits" who ever laughed and cried over the adventures of Anne Shirley, the little freckle-faced, red-haired orphan, a visit to Green Gables House is a must. L. M. Montgomery, author of *Anne of Green Gables* and 22 other books, never lived at Green Gables, but she visited there often (it belonged to David and Margaret MacNeill, elderly cousins of Montgomery) and it provided her with the setting and the inspiration for *Anne*. L. M. Montgomery was born at New London, Prince Edward Island, in 1874 and died in 1942. The house has been restored and furnished to the 1890 period, the time when Anne would have lived there. Take some time to walk around the grounds. "Lovers Lane" is located behind the house, and you can see the "Haunted Wood" quite easily.

▲ ■ on-site; teaching materials

Basin Head Fisheries Museum 10

✉
P.O. Box 238
Souris, PE C0A 2B0

☎ (902) 357-2966

Want to hear a fish story? Then come to Basin Head Fisheries Museum. For eons this part of the Atlantic Ocean has teemed with marine life, and the museum tells that story. History here begins more than 10 000 years ago, when the Paleo-Indian tribes came here to fish, hunt seals, and gather shellfish. They were followed some 8000 years later by the Micmacs, as the spearpoints, arrowheads, and stone tools exhibited in the museum prove. The Europeans, too, benefited from the sea's rich bounty when they came as long ago as the 16th century. After the British conquest in 1758, fishing blossomed into a major industry. The museum offers reconstructed fish stages and fishermen's huts, along with a series of dioramas to describe how various species were caught. With the growth of industrialization, canning became a major occupation, and the museum displays early canning equipment and labels. See the different tools of the fisherman's trade, from simple ropes, buoys, and lobster traps to boats and engines. Fishing of course spawned a number of secondary industries. On the site is a salt-box factory, where replicas of the original containers used to pack salt fish were manufactured.

■ guided tours

NEWFOUNDLAND

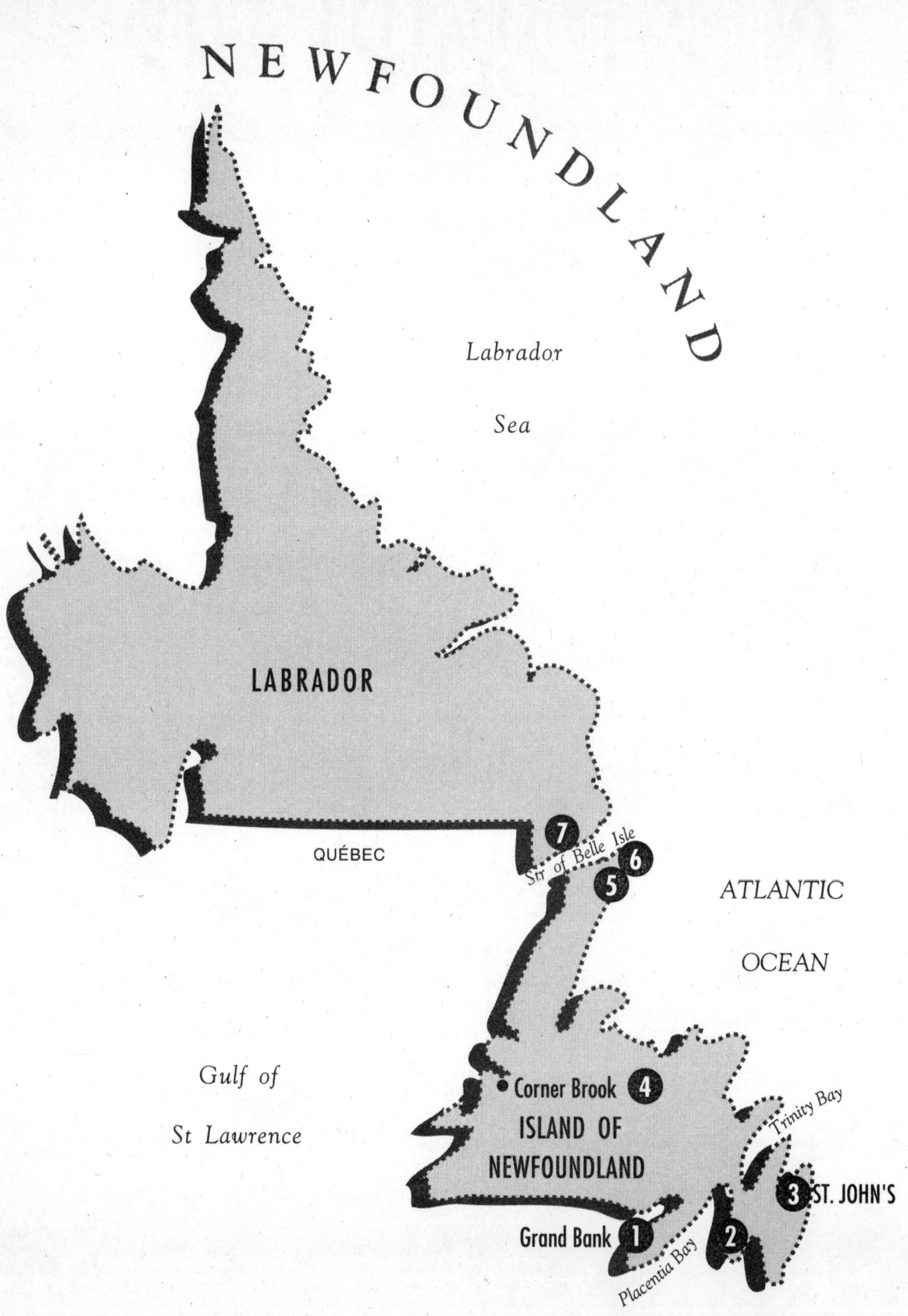

1   Southern Newfoundland Seamen's Museum
2   Castle Hill National Historic Site
3a Beothuk Provincial Park
3b Commissariat House
3c Ocean Sciences Centre, Memorial University of Newfoundland
3d Newfoundland Freshwater Resource Centre
3e Newfoundland Museum
3f Newfoundland Museum at the Murray Premises
3g Hiscock House Provincial Historic Site
3h Cape Bonavista Lighthouse Provincial Historic Site
3i Signal Hill National Historic Site
3j Cape Spear National Historic Site
4   Mary March Regional Museum
5   Grenfell House Museum
6   L'Anse-aux-Meadows National Historic Park
7   World Whaling Capital AD 1550-1600

In the site descriptions, note that:
▲ indicates that second language services are available: English in Quebec and French elsewhere in Canada. Where "limited service" is given, it would be wise to call ahead for specifics
■ indicates that educational services are available

Southern Newfoundland Seamen's Museum 1

Marine Dr.
Grand Bank, NF A0E 1W0

☎ (709) 832-1484

Grand Bank, a fishing town, is about 300 years old. The Southern Newfoundland Seamen's Museum scrutinizes life at sea in two permanent galleries. Examine the era of the banking schooner, as shown through photographs, documents, a collection of model ships and other artifacts. Then proceed to see how the fishing industry on the Grand Banks has been revolutionized through changes in technology — from hand-held fishing lines to modern trawlers. Note that this museum was built as a memorial to the many Newfoundlanders who have lost their lives at sea.

■ on-site

Castle Hill National Historic Site 2

✉
P.O. Box 10
Jerseyside, NF A0B 2G0

☎ (709) 227-2401

In the 16th century, Basque fishermen came to Newfoundland, lured by its rich cod stocks. A settlement sprang up at Placentia (originally called Plaisance), an ideal spot because of its stony beach for drying cod and its protected harbour that never froze over. To protect their position, the French built a fortification called Le Gaillardin (a picketed palisade that could hold up to a hundred men), and then, in 1693, constructed Fort Royal. The Treaty of Utrecht ceded Newfoundland to the British in 1713, and the French were moved to Cape Breton. The British had no particular use for Fort Royal in peacetime, so they allowed it to deteriorate. The remains of the fortifications built by the French are preserved at Castle Hill National Historic Site. The visitor centre has displays, models, and dioramas recounting the history of Fort Royal and Placentia. Visitors may follow the interpretive trails and see the redoubt, which served as an observation post, the walls of the fort, and Le Gaillardin.

▲ ■ guided tours

Beothuk Provincial Park 3a

✉

Department of Tourism
and Culture, P.O. Box 8700
St. John's, NF A1B 4J6

☎ (709) 729-0862

The name of Beothuk Provincial Park commemorates the Beothuck people, an aboriginal nation that perished from the twin evils of settler warfare and imported European diseases and is now completely extinct. Because the forest industry has been so important to the economy of Newfoundland, the park contains a full-scale replica of an old-time logging camp complete with bunkhouse, cookhouse, forepeak (foreman's shack or office), filing shack, privy, and barn. See the display of artifacts related to the logging industry. Park interpreters will provide information and answer questions.

Commissariat House

King's Bridge Rd., St. John's
✉
c/o Newfoundland Historic Sites
P.O. Box 8700
St. John's, NF A1B 4J6

☎ (709) 729-6730/576-2460

Every army has to be clothed, fed, armed, and housed. During the 18th century, the British military presence in North America increased steadily as Britain competed with France for supremacy in the New World. And so it was that in 1820 they finished construction on a building in St. John's to house the Commissariat Department, the body responsible for provisioning troops. The department occupied the building until 1870, when there was no longer any need for it, but during its tenure one of its more noteworthy occupants was Oliver Goldsmith. Goldsmith, a writer born in New Brunswick, was the grand-nephew of the celebrated Anglo-Irish author Oliver Goldsmith and is considered to be one of British North America's first native-born, English-language poets. Commissariat House has been restored and furnished to the 1830 period. Costumed interpreters will greet you. The house contains an elegant dining room with the table set, bedrooms complete with four-poster beds, a fully equipped kitchen, and a beautiful drawing room. The former coach house, to the rear of the building, now serves as the visitor centre and contains a number of displays and artifacts.

■ guided tours

Ocean Sciences Centre, Memorial University of Newfoundland 3c

4 Clark Place, Logy Bay Lab
St. John's, NF A1C 5S7

☎ (709) 737-3709 or 737-8833

As you approach Memorial University's Ocean Sciences Centre, you notice that it looks like a large circular spaceship, complete with portholes. In fact, the structure of the building was designed to resemble the internal anatomy of the sea anemone. Although primarily a major research facility, the centre also promotes public awareness of ocean sciences and welcomes visitors. And what an interesting and entertaining place it is. Be sure to stop in at the Discovery Room, which contains aquaria filled with a variety of coldwater ocean fish, displays, and a touch tank. Reach your hand in and make friends with a living sea creature. See the decompression chamber, and outside, in an enclosure, a friendly group of harbour seals, who entertain visitors with their antics, particularly when they sense that a snack of herring might be at hand.

■ on-site

Newfoundland Freshwater Resource Centre 3d

Box 5, Nagle's Place
St. John's, NF A1B 2Z2

☎ (709) 754-FISH (3474)

What on earth is a fluvarium? You can see one at the Newfoundland Freshwater Centre. It's on the first floor: a window that allows you to see the underwater world of Nagle's Hill Brook, which flows around the outside of the building. Here you will see brown trout, brook trout, arctic char, and three types of river habitats: deep holding pools, fast-flowing riffles, and shallow, slow-moving streams. You will learn why all three environments are important to marine life, and how fish and other water creatures adapt to the changing seasons. On the second floor, you can watch a slide presentation and explore the world of the Atlantic salmon. Outside the building, take a stroll along the walking trails through Pippy Park.

■ on-site; all grades

Newfoundland Museum 3e

285 Duckworth St.
St. John's, NF A1C 1G9

☎ (709) 729-2329

The Newfoundland Museum consists of four branches, each with its own area of emphasis. The focus at the Duckworth Street facility, which consists of two permanent galleries, is the 9000-year prehistory and history of Newfoundland and Labrador. One gallery presents the cultures and traditions of the six groups of Maritime First Nations: Maritime Archaic, Dorset, Beothuk, Micmac, Montagnais/Naskapi, and Labrador Inuit. The second gallery explores the way of life that developed in the towns and outports of 19th-century Newfoundland. The Duckworth Street museum also offers a series of temporary exhibits.

■ on-site

Newfoundland Museum at the Murray Premises 3f

Beck's Cove
St. John's, NF A1C 1G9

☎ (709) 729-5044

You'll find this branch of the Newfoundland Museum in the restored property of a 19th-century fish merchant. This location seems quite appropriate when you realize that one of the two permanent exhibits explores the theme "Business in Great Waters." The exhibit presents the fishery workers of Newfoundland, from 16th-century Basque whalers and cod-fishers in Labrador to the fish merchants of the early 20th century. The second gallery, "For King and Country," presents Newfoundland's involvement in military events from 1689 to the end of World War II.

■ on-site

Hiscock House Provincial Historic Site 3g

Trinity
✉

c/o Historic Resources Division
P.O. Box 8700
St. John's, NF A1B 4J6

☎ (709) 464-2042

At the restored Hiscock House in Trinity, you can experience

the way of life of a rural Newfoundland family engaged in small business. The house was built in 1881 for Richard and Emma Hiscock. After Richard's death in 1893, Emma managed in various ways. Richard had left her the family business: a forge, a garden, and a shop. She rented her house to a local magistrate, continued to run the shop, and set herself up as the town's postmistress. Emma Hiscock died in 1936. The house has been restored to the 1910 period, when Emma lived there with her teenage daughters. The furniture and artifacts are primarily those used by the family, and together represent a typical local Newfoundland merchant's household during the early 20th century. Costumed staff interpret the house for visitors.

■ guided tours

Cape Bonavista Lighthouse Provincial Historic Site 3h

Bonavista

✉

c/o Historic Resources Division
P.O. Box 8700
St. John's, NF A1B 4J6

☎ (709) 468-7444 or 729-0862

Discover what the life of a 19th-century lighthouse keeper was like at the Cape Bonavista Lighthouse. Operational from 1843 to 1895, it was the fourth lighthouse to be built in Newfoundland. Life for the lighthouse keeper was not easy. A great number of ships sailed in the waters off Cape Bonavista. The light's mechanism had to be wound every two hours, and the reflectors required continual cleaning and polishing. The keeper maintained a daily record of all activities. The lighthouse has been restored to the 1870 period. The living quarters have been furnished as they were when Jeremiah White lived there, still the lighthouse keeper at the age of 80. An interpretive display on the second floor recounts the history of the lighthouse and its keepers.

■ on-site

Signal Hill National Historic Site 3i

P.O. Box 5879
St. John's, NF A1C 5X4

☎ (709) 772-5367

In the 18th century, Newfoundland was coveted by both England and France for its rich fishery. Signal Hill, standing 183 m (600 ft.) above the entrance to St. John's Harbour, was the site of many battles between these bitter rivals. The last battle was fought in 1762, when the British established themselves for good. Because of its height and position at the mouth of the harbour, the site was also an important communications post. Known in the 18th century as the Lookout, residents would watch for flags hoisted on incoming ships and inform harbour pilots and customs officials. Communication at Signal Hill took on a new dimension in 1901, when inventor Guglielmo Marconi received the first wireless signal there. During the summer months, army cadets, dressed in authentic uniforms of the period, perform 19th-century military drills on the site. A visitor centre contains informative displays that give the history of the site.

▲ ■ guided tours

Cape Spear National Historic Site 3i

P.O. Box 5879
St. John's, NF A1C 5X4

☎ (709) 772-5367

For more than a century, ships entering St. John's harbour depended on the Cape Spear Lighthouse to guide them safely past the rocks. Built in 1836, Cape Spear Lighthouse, which functioned until 1955, is the oldest surviving lighthouse in Newfoundland. The lighthouse, which has been restored to the 1839 period, recalls how a lighthouse keeper and his family would have lived at that time. It was a lonely but busy life. The oil lamps had to be kept filled and the wicks trimmed because the light could not be allowed to go out. The reflectors had to be cleaned and polished constantly — soot would dim the light. The lighthouse keeper was also responsible for operating a fog alarm. Cape Spear assumed a new importance during World War II, when the military was concerned about the presence of German submarines off the east coast of Canada. Gun emplacements were constructed at the site and were connected to magazines and equipment rooms by a series of underground passages. A visitor centre presents informative exhibits on the history of lighthouses and the traditions of lighthouse keeping.

▲ ■ on-site

Mary March Regional Museum 4

St. Catherine St.
Grand Falls–Windsor, NF A2A 1W9

☎ (709) 489-9331

The Mary March Regional Museum is named for Mary March (Demasduit), one of the last of the Beothuk Nation. The museum presents three permanent displays. One gallery explores the natural history of the Grand Falls–Windsor area, focusing on its geological formation 500 million years ago. In the second gallery, learn about the history and traditions of the many diverse groups of Native people who have inhabited central Newfoundland. The third gallery concentrates on the story of European exploration and settlement, and the subsequent development of central Newfoundland's fishing, mining, and forestry resources.

■ on-site

Grenfell House Museum 5

c/o The Sir Wilfred Thomason
Grenfell Historical Society
P.O. Box 93
St. Anthony, NF A0K 4S0

☎ (709) 454-3333

Born in England in 1865, Sir Wilfred Grenfell trained as a medical doctor. A member of the National Mission to Deep Sea Fishermen, he travelled to Newfoundland in 1892 to investigate conditions in the Labrador fishery. The poverty he saw appalled him. He returned a year later with two doctors and two nurses to establish a hospital at Battle Harbour. A few years later he established another hospital at St. Anthony. His efforts were unflagging. He initiated a cash-only co-operative system to reduce the fishermen's debt to the merchants; he developed farms and gardens; and he even built a greenhouse in St. Anthony. He attracted doctors, nurses, dentists, teachers, and other professionals to his hospitals, clinics, and other facilities. The Grenfell House, built in 1909, was the home of Grenfell and his family for a number of years; it then became a residence for mission workers before being restored and opened as a museum honouring one of Canada's great humanitarians. "Real joy comes not from ease or riches or from the praise of men but from doing something worthwhile." — Wilfred T. Grenfell

▲ ■ guided tours

L'Anse-aux-Meadows National Historic Park 6

P.O. Box 70
St. Lunaire–Griquet, NF A0K 2X0

☎ (709) 623-2608

For a long time, the inhabitants of L'Anse-aux-Meadows puzzled over the grass-covered bumps and ridges that dotted the landscape. In 1960, a Norwegian explorer and writer, Helge Ingstad, and his wife, archaeologist Anne Stine Ingstad, excavated the bumps and ridges and made the discovery they were hoping for: the grassy ridges were actually the lower courses of the walls of eight Norse buildings from the 11th century. The Ingstads unearthed several artifacts that revealed a great deal about the settlement: a bronze pin, used by the Norsemen to fasten their capes, a stone oil lamp, a small spindle whorl, a bone knitting needle, a small whetstone, iron boat nails, and a lot of slag from the smelting of iron. The Ingstads found that the settlement had been organized into three complexes, each with a dwelling and a workshop for smiths, carpenters, and shipwrights. The settlement was founded by Leif Eriksson, whose first arrival in North America, five centuries before Columbus, is described in the 13th-century Greenlander's Saga. L'Anse-aux-Meadows has been declared a World Heritage Site. The visitors' centre has a video giving the history of the site, informative displays, and exhibits of the artifacts found. On leaving the centre, visitors may walk about the site to see both the original ruins and the reconstructed sod huts.

▲ ■ guided tours

World Whaling Capital A.D. 1550–1600
7

Red Bay, LB/NF

☎ (709) 920-2154/737-8872

Canada's first real oil boom took place between the years 1550 and 1600, when Basque sailors from France and Spain discovered that the Strait of Belle Isle was a fertile hunting ground for bowhead whales, a sought-after source of whale oil, used in Europe as fuel for heat and light. Every spring the whalers arrived at Red Bay to hunt; in late fall, their ships would set sail again for Europe, laden with barrels of the coveted oil. There arose around the Red Bay site what might be described as Canada's first industrial complex: comprising dwellings, workshops for equipment repair, tryworks for "trying," or rendering, the whale blubber into oil, and cooperages, where barrels were made. Excavations by archaeologists at the Red Bay site have resulted in some significant finds. A number of boats have been recovered, including a 16th-century whale ship, probably the *San Juan*, which was sunk in a storm in 1565. Skeletons, remnants of clothing, tools, and personal effects have all helped tell the story of the World Whaling Capital of A.D. 1550–1600. A visitors' centre displays many of the artifacts found, along with life-size reproductions and scale models.

North West Territories

NORTHWEST TERRITORIES

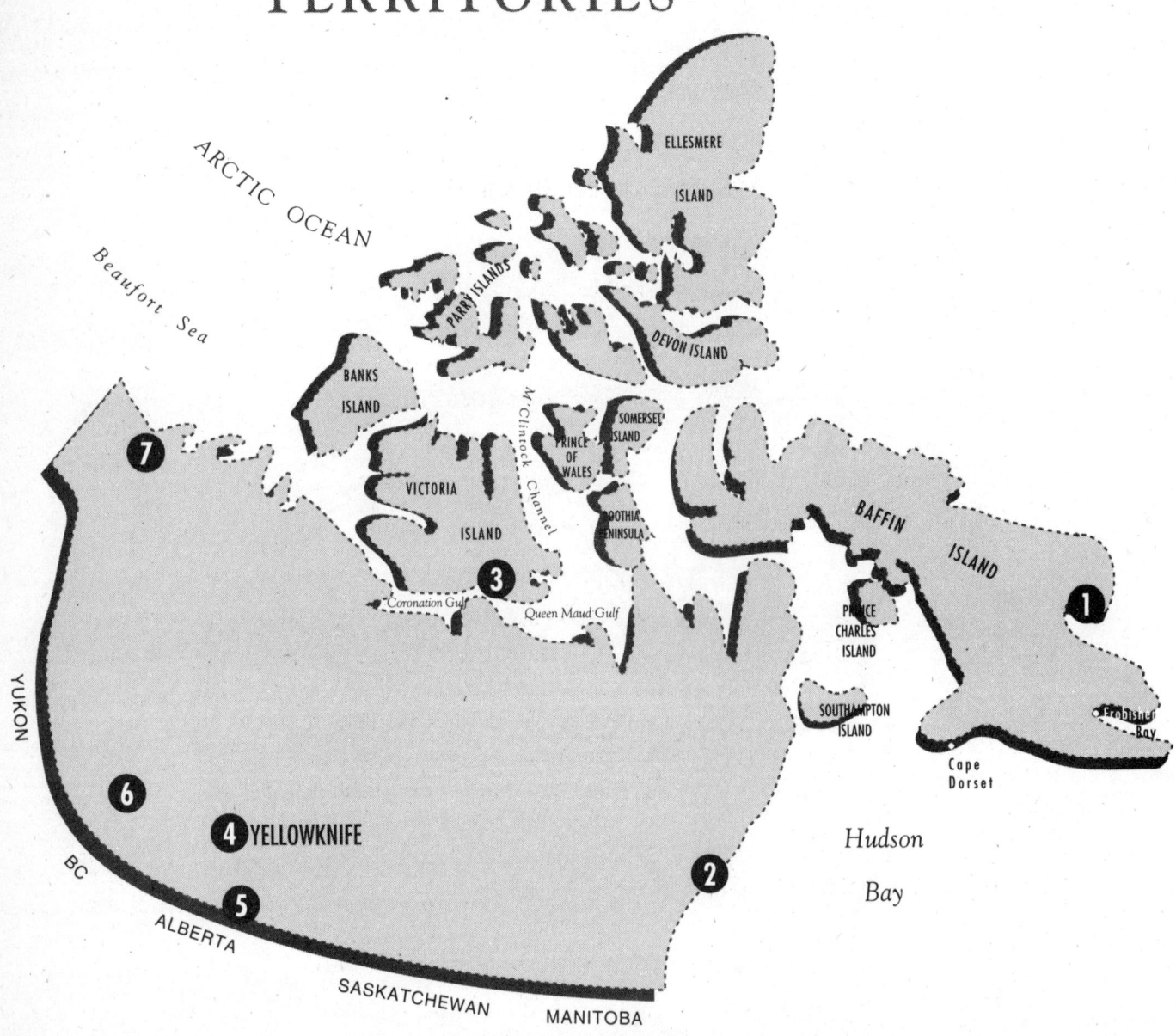

1   Pangnirtung

2   Rankin Inlet

3   Cambridge Bay

4a Prince of Wales Northern Heritage Centre

4b Ndilo Cultural Village

5   Wood Buffalo National Park

6   Fort Simpson

7   Aklavik

In the site descriptions, note that:
▲   indicates that second language services are available: English in Quebec and French elsewhere in Canada. Where "limited service" is given, it would be wise to call ahead for specifics
■   indicates that educational services are available

Pangnirtung

Cumberland Peninsula

Baffin Tourism Association
P.O. Box 1450
Iqualuit, NT X0A 0H0

☎ (819) 979-6551

Pangnirtung is a fishing, arts, and tourism centre on the Cumberland Peninsula, northeast of Iqualuit. Visitors may explore former whaling stations in Kekerten Historic Park, which is the site of the first permanent land-based whaling station in the eastern Arctic (established during the 1850s). Also see the stone foundations and the remains of Inuit sod houses. The Inuit people welcome visitors to their camps. At the Angmarlik Interpretive Centre, the Elders will share their history and traditions.

Rankin Inlet

Baffin Tourism Association
P.O. Box 1450
Iqualuit, NT X0A 0H0

☎ (819) 979-6551

The Inuit Cultural Institute in Rankin Inlet has one of the world's largest collections of Arctic resource materials, including historic films made early in the 20th century. While in Rankin Inlet, visit nearby Marble Island. This was the final resting place for several 19th-century whaling ships. Also in the neighbourhood of Rankin Inlet, at the mouth of the Meliadine River, find a number of 15th-century Thule subterranean houses at the Ijiraliq Archaeological Site.

Syllabics
Titirausiq nutaaq

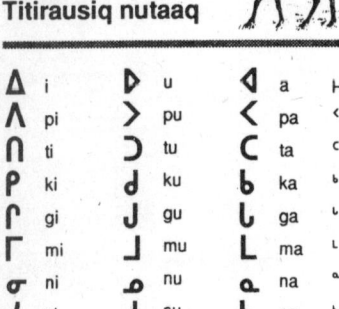

Cambridge Bay 3

✉ Arctic Coast Tourism Association
Dept. EG, Box 9
Cambridge Bay, NT X0E 0C0

☎ (403) 983-2224/800-661-0788

See the remains of *Maude*, the ship belonging to explorer Roald Amundsen. Amundsen was the first man to reach the South Pole (1911), the first to sail through the Northwest Passage (1903–06), and the first to sail through the Northeast Passage (1918–20). Amundsen was lost while attempting to rescue the Italian explorer Umberto Nobile, who crashed while crossing the North Pole in an airship in 1928.

Prince of Wales Northern Heritage Centre 4a

✉ Box 1320
Yellowknife, NT X1A 2L9

☎ (403) 873-7551

For a comprehensive look at the Northwest Territories and the forces that have shaped the region over the centuries, come to the Prince of Wales Northern Heritage Centre. 7000 years of habitation come to light through displays showing the way of life of Dene, Inuit, Métis, and Canadians of European origin, and through its collection of more than 5000 pieces of fine art. The

Courtesy Prince of Wales Northern Heritage Centre

South Gallery portrays the Arctic before recorded history, including the natural environment, the arrival of the first inhabitants, and the culture of the Dene and Inuit. The North Gallery focuses on events and developments since the arrival of the Europeans, including exploration, whaling, the fur trade, the North-West Mounted Police, the missions, and the growth of gold mining and other industries. The Wings of Change Gallery illustrates more than 60 years of Northern aviation history. The centre includes several items of particular interest. These include a small wooden carving discovered on Baffin Island of a man believed to be clad in 13th-century Viking dress. An original sled from the 1913–18 Arctic expedition of anthropologist Vilhjalmur Stefansson is on display, as well as items originally cached in 1845 for the lost Sir John A. Franklin expedition.

▲ ■ on-site; outreach; teaching materials; all grades

Ndilo Cultural Village 4b

Yellowknife

✉

c/o Yellowknife Band Office
P.O. Box 2514
Yellowknife, NT X1A 2P8

☎ (403) 873-2869 (summer only)
(403) 873-8951 (Band office)

The Dene people of the Mackenzie District of Canada's Northwest Territories have occupied a vast area of land, covering some 1 165 500 km^2 (450 000 sq. mi.), for the past 25 000 to 30 000 years. The Ndilo Cultural Village invites you to learn the Dene ways and traditions in a recreated family bush camp. At the village, you will see Elders engaged in such daily activities as tanning hides, crafting tools, or drying fish or caribou. You will have an opportunity to try your hand at drumming, making a rattle, sharing Dene legends around a campfire, and tasting traditional foods. On-site interpreters offer tours.

■ on-site

Wood Buffalo National Park 5

✉
Box 750
Fort Smith, NT X0E 0P0

☎ (403) 872-2349

Although the park address given above suggests that Wood Buffalo National Park lies in the Northwest Territories, it actually extends far into Alberta as well. One of the largest national parks in the world, Wood Buffalo is almost as big as the province of Nova Scotia. Established originally to protect the last remaining herd of wood bison, it has since gone on to establish a reputation for itself as a safe environment for other endangered species, such as the Whooping Crane and the Northern Alberta Peregrine. One of the park's outstanding features is the Salt Plains. Because the area was flooded with salt water for thousands of years, salt-tolerant vegetation evolved. Prior to the arrival of the Europeans, the Natives would collect salt for curing and preserving food and hides. Later the Europeans collected salt as a trade commodity. In the 1970s, park management recognized the need for conservation, and now the Salt Plains are recognized as a fragile environment, the only one of its kind in Canada. Interpreters are available and provide a number of interesting and informative programs. Wood Buffalo National Park has been designated a UNESCO World Heritage Site.

▲ ■

Fort Simpson 6

✉ c/o Nahanni-Ram
Tourism Association
Dept. EG, Box 177
Fort Simpson, NT X0E 0N0

☎ (403) 695-3182/
1-800-661-0788

When built in 1804, Fort Simpson was known as "Fort of the Forks." Later, its name was changed to Fort Simpson in honour of George Simpson, the first governor of the newly-combined North West and Hudson's Bay Companies. Be sure to see the Papal Site commemorating the visit of Pope John Paul II. Fine Native products, including quillwork, beading, and birchbark baskets, are for sale in the craft shop. Fort Simpson acts as headquarters for the spectacular Nahanni National Park Reserve.

Aklavik 7

✉ c/o Western Arctic Tourism Association
Dept. EG, Box 2600
Inuvik, NT X0E 0T0

☎ (403) 979-4321/2434

Here in Aklavik, the Mad Trapper of Rat River lies buried. Albert Johnson, the so-called Mad Trapper, was the object of the first aerial manhunt in Canadian history. Nobody knew much about the eccentric hermit, who lived alone in a cabin near the Mackenzie River delta. Then one day in 1932 he shot and wounded a police officer who was investigating a complaint that Johnson was disturbing Native traplines. A posse of trappers and

RCMP officers pursued him for 48 days; several gun battles took place and Johnson shot one police officer dead before vanishing again. He was shadowed from the air by the famous bush pilot "Wop" May, and when the posse caught up to him he wounded yet another police officer before dying in a hail of gunfire.

YUKON

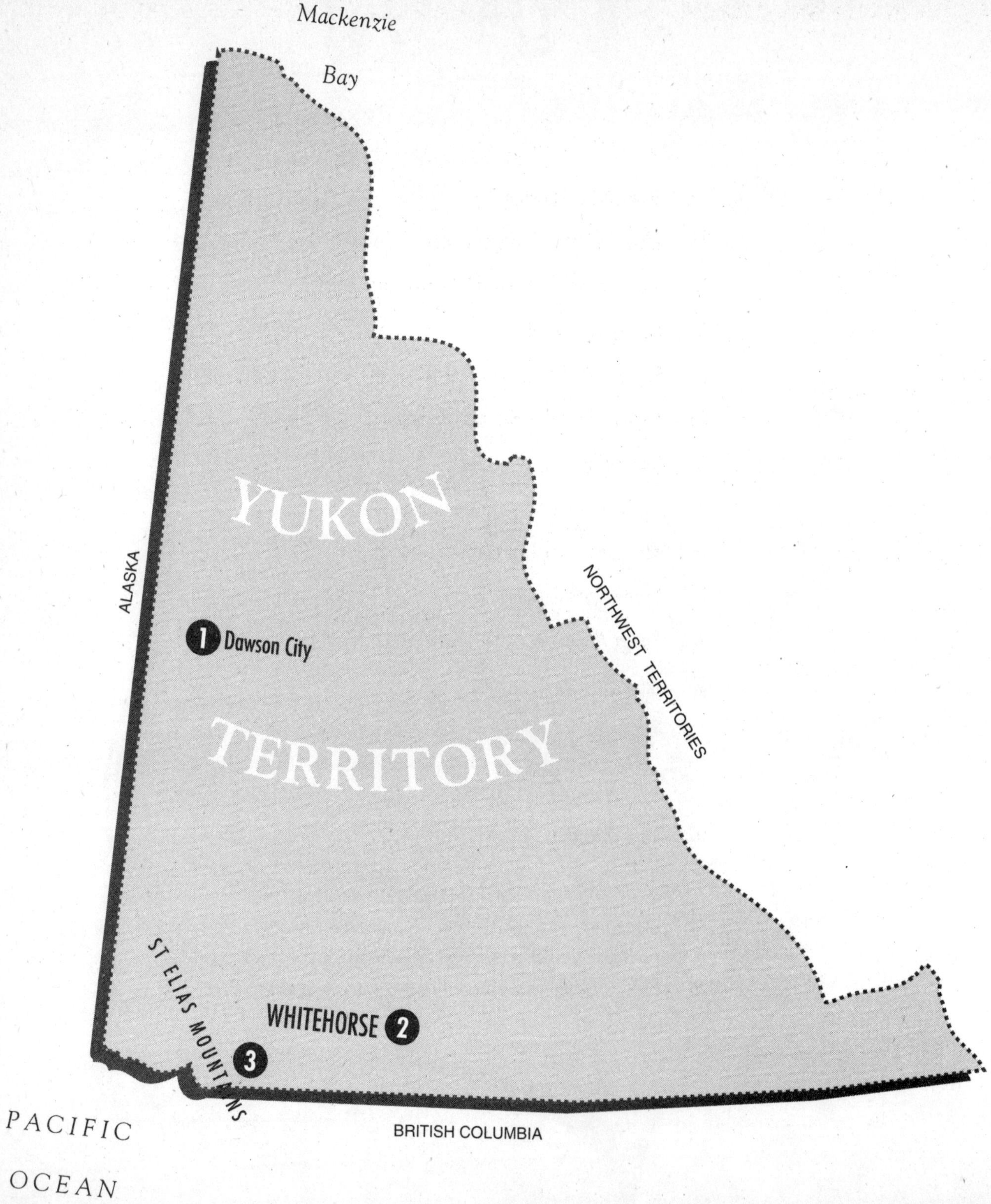

Mackenzie Bay

YUKON

ALASKA

1 Dawson City

TERRITORY

NORTHWEST TERRITORIES

ST ELIAS MOUNTAINS

WHITEHORSE 2

3

PACIFIC OCEAN

BRITISH COLUMBIA

1a   Dawson City Museum

1b   Klondike National Historic Sites

1c   Jack London's Cabin and Interpretation Centre

1d   Robert Service Cabin

2a   SS Klondike National Historic Site

2b   Chilkoot Trail National Historic Site

2c   Sam McGee's Cabin

2d   MacBride Museum and Historical Society

2e   Alaska Highway Interpretive Centre

2f   Yukon Transportation Museum

2g   Yukon Wildlife Preserve

3   Kluane National Park Reserve

In the site descriptions, note that:

▲ indicates that second language services are available: English in Quebec and French elsewhere in Canada. Where "limited service" is given, it would be wise to call ahead for specifics

■ indicates that educational services are available

Dawson City Museum 1a

✉ Box 303
Dawson City, YT Y0B 1G0

☎ (403) 993-5291

To get a feel for the turbulent history of the Yukon, visit the Dawson City Museum. The South Gallery, entitled "Kings of the Klondike," was created as a tribute to the unsung heroes of the Klondike: the flora and fauna, and the Native people. The gold rush is chronicled here as well. The North Gallery, entitled "From Moose Pasture to Metropolis," recounts the growth of Dawson City from 1898 to 1903. See how the gold rush and the sudden influx of people caused Dawson, a mining camp, to grow into a capital city. Be sure to examine the working model of a section of the Klondike Mines Railway; it includes four functioning locomotives. On display as well are mammoth and mastodon bones, an early log cabin, and many other items of interest.

▲ ■ guided tours

Klondike National Historic Sites 1b

✉ Box 390
Dawson City, YT Y0B 1G0

☎ (403) 993-5462

On August 17, 1896, George Washington Carmack and two Natives, Skookum Jim and Tagish Charlie, discovered gold in Rabbit Creek (later named Bonanza Creek), a tributary of the Klondike River. This brought thousands of treasure-hunters to the Yukon and established Dawson City. There are numerous sites in and around Dawson City that are associated with the Klondike gold rush.

Dredge No. 4 (on Bonanza Creek Road). This huge structure has the distinction of being the largest wooden hull dredge in

North America. Its huge buckets ripped up the Klondike Valley, leaving massive piles of tailings.

Bear Creek Gold Dredge Support Camp. This community supported the Klondike gold dredges until 1966. It contained the most modern blacksmith and machine shops north of Vancouver.

Fort Herchmer Tour. This tour takes visitors to historic buildings; these include the North-West Mounted Police barracks and administrative buildings.

Palace Grand Theatre (Third Ave. and King St.). The Palace Grand Theatre, opened in 1899, offered exciting entertainment over many years. It has now been reconstructed, and visitors are welcome.

1901 Post Office (Third Ave. and King St.). This historic post office still functions; anyone may drop off mail here or purchase stamps. Special commemorative stamps are for sale.

Steamer *Keno* (Front St.). The steamer *Keno*, one of the last sternwheelers to travel the Yukon and Stewart rivers, is now a National Historic Site.

Jack London's Cabin and Interpretation Centre 1c

c/o Klondike Visitors Association,
Front and King St.

Box 389
Dawson City, YT Y0B 1G0

☎ (403) 993-5575

For anyone who has ever thrilled to the adventure of the Far North as recounted in *White Fang* or *The Call of the Wild*, a stop at Jack London's Cabin and Interpretation Centre should head the itinerary. Lured by the promise of gold, London hiked the Chilkoot Pass, ran the rapids through Miles Canyon, and eventually made it to Dawson City where he lived briefly in 1898.

He never found gold, but he did find enough material to fuel his novels and short stories for many years to come. The cabin contains some of the original logs from his place on Henderson Creek. See the extensive photo exhibit at the site, and, during the summer months, attend the daily readings from his works.

- on-site

Robert Service Cabin 1d

Eighth Ave.

c/o Klondike National Historic Sites
Box 390
Dawson City, YT Y0B 1G0

☎ (403) 993-5462

"A bunch of the boys were whooping it up in the Malamute Saloon..." *The Shooting of Dan McGrew* is one of Robert Service's classic ballads about life during the wild days of the Klondike gold rush. Robert Service, born in Scotland in 1874, arrived in the Yukon in 1904 as an employee of the Canadian Imperial Bank of Commerce, and stayed until 1912. His Yukon poetry, *Songs of a Sourdough* and *Ballads of a Cheechako* have immortalized him and made the Klondike gold rush part of Canadian folklore. The cabin where he lived is open to visitors. Twice daily during the summer months, recitals of his poetry are held there.

- guided tours

Ss Klondike National Historic Site 2a

c/o Yukon National Historic Sites
205–300 Main St.
Whitehorse, YT Y1A 2B5

☎ (403) 667-3910

From the 1860s until the 1950s, river navigation was the key to transportation in the Yukon, and sternwheelers were the vessels of choice. The original SS *Klondike* was built in 1929. Its innovative design meant that it could carry 50 percent more cargo than other boats on the river. Unfortunately it ran aground in 1936. The British Yukon Navigation Company immediately built a virtual carbon copy, naming the vessel *Klondike II*. The *Klondike II* carried cargo and passengers from 1937 until 1952, after which it sailed as a cruise ship. Tourism was not a major industry in the Yukon at the time, so in 1955 the *Klondike II* made its last trip. Now a National Historic Site, the vessel has been restored to the 1937-40 period and welcomes visitors.

▲

Chilkoot Trail National Historic Site 2b

✉

c/o Yukon National Historic Sites
205–300 Main St.
Whitehorse, YT Y1A 2B5

☎ (403) 667-3910

The Chilkoot Trail has been called "the meanest 33 miles of history." During the winter of 1897-98, thousands rushed north to cash in on the discovery of gold in the Klondike. Many were ill-prepared for the journey that awaited them in the Far North and didn't make it. Today the Chilkoot Trail follows the actual path of the adventurers of that extraordinary time in our history. The trail is dotted with historic artifacts and archaeological features, mute testimony to the past. While the trail is open to hikers, many would find the going tough: the terrain is rough and weather conditions can be poor. Train excursions are available.

▲

Sam McGee's Cabin 2c

c/o McBride Museum Society
P.O. Box 4037
Whitehorse, YT Y1A 3S9

☎ (403) 667-2709

"There are strange things done in the midnight sun by the men who moil for gold . . . ." So go the opening lines to Robert Service's classic poem, *The Cremation of Sam McGee*. The real Sam McGee was an entrepreneur born near Peterborough, Ontario. Among other things, he prospected for gold, mined, and built roads and bridges. McGee was in Whitehorse, living in a one-room cabin he built in 1899, at the same time that Robert Service was there, working as a clerk at the Bank of Commerce. It was at this time that Service wrote his most famous poem. Visitors are welcome to see Sam McGee's cabin and to participate in a program entitled "Sam McGee: The Making of a Legend."

MacBride Museum and Historical Society 2d

First Ave and Wood St., Whitehorse

c/o McBride Museum Society
P.O. Box 4037
Whitehorse, YT Y1A 3S9

☎ (403) 667-2709

With over 465 m^2 (5000 sq. ft.) of exhibition space, the MacBride Museum presents the history of the Yukon through a series of exhibits that explores prehistory, history, culture, transportation, and mining. These exhibits include ones on prehistoric mammals, Native cultures, the gold rush, the construction of the Alaska Highway, a wildlife collection, and historical photography of the Yukon peoples. An audio-visual presentation supplements the displays.

Alaska Highway Interpretive Centre 2e

Junction of Alaska Hwy. and Robert Campbell Hwy., Watson Lake

c/o Tourism Yukon
P.O. Box 2703
Whitehorse, YT Y1A 2C6

☎ (403) 536-7469/667-5340

The Alaska Highway begins in British Columbia at Dawson Creek, crosses the Yukon, and ends in Alaska at Delta Junction. Travelling this historic highway is an experience. The highway was a joint American and Canadian project, started in 1942 in response to American fears of an enemy attack from the Far North. The construction of the highway had a devastating effect on the Native people; new diseases carried into the region by construction workers caused decimating epidemics. However, the Alaska Highway is considered to be one of the greatest engineering achievements of the 20th century. Many significant events were connected with its construction and operation. There are markers and interpretive panels at mileposts along the way; these explain various points of interest and significance.

Yukon Transportation Museum 2f

Whitehorse Airport

Box 5867
Whitehorse, YT Y1A 4A2

☎ (403) 668-4191

Transportation was essential to the opening of the Yukon. In this museum you can see exhibits such as *The Queen of the Yukon*, which was the sister aircraft to the *Spirit of St. Louis*, and many artifacts that were donated by the WP & YR Railroad.

Yukon Wildlife Preserve 2g

c/o Gray Line Yukon
208G Steele St.
Whitehorse, YT Y1A 2C4

☎ (403) 668-3225

The Yukon's abundant wildlife attracts many visitors. The Yukon Wildlife Preserve consists of a huge expanse of forest, meadow and marshland, where animals roam unhindered. Look for elk, caribou, bison, moose, mountain goats, sheep, musk-ox, mule deer, snowy owls, rare peregrine falcons, and much more. Guided tours are offered. Don't forget your camera.

Kluane National Park Reserve 3

✉
P.O. Box 5495
Haines Junction, YT Y0B 1L0

☎ (403) 634-2251

Beautiful Kluane Park has been declared a UNESCO World Heritage Site. Home to Mount Logan, Canada's highest mountain, it also contains the world's largest ice fields outside the polar regions, wide valleys, mountain lakes, alpine meadows, and tundra. Visitors to the park see excellent examples of how glaciers have determined the shape of the land. Wildlife and plants in Kluane have also had to adapt to extremes of climate and diverse topography in order to survive. The park contains a wide variety of wildlife, including moose, Dall sheep, mountain goats, caribou, and bears. Both black bears and grizzlies make their home in Kluane. The park is a paradise for naturalists and amateur photographers. Excellent interpretation programs are available for visitors.

Index

A

Acadian Mus. (PE) 276
Addiction Research Foundation Mus. (ON) 148
Aero Space Mus. (AB) 51
African Lion Safari (ON) 131

Agriculture & Farming
   Central Experimental Farm (ON) 180
   Manitoba Agricultural Mus. (MB) 98
   North Battleford Western Development Mus. (SK) 88
   Ontario Agricultural Mus. (ON) 143
   Puck's Farm (ON) 147
   Reynolds–Alberta Mus. (AB) 58

Ukrainian Cultural Heritage Village (AB) 60
Aklavik (NT) 304
Alaska Highway Interpretive Ctr. (YT) 315
Alberta Railway Mus. (AB) 63
Alberta Science Ctr. (AB) 46
Alexander Graham Bell National Historic Pk. (NS) 269
Algonquin Pk. (ON) 187
Amethyst Mine Panorama (ON) 192

Amusement
   African Lion Safari (ON) 131
   Biscuit Puppet Theatre and Mus. (PQ) 220
   Calgary Exhibition and Stampede (AB) 47
   CN Tower (ON) 152
   London Regional Children's Mus. (ON) 127
   Manitoba Children's Mus. (MB) 104
   Marineland (ON) 135
   Miniature World (BC) 5
   Niagara Falls IMAX Theatre and Daredevil Gallery
      and Mus. (ON) 136
   Norman Elder Mus. (ON) 156
   Ontario Place (ON) 157
   Paramount Canada's Wonderland (ON) 147
   Pays de la Sagouine (NB) 252
   Philip's Magical Paradise Mus. of Magic and Illusion (MB) 100
   Royal London Wax Mus. (BC) 5
   Storyland (ON) 85
   Tivoli Miniature World (ON) 136
   West Edmonton Mall (AB) 59

Anne of Green Gables Mus. at Silver Bush (PE) 277
Archelaus Smith Mus. (NS) 258

Archaeology & Paleontology
   Bon Echo Provincial Pk. (ON) 185
   Bonnechere Caves (ON) 185
   Calgary Zoo, Botanical Gdns. and Prehistoric Pk. (AB) 48
   Charlie Lake Cave (BC) 37
   Chilkoot Trail N.H.S. (YT) 313
   Dinosaur Provincial Pk. (AB) 45
   Forks, The (MB) 102
   Fundy Geological Mus. (NS) 265
   Head-Smashed-In Buffalo Jump (AB) 43
   L'Anse-aux-Meadows National Historic Pk. (NF) 294
   McCord Mus. of Canadian History (PQ) 211
   Petroglyphs Provincial Pk. (ON) 186
   Pointe-à-Callière Mus. of Archaeology and History (PQ) 213
   Royal Ontario Mus. (ON) 157
   Royal Saskatchewan Mus. (SK) 75
   Royal Tyrrell Mus. of Palaeontology (AB) 56
   Serpent Mounds Provincial Pk. (ON) 166
   Simcoe County Mus. (ON) 198
   World Whaling Capital AD 1550-1600 (NF) 295

Ardgowan National Historic Pk. (PE) 279
Art Gallery of Hamilton (ON) 139
Art Gallery of Ontario (ON) 149
Artillery Pk. N.H.S. (PQ) 229

Arts
   Anne of Green Gables Mus. at Silver Bush (PE) 277
   Art Gallery of Hamilton (ON) 139
   Art Gallery of Ontario (ON) 149
   Beaverbrook Art Gallery (NB) 249
   Biscuit Puppet Theatre and Mus. (PQ) 220
   Bottle Houses (PE) 275
   Canadian Mus. of Caricature (ON) 177
   Canadian Ctr. for Architecture (PQ) 219
   Carr House (BC) 4
   Centre Culturel Franco-Manitobain (MB) 108
   Cinémathèque Québécoise and Cinema Mus. (PQ) 213
   Edmonton Art Gallery (AB) 63
   Elizabeth Lefort Gallery (NS) 270
   Emily Carr Gallery (BC) 8
   Gabrielle Roy House (MB) 107
   Green Gables House (PE) 281
   International Mus. of Humour (PQ) 218
   Jack London's Cabin and Interpretation Ctr. (YT) ... 311
   Leo Mol Sculpture Gdn. (MB) 106
   L. M. Montgomery Birthplace (PE) 277
   MacKenzie Art Gallery (SK) 73
   Margaret Laurence Home (MB) 97
   McMichael Canadian Art Collection (ON) 145
   Mendel Art Gallery and Civic Conservatory (SK) 83
   Montreal Mus. of Fine Arts (PQ) 210
   Mus. of Contemporary Art (PQ) 212
   Mus. of Decorative Arts (PQ) 215
   Mus. of Movie Art (AB) 50
   National Circus School (PQ) 217
   National Gallery of Canada (ON) 182
   Pangnirtung (NT) 300
   Pays de la Sagouine (NB) 252

... Arts
    Petroglyphs Provincial Pk. (ON) 186
    Robert Service Cabin (YT) 312
    Sam McGee's Cabin (YT) 314
    Shaw Festival (ON) 138
    Stephen Leacock Mus. (ON) 196
    Stratford Festival (ON) 128
    Todmorden Mills Heritage Mus. and Arts Ctr. (ON) 163
    Village Mont-Carmel (PE) 276
    Woodland Cultural Heritage Ctr. (ON) 133
Atlas Coal Mine Mus. (AB) 55
Atomic Energy of Canada Limited Research Laboratories (ON) 187

B

Bank of Canada's Currency Mus. (ON) 178
Bank of Montreal Mus. (PQ) 212
Banting Mus. and Education Ctr. (ON) 125
Barkerville Historic Town (BC) 34
Basin Head Fisheries Mus. (PE) 282
Bata Shoe Mus. (ON) 150
Batoche National Historic Pk. (SK) 88
Battle of the Chateauguay N.H.S. (PQ) 206
Battle of the Restigouche N.H.S. (PQ) 238
Battle of the Windmill Historic Site (ON) 174
Bay of Fundy Tides and Reversing Falls (NB) 247
Beaulne Mus. (PQ) 223
Beaverbrook Art Gallery (NB) 249
Bee Mus. (PQ) 235
Bell Homestead (ON) 132
Bellevue House N.H.S. (ON) 169
Beothuk Provincial Pk. (NF) 287
Bethune Memorial House (ON) 195
Billy Bishop Mus. (ON) 199
Biodôme (PQ) 218
Biscuit Puppet Theatre and Mus. (PQ) 220
Black Creek Pioneer Village (ON) 150
Black Cultural Ctr. for Nova Scotia (NS) 263
Bloedel Conservatory (BC) 17
Bon Echo Provincial Pk. (ON) 185
Bonnechere Caves (ON) 185
Bottle Houses (PE) 275
British Columbia Forest Mus. (BC) 12
British Columbia Legislature (BC) 6
British Columbia Sports Hall of Fame and Museum (BC) 19
Brooks Aqueduct N.H.S. (AB) 45
Butchart Gdns. (BC) 9
Bytown Mus. (ON) 176

C

Calgary Exhibition and Stampede (AB) 47
Calgary Zoo, Botanical Gdns. and Prehistoric Pk. (AB) 48
Cambridge Bay (NT) 301
Canada Olympic Pk. (AB) 50
Canada's Sports Hall of Fame (ON) 151
Canadian Ctr. for Architecture (PQ) 219
Canadian Craft Mus. (BC) 22
Canadian Football Hall of Fame and Mus. (ON) 140
Canadian Forces Communications and Electronics Mus. (ON) 170
Canadian Mus. of Caricature (ON) 177
Canadian Mus. of Civilization (PQ) 204
Canadian Mus. of Nature (ON) 178
Canadian Mus. of Rail Travel (BC) 29
Canadian Ski Mus. (ON) 178
Canadian War Mus. (ON) 179
Canadian Western Natural Gas, Light, Heat
    and Power Mus. (AB) 49
Canadiana Costume Mus. and Archives
    of British Columbia (BC) 7
Cannington Manor Provincial Historic Pk. (SK) 78
Cape Bonavista Lighthouse P.H.S (NF) 291
Cape Merry N.H.S. (MB) 114
Cape Spear N.H.S. (NF) 292
Capilano Suspension Bridge and Pk. (BC) 23
Carleton Martello Tower N.H.S. (NB) 246
Carr House (BC) 4
Cartier-Brébeuf N.H.S. (PQ) 232
Casa Loma (ON) 152
Castle Hill N.H.S. (NF) 286
Cave and Basin N.H.S. (AB) 53
Central Experimental Farm (ON) 180
Central New Brunswick Woodmen's Mus. (NB) 252
Centre Culturel Franco-Manitobain (MB) 108
Centre d'histoire de Montréal (PQ) 214
Charlie Lake Cave (BC) 37
Chilkoot Trail N.H.S. (YT) 313
Churchill, Manitoba "Polar Bear Capital of the World" (MB) 116
Cinémathèque Québécoise and Cinema Mus. (PQ) 213
Citadel of Quebec (PQ) 228
CN Tower (ON) 156
Cobalt's Northern Ontario Mining Mus. (ON) 190
Cochrane Ranche P.H.S (AB) 54
Colborne Lodge (ON) 153
Columbia Icefield Athabaska Glacier (AB) 54
Commissariat House (NF) 287

Comox Air Force Mus. (BC) 14
Coteau-du-Lac National Historic Pk. (PQ) 206
Cowichan and Chemainus Valleys Ecomuseum (BC) 13

Crafts
    Canadian Craft Mus. (BC) 22
    Elizabeth Lefort Gallery (NS) 270
    Native Heritage Ctr. (BC) 10

Crawford Lake Conservation Area (ON) 143
Cullen Gdns. and Miniature Village (ON) 164
Cumberland House Provincial Historic Pk. (SK) 76
Cypress Hills Massacre N.H.S. (SK) 71

D

Dalnavert Provincial and N.H.S. (MB) 101
Darlington Generating Station (ON) 165
David Dunlap Observatory (ON) 148
David M. Stewart Mus.: Mus. of Discoveries (PQ) 216
Dawson City Mus. (YT) 310
Diefenbaker Homestead (SK) 76
Dinosaur Provincial Pk. (AB) 45
Dionne Quints Mus. (ON) 189
Dominion Astrophysical Observatory (BC) 4
Doon Heritage Crossroads (ON) 129
Dr. Sun Yat-Sen Classical Chinese Gdn. (BC) 21
Duck Lake Regional Interpretive Ctr. (SK) 89
Dugald Costume Mus. (MB) 108
Duncan, City of Totems (BC) 11
Dundurn Castle (ON) 140

E

Edmonton Art Gallery (AB) 63
Elizabeth Lefort Gallery (NS) 270
Emily Carr Gallery (BC) 8
Energeum (AB) 49

Environment & Ecology
    Algonquin Pk. (ON) 187
    Bay of Fundy Tides and Reversing Falls (NB) 247
    Bloedel Conservatory, Queen Elizabeth Pk. (BC) 17
    British Columbia Forest Mus. (BC) 12
    Biodôme (PQ) 218
    Canadian Mus. of Nature (ON) 178
    Cave and Basin N.H.S. (AB) 53
    Columbia Icefield Athabaska Glacier (AB) 54
    Cowichan and Chemainus Valleys Ecomuseum (BC) 13
    Crawford Lake Conservation Area (ON) 143
    Forillon N.H.S. (PQ) 238
    Ft. Simpson (NT) 304

    Ft. Whyte Ctr. for Environmental Education (MB) 103
    Grasslands National Pk. (SK) 71
    Insectarium (PQ) 210
    Kluane National Pk. Reserve (YT) 316
    Kortright Ctr. for Conservation (ON) 146
    Living Prairie Mus. (MB) 105
    Lynn Canyon Suspension Bridge and Ecology Ctr. (BC) ... 24
    Petawawa National Forest Institute (ON) 188
    Point Pelee National Pk. (ON) 121
    Prince Albert National Pk. (SK) 92
    Royal British Columbia Mus. (BC) 9
    Saguenay Marine Pk. (PQ) 237
    Spruce Woods Provincial Heritage Pk. (MB) 97
    Undersea Gdns. of Victoria (BC) 7
    Wickaninnish Interpretive Ctr. (BC) 13
    Wildcare Wildlife Rehabilitation Ctr. (ON) 145
    Wood Buffalo National Pk. (NT) 303
    Yukon Wildlife Preserve (YT) 316

F

Famous People
    Alexander Graham Bell National Historic Pk. (NS) 269
    Anne of Green Gables Mus. at Silver Bush (PE) 277
    Banting Mus. and Education Ctr. (ON) 125
    Bell Homestead (ON) 132
    Bellevue House N.H.S. (ON) 169
    Bethune Memorial House (ON) 195
    Billy Bishop Mus. (ON) 199
    Bytown Mus. (ON) 176
    Carr House (BC) 4
    Colborne Lodge (ON) 153
    Dalnavert P. and N.H.S. (MB) 101
    Diefenbaker Homestead (SK) 76
    Dionne Quints Mus. (ON) 189
    Dundurn Castle (ON) 140
    Emily Carr Gallery (BC) 8
    Gabrielle Roy House (MB) 107
    George Brown House (ON) 154
    Gilles Villeneuve Mus. (PQ) 226
    J. Armand Bombardier Mus. (PQ) 224
    Jack London's Cabin and Interpretation Ctr. (YT) 311
    Laurier House N.H.S. (ON) 180
    L. M. Montgomery Birthplace (PE) 277
    Louis S. St-Laurent N.H.S. (PQ) 224
    Mackenzie Heritage Printery (ON) 137
    Margaret Laurence Home (MB) 97
    Mackenzie House (ON) 155
    Mackenzie King Estate (PQ) 205
    McCrae House (ON) 130
    Prince Albert National Pk. (SK) 92
    Riel House National Historic Pk. (MB) 107

... Famous People
- Rt. Hon. J. G. and Olive Diefenbaker Mus. (SK) 90
- Rt. Hon. J. G. Diefenbaker Ctr. Mus. and Archives (SK) 84
- Robert Service Cabin (YT) 312
- Royal London Wax Mus. (BC) 5
- Rutherford House Provincial Site (AB) 64
- Sam McGee's Cabin (YT) 314
- Samuel de Champlain Provincial Pk. (ON) 189
- Sir George-Étienne Cartier House N.H.S. (PQ) 216
- Sir Wilfrid Laurier N.H.S. (PQ) 225
- Stephansson House Historic Site (AB) 57
- Stephen Leacock Mus. (ON) 196
- Woodside N.H.S. (ON) 129

Fanshawe Pioneer Village (ON) 126
Fathom Five National Marine Pk. (ON) 200
Fisheries Mus. of the Atlantic (NS) 259
Fleming Mill (PQ) 208
Forges of St-Maurice N.H.S. (PQ) 226
Forillon National Pk. (PQ) 238
Forks, The (MB) 102
Ft. Amherst/Port La Joye N.H.S. (PE) 279
Ft. Anne N.H.S. (NS) 258
Ft. Battleford National Historic Pk. (SK) 87
Ft. Beauséjour N.H.S. (NB) 251
Ft. Calgary Historic Pk. (AB) 52
Ft. Carlton Historic Pk. (SK) 91
Ft. Chambly N.H.S. (PQ) 221
Ft. Edmonton Pk. (AB) 60
Ft. Edward N.H.S. (NS) 265
Ft. George (ON) 138
Ft. George—Buckingham House P.H.S (AB) 64
Ft. Henry (ON) 170
Ft. Ingall (PQ) 236
Ft. Kente (ON) 167
Ft. La Reine Mus. and Pioneer Village (MB) 99
Ft. Langley National Historic Pk. (BC) 27
Ft. Lennox N.H.S. (PQ) 222
Ft. Macleod (AB) 43
Ft. Malden N.H.S. (ON) 120
Ft. McMurray Oil Sands Interpretive Ctr. (AB) 65
Ft. Nelson's Welcome Visitor Program (BC) 38
Ft. No. 1 at Point Lévis N.H.S. (PQ) 234
Ft. Rodd Hill and Fisgard Lighthouse N.H.S. (BC) 8
Ft. Simpson (NT) 304
Ft. St. James N.H.S. (BC) 35
Ft. St. Joseph N.H.S. (ON) 193
Ft. Steele Heritage Town (BC) 30
Ft. Temiscamingue N.H.S. (PQ) 239

Ft. Whyte Ctr. for Environmental Education (MB) 103
Ft. Walsh National Historic Pk. (SK) 70
Ft. Wellington N.H.S. (ON) 174
Ft. Whoop-Up Interpretive Ctr. (AB) 42
Fortress of Louisbourg (NS) 268
Fortifications of Quebec N.H.S. (PQ) 229
Frank Slide Interpretive Ctr. (AB) 42
Fundy Geological Mus. (NS) 265
Fur Trade at Lachine National Historic Pk. (PQ) 207

G

Gabrielle Roy House (MB) 107

Gardens
- Butchart Gdns. (BC) 9
- Calgary Zoo, Botanical Gdns. and Prehistoric Pk. (AB) 48
- Cullen Gdns. and Miniature Village (ON) 164
- Dr. Sun Yat-Sen Classical Chinese Gdn. (BC) 21
- International Peace Gdn. (MB) 96
- Minter Gdns. (BC) 27
- Montreal Botanical Gdn. (PQ) 209
- Royal Botanical Gdns. (ON) 142
- University of British Columbia Botanical Gdns. (BC) 16

George Brown House (ON) 154
Gilles Villeneuve Mus. (PQ) 226
Glenbow Mus. (AB) 51
Grand-Pré N.H.S. (NS) 264
Grant's Old Mill (MB) 106
Grasslands National Pk. (SK) 71
Grassy Island National Historic Pk. (NS) 266
Green Gables House (PE) 281
Green Park Shipbuilding Mus. (PE) 275
Grenfell House Mus. (NF) 294
Grist Mill at Keremeos P.H.S (BC) 28
Grocery Hall of Fame (BC) 25
Grosse-Île N.H.S. (PQ) 231

H

Halifax Citadel N.H.S. (NS) 261
Hamilton Children's Mus. (ON) 141
Hamilton Mus. of Steam and Technology (ON) 141
Harris & District Mus. (SK) 82
Hat Creek Ranch (BC) 32
Head-Smashed-In Buffalo Jump (AB) 43
Heritage Pk. Historical Village (AB) 47
Hiscock House P.H.S (NF) 290

Historic – Fur Trade
- Ft. George—Buckingham House P.H.S (AB) 64
- Ft. Carlton Historic Pk. (SK) 91

Ft. Langley National Historic Pk. (BC) 27
Ft. Temiscamingue N.H.S. (PQ) 239
Fur Trade at Lachine National Historic Pk. (PQ) 207
Lower Ft. Garry National Historic Pk. (MB) 109
Old Ft. William (ON) 192
Prince of Wales Ft. National Historic Pk. (MB) 113
Rocky Mountain House N.H.S. (AB) 58
Samuel de Champlain Provincial Pk. (ON) 189
York Factory N.H.S. (MB) 115

Historic – General

Acadian Mus. (PE) 276
Aklavik (NT) 304
Alaska Highway Interpretive Ctr. (YT) 315
Alexander Graham Bell National Historic Pk. (NS) 269
Archelaus Smith Mus. (NS) 258
Bank of Canada's Currency Mus. (ON) 178
Banting Mus. and Education Ctr. (ON) 125
Basin Head Fisheries Mus. (PE) 282
Bata Shoe Mus. (ON) 150
Beaulne Mus. (PQ) 223
Beothuk Provincial Pk. (NF) 287
Black Cultural Ctr. for Nova Scotia (NS) 263
Brooks Aqueduct N.H.S. (AB) 45
Bytown Mus. (ON) 176
Cambridge Bay (NT) 301
Canadiana Costume Mus. and Archives
  of British Columbia (BC) 7
Canadian Mus. of Civilization (PQ) 204
Canadian Mus. of Nature (ON) 178
Cape Bonavista Lighthouse P.H.S (NF) 291
Cape Spear N.H.S. (NF) 292
Centre d'histoire de Montréal (PQ) 214
Chilkoot Trail N.H.S. (YT) 313
Cochrane Ranche P.H.S. (AB) 54
Coteau-du-Lac National Historic Pk. (PQ) 206
Cumberland House Provincial Historic Pk. (SK) 76
Cypress Hills Massacre N.H.S. (SK) 71
David M. Stewart Mus.: Mus. of Discoveries (PQ) 216
Dionne Quints Mus. (ON) 189
Dugald Costume Mus. (MB) 108
Fleming Mill (PQ) 208
Forillon National Pk. (PQ) 238
Forks, The (MB) 102
Ft. Calgary Historic Pk. (AB) 52
Ft. Ingall (PQ) 236
Ft. Simpson (NT) 304
Ft. St. James N.H.S. (BC) 35
Ft. Whoop-Up Interpretive Ctr. (AB) 42
Ft. Walsh National Historic Pk. (SK) 70
Fortress of Louisbourg (NS) 268
Fundy Geological Mus. (NS) 265

Glenbow Mus. (AB) 51
Grand-Pré N.H.S. (NS) 264
Green Pk. Shipbuilding Mus. (PE) 275
Grosse-Île N.H.S. (PQ) 231
Hamilton Mus. of Steam and Technology (ON) 141
Head-Smashed-In Buffalo Jump (AB) 43
Historic Acadian Village (NB) 253
Holocaust Education and Memorial Ctr. of Toronto (ON) 162
Hôtel-Dieu Mus. (PQ) 234
Huron Historic Gaol (ON) 125
Île-aux-Basques Excursion (PQ) 237
Ingersoll Cheese Factory Mus. (ON) 127
J. Armand Bombardier Mus. (PQ) 224
Last Mountain House Provincial Historic Pk. (SK) 81
Little Stone School (SK) 85
Louis S. St-Laurent N.H.S. (PQ) 224
Loyalist Cultural Ctr. (ON) 168
MacBride Mus. and Historical Society (YT) 314
MacKenzie Heritage Printery (ON) 137
MacLachlan Woodworking Mus. (ON) 171
Manitoba Agricultural Mus. (MB) 98
Manitoba Mus. of Man and Nature (MB) 105
Marine Mus. (ON) 156
Marine Mus. of the Great Lakes at Kingston (ON) 172
Maritime Mus. of the Atlantic (NS) 262
Mary March Regional Mus. (NF) 293
McCord Mus. of Canadian History (PQ) 211
McNab's Island (NS) 262
Montgomery's Inn (ON) 160
Montreal Holocaust Memorial Ctr. (PQ) 219
Musée Amérindien de Pointe-Bleue (PQ) 240
Musée de l'Amérique française (PQ) 227
Musée du Québec (PQ) 227
Mus. of Antiquities (SK) 85
Mus. of Canadian Scouting (ON) 181
Mus. of Decorative Arts (PQ) 215
National Aviation Mus. (ON) 182
Newfoundland Mus. (NF) 289
North American Black Historical Mus.
  and Cultural Ctr. (ON) 121
North Pacific Cannery Village and Mus. N.H.S. (BC) ... 36
Ontario Agricultural Mus. (ON) 143
Partridge Island N.H.S. (NB) 248
Peel Heritage Complex (ON) 144
Pointe-à-Callière Mus. of Archæology and History (PQ) 213
Prince of Wales Northern Heritage Ctr. (PE) 301
Province House N.H.S. (PE) 278
Provincial Mus. of Alberta (AB) 61
Rankin Inlet (NT) 300
Reynolds–Alberta Mus. (AB) 58
Royal British Columbia Mus. (BC) 9

...Historic – General

- Royal Ontario Mus. (ON) 157
- Royal Saskatchewan Mus. (SK) 75
- Sandon Historic Site and Mus. (BC) 32
- Saskatoon Western Development Mus. (SK) 86
- Simcoe County Mus. (ON) 198
- Sir Wilfrid Laurier N.H.S. (PQ) 225
- Sloop's Cove N.H.S. (MB) 114
- Sooke Region Mus. (BC) 10
- S.S. Klondike N.H.S. (YT) 312
- St. Andrew's Rectory National Historic Pk. (MB) 111
- St. Roche N.H.S. (BC) 19
- Steele Narrows Provincial Historic Pk. (SK) 77
- Steveston Mus. (BC) 24
- Survival of the Acadians N.H.S. (NB) 250
- Toronto's First Post Office (ON) 159
- Trait-Carré Historic Site (PQ) 235
- Uncle Tom's Cabin (ON) 123
- Vancouver Mus. (BC) 22
- Wanuskewin Heritage Pk. (SK) 82
- Watson's Mill (ON) 176
- West Point Lighthouse (PE) 274
- Western Development Mus. (SK) 86
- Winnie-the-Pooh Statue (ON) 193
- Woodland Cultural Ctr. (ON) 133
- Wood Mountain Provincial Pk. (SK) 72
- Yorkton Western Development Mus. (SK) 80
- Yukon Transportation Mus. (YT) 315

Historic – Gold Rush & Mining

- Atlas Coal Mine and Mus. (AB) 55
- Barkerville Historic Town (BC) 34
- Dawson City Mus. (YT) 310
- Frank Slide Interpretive Ctr. (AB) 42
- Harris & District Mus. (SK) 82
- Hat Creek Ranch (BC) 32
- Klondike N.H.S. (YT) 310
- Lillooet Mus. (BC) 33
- Sandon Historic Site and Mus. (BC) 32

Historic – Homes and Settlements

- Ardgowan National Historic Pk. (PE) 279
- Barkerville Historic Town (BC) 34
- Bell Homestead (ON) 132
- Bellevue House N.H.S. (ON) 169
- Bethune Memorial House (ON) 195
- Black Creek Pioneer Village (ON) 150
- Cannington Manor Provincial Historic Pk. (SK) 78
- Cartier-Brébeuf N.H.S. (PQ) 232
- Casa Loma (ON) 152
- Centre d'histoire de Montréal (PQ) 214
- Citadel of Quebec (PQ) 228
- Colborne Lodge (ON) 153
- Crawford Lake Conservation Area (ON) 143
- Dalnavert P. and N.H.S. (MB) 101
- Diefenbaker Homestead (SK) 76
- Doon Heritage Crossroads (ON) 129
- Dundurn Castle (ON) 140
- Fanshawe Pioneer Village (ON) 126
- Ft. Edmonton Pk. (AB) 60
- Ft. la Reine Mus. and Pioneer Village (MB) 99
- Ft. Steele Heritage Town (BC) 30
- George Brown House (ON) 154
- Grassy Island National Historic Pk. (NS) 266
- Grenfell House Mus. (NF) 294
- Heritage Pk. Historical Village (AB) 47
- Hiscock House P.H.S (NF) 290
- Historic Naval and Military Establishments (ON) 197
- Huronia Mus. and Huron Indian Village (ON) 196
- Hutchison House (ON) 167
- J. R. Park Homestead & Essex Region Conservation Authority (ON) 122
- Joseph Schneider Haus (ON) 130
- Kings Landing Historical Settlement (NB) 250
- Lang Pioneer Village (ON) 165
- Laurier House N.H.S. (ON) 180
- Louis S. St-Laurent N.H.S. (PQ) 224
- L. M. Montgomery Birthplace (PE) 277
- Mackenzie House (ON) 155
- Mackenzie King Estate (PQ) 205
- Manoir Louis-Joseph Papineau (PQ) 205
- McCrae House (ON) 130
- Motherwell Homestead National Historic Pk. (SK) 79
- National Doukhobour Heritage Village (SK) 80
- North Battleford Western Development Mus. (SK) 88
- Nova Scotia Highland Village (NS) 267
- Port Royal Habitation N.H.S. (NS) 259
- Post House Mus. (PQ) 214
- Province House N.H.S. (PE) 278
- Riel House National Historic Pk. (MB) 107
- Robert Service Cabin (YT) 312
- Rocky Mountain House N.H.S. (AB) 58
- Roosevelt Campobello Intl. Pk. and Natural Area (NB) 244
- Rutherford House Provincial Site (AB) 64
- Sam McGee's Cabin (YT) 314
- Sherbrooke Village (NS) 266
- Sir George-Étienne Cartier House N.H.S. (PQ) 216
- Sir Wilfrid Laurier N.H.S. (PQ) 225
- Spadina (ON) 159
- Ste-Marie Among the Hurons (ON) 197
- Stephansson House Historic Site (AB) 57
- Todmorden Mills Heritage Mus. and Arts Ctr. (ON) 163
- Upper Canada Village (ON) 175

Village Mont-Carmel (PE) 276
White Otter Castle (ON) 191
Woodside N.H.S. (ON) 129

Historic – Military (*see also* **Police and Military**)
   Artillery Pk. N.H.S. (PQ) 229
   Batoche National Historic Pk. (SK) 88
   Battle of the Chateauguay N.H.S. (PQ) 206
   Battle of the Restigouche Historic Site (PQ) 238
   Battle of the Windmill Historic Site (ON) 174
   Billy Bishop Mus. (ON) 199
   Canadian War Mus. (ON) 179
   Cape Merry N.H.S. (MB) 114
   Carleton Martello Tower N.H.S. (NB) 246
   Castle Hill N.H.S. (NF) 286
   Commissariat House (NF) 287
   Comox Air Force Mus. (BC) 14
   Duck Lake Regional Interpretive Ctr. (SK) 89
   Ft. Anne N.H.S. (NS) 258
   Ft. Battleford National Historic Pk. (SK) 87
   Ft. Beauséjour N.H.S. (NB) 251
   Ft. Chambly N.H.S. (PQ) 221
   Ft. Edward N.H.S. (NS) 265
   Ft. George (ON) 138
   Ft. Henry (ON) 170
   Ft. Kente (ON) 167
   Ft. Lennox N.H.S. (PQ) 222
   Ft. Macleod (AB) 43
   Ft. Malden N.H.S. (ON) 120
   Ft. No. 1 at Point Lévis (PQ) 234
   Ft. Rodd Hill and Fisgard Lighthouse N.H.S. (BC) .. 8
   Ft. St. Joseph N.H.S. (ON) 193
   Ft. Wellington N.H.S. (ON) 174
   Fortifications of Quebec N.H.S. (PQ) 229
   Halifax Citadel N.H.S. (NS) 261
   Historic Ft. Erie (ON) 134
   Historic Ft. York (ON) 154
   Historic Naval and Military Establishments (ON) .. 197
   Kingston Mills Blockhouse (ON) 173
   Kitwanga Ft. N.H.S. (BC) 35
   Lundy's Lane Historical Mus. (ON) 135
   Nancy Island Historic Site (ON) 199
   Nanton Lancaster Air Mus. (AB) 44
   National Battlefields Pk. (PQ) 233
   Signal Hill N.H.S. (NF) 292
   St. Andrews Blockhouse N.H.S. (NB) 245

Historic Acadian Village (NB) 253
Historic Babcock Mill (ON) 168
Historic Ft. Erie (ON) 134
Historic Ft. York (ON) 154
Historic Naval and Military Establishments (ON) .. 197

Hockey Hall of Fame (ON) 155
Holocaust Education and Memorial Ctr. of Toronto (ON) 162
Hôtel-Dieu Mus. (PQ) 234
Huntsman Marine Science Ctr. (NB) 245
Huron Historic Gaol (ON) 125
Huronia Mus. and Huron Indian Village (ON) 196
Hutchison House (ON) 167

I

Île-aux-Basques Excursion (PQ) 237
Images of the Future (PQ) 220

Industry
   Addiction Research Foundation Mus. (ON) 148
   Amethyst Mine Panorama (ON) 192
   Atlas Coal Mine and Mus. (AB) 55
   Atomic Energy of Canada Ltd. Research Laboratories (ON) 187
   Bank of Montreal Mus. (PQ) 212
   Basin Head Fisheries Mus. (PE) 282
   Bata Shoe Mus. (ON) 150
   Beothuk Provincial Pk. (NF) 287
   Canadian Western National Gas, Light, Heat
     and Power Mus. (AB) 49
   Central New Brunswick Woodmen's Mus. (NB) ... 252
   Cobalt's Northern Ontario Mining Mus. (ON) ... 190
   Darlington Generating Station (ON) 165
   Energeum (AB) 49
   Fleming Mill (PQ) 208
   Fisheries Mus. of the Atlantic (NS) 259
   Forges of St-Maurice N.H.S. (PQ) 226
   Ft. MacMurray Oil Sands Interpretive Ctr. (AB) ... 65
   Grant's Old Mill (MB) 106
   Green Pk. Shipbuilding Mus. (PE) 275
   Grist Mill at Keremeos Provincial Site (BC) 28
   Grocery Hall of Fame (BC) 25
   Hamilton Mus. of Steam and Technology (ON) .. 141
   Historic Babcock Mill (ON) 168
   Ingersoll Cheese Factory Mus. (ON) 127
   Mackenzie Heritage Printery (ON) 137
   Marine Mus. of Manitoba (MB) 110
   Marine Mus. of the Great Lakes at Kingston (ON) .. 172
   Newfoundland Mus. at the Murray Premises (NF) .. 290
   North Pacific Cannery Village and Mus. N.H.S. (BC) .. 36
   Old Stone Mill (ON) 173
   Oil Mus. of Canada (ON) 123
   Old Port of Quebec (PQ) 230
   Pangnirtung (NT) 300
   Petrolia Discovery (ON) 124
   Port of Vancouver Public Viewing Ctr. (BC) 21
   Post House Mus. (PQ) 214

Quarry Pk. Provincial Heritage Site (MB) 109
Reynolds—Alberta Mus. (AB) 58
Royal Canadian Mint (ON) 183
Science North (ON) 194
Sherbrooke Village (NS) 266
Southern Newfoundland Seamen's Mus. (NF) 286
Steveston Mus. (BC) 24
St. Catharines Mus. and Welland Canal
    Viewing Complex (ON) 139
Todmorden Mills Heritage Museum and Arts Centre (ON) 163
Toronto Stock Exchange (ON) 160
Underground Gold Mine Tour (ON) 190
Watson's Mill (ON) 176
Whiteshell Laboratories (MB) 112
Ingersoll Cheese Factory Mus. (ON) 127
Insectarium (PQ) 210
International Buddhist Society (BC) 26
International Mus. of Humour (PQ) 218
International Peace Gdn. (MB) 96

J

J. Armand Bombardier Mus. (PQ) 224
Jack London's Cabin and Interpretation Ctr. (YT) 311
John R. Park Homestead and Essex Region
  Conservation Authority (ON) 122
Joseph Schneider Haus (ON) 130

K

Kings Landing Historical Settlement (NB) 250
Kingston Mills Blockhouse (ON) 173
Kitwanga Ft. N.H.S. (BC) 35
Klondike N.H.S. (YT) 310
Kluane National Pk. Reserve (YT) 316
Kortright Ctr. for Conservation (ON) 146

L

L'Anse-aux-Meadows National Historic Pk. (NF) 294
Lang Pioneer Village (ON) 165
Last Mountain House P.H.S. (SK) 81
Laurier House N.H.S. (ON) 180
Leo Mol Sculpture Gdn. (MB) 106
Lillooet Mus. (BC) 33
Little Qualicum Spawning Channel (BC) 15
Little Stone School (SK) 85
Living Prairie Mus. (MB) 105
London Regional Children's Mus. (ON) 127
Louis S. St-Laurent N.H.S. (PQ) 224
Lower Ft. Garry National Historic Pk. (MB) 109

Loyalist Cultural Ctr. (ON) 168
L. M. Montgomery Birthplace (PE) 277
Lundy's Lane Historical Mus. (ON) 135
Lynn Canyon Suspension Bridge and Ecology Ctr. (BC) 24

M

MacBride Mus. and Historical Society (YT) 314
MacKenzie Art Gallery (SK) 73
Mackenzie Heritage Printery (ON) 137
Mackenzie House (ON) 155
Mackenzie King Estate (PQ) 205
MacLachlan Woodworking Mus. (ON) 171
Manitoba Agricultural Mus. (MB) 98
Manitoba Children's Mus. (MB) 104
Manitoba Mus. of Man and Nature (MB) 105
Manoir Louis-Joseph Papineau (PQ) 205

Many Cultures
Batoche National Historic Pk. (SK) 88
Black Cultural Ctr. for Nova Scotia (NS) 263
Centre Culturel Franco-Manitobain (MB) 108
Duck Lake Regional Interpretive Ctr. (SK) 89
Duncan, City of Totems (BC) 11
Dr. Sun Yat-Sen Classical Chinese Gdn. (BC) 21
Elizabeth Lefort Gallery (NS) 270
Head-Smashed-In Buffalo Jump (AB) 43
Historic Acadian Village (NB) 253
Huronia Mus. and Huron Indian Village (ON) 196
International Buddhist Society (BC) 26
Joseph Schneider Haus (ON) 130
Mennonite Heritage Village (MB) 100
Musée Amérindien de Pointe-Bleue (PQ) 240
Musée de l'Amérique française (PQ) 227
Musée du Québec (PQ) 227
Mus. of Anthropology (BC) 20
Native Heritage Ctr. (BC) 10
Ndilo Cultural Village (NT) 302
North American Black Historical Mus.
  and Cultural Ctr. (ON) 121
Nova Scotia Highland Village (NS) 267
Pangnirtung (NT) 300
Petroglyphs Provincial Pk. (ON) 186
Prince Albert National Pk. (SK) 92
Prince of Wales Northern Heritage Ctr. (NT) 301
Rankin Inlet (NT) 300
Royal Saskatchewan Mus. (SK) 75
Six Nations Tourist Sites (ON) 132
Sooke Region Mus. (BC) 10
Ste-Marie Among the Hurons (ON) 197
Survival of the Acadians N.H.S. (NB) 250

Ukrainian Cultural Heritage Village (AB) 60
Ukrainian Mus. of Canada (SK) 83
Wanuskewin Heritage Pk. (SK) 82
Woodland Cultural Centre (ON) 133
Yorkton Western Development Mus. (SK) 80
Zuckerburg Island Heritage Pk. (BC) 29
Maple Syrup Mus. (ON) 128
Margaret Laurence Home (MB) 97
Marine Mus. (ON) 156
Marine Mus. of Manitoba (MB) 110
Marine Mus. of the Great Lakes at Kingston (ON) 172
Marineland (ON) 135
Maritime Command Mus. (NS) 260
Maritime Mus. of the Atlantic (NS) 262
Mary March Regional Mus. (NF) 293
McCord Mus. of Canadian History (PQ) 293
McCrae House (ON) 211
McMichael Canadian Art Collection (ON) 130
McNab's Island, Halifax Harbour (NS) 262
Mendel Art Gallery and Civic Conservatory (SK) 83
Mennonite Heritage Village (MB) 100
Metro Toronto Zoo (ON) 164
Mildred M. Mahoney Silver Jubilee Doll's House Gallery (ON) 133
Mingan Archipelago National Pk. Reserve (PQ) 239
Miniature World (BC) 5
Minter Gdns. (BC) 27
Montgomery's Inn (ON) 160
Montreal Botanical Gdn. (PQ) 209
Montreal Holocaust Memorial Ctr. (PQ) 219
Montreal Mus. of Fine Arts (PQ) 210
Montreal Planetarium (PQ) 221
Moose Jaw Western Development Mus. (SK) 73
Motherwell Homestead National Historic Pk. (SK) 79
Musée Amérindien de Pointe-Bleue (PQ) 240
Musée de l'Amérique française (PQ) 227
Musée du Québec (PQ) 227
Mus. of Anthropology (BC) 20
Mus. of Antiquities (SK) 85
Mus. of Canadian Scouting (ON) 181
Mus. of Contemporary Art (PQ) 212
Mus. of Decorative Arts (PQ) 215
Mus. of Discoveries (PQ) 216
Mus. of Exotic World (BC) 23
Mus. of Movie Art (AB) 50

N

Nancy Island Historic Site (ON) 199
Nanton Lancaster Air Mus. (AB) 44
Narcisse Wildlife Management Area (MB) 112
National Aviation Mus. (ON) 182
National Battlefields Pk. (PQ) 233
National Circus School (PQ) 217
National Doukhobour Heritage Village (SK) 80
National Gallery of Canada (ON) 182
National Mus. of Science and Technology (ON) 183
Native Heritage Ctr. (BC) 10
Ndilo Cultural Village (NT) 302
Newfoundland Freshwater Resource Ctr. (NF) 289
Newfoundland Mus. (NF) 289
Newfoundland Mus. at the Murray Premises (NF) 290
Niagara Falls IMAX Theatre and Daredevil Gallery
    and Mus. (ON) 136
Norman Elder Mus. (ON) 156
North American Black Historical Mus. and Cultural Ctr. (ON) 121
North Battleford Western Development Mus. (SK) 88
North Pacific Cannery Village and Mus. N.H.S. (BC) ... 36
Nova Scotia Highland Village (NS) 267

O

Ocean Sciences Ctr., Memorial University
    of Newfoundland (NF) 288
Oil Mus. of Canada (ON) 123
Old Ft. William (ON) 192
Old Port of Quebec N.H.S. (PQ) 230
Old Stone Mill (ON) 173
Old Strathcona Model and Toy Mus. (AB) 62
Ontario Agricultural Mus. (ON) 143
Ontario Place (ON) 157
Ontario Science Ctr. (ON) 161

P

Pacific Space Ctr. (BC) 15
Pangnirtung (NT) 300
Paramount Canada's Wonderland (ON) 147
Parliament Hill (ON) 184
Partridge Island N.H.S. (NB) 248
Pays de la Sagouine (NB) 252
Peel Heritage Complex (ON) 144
Petawawa National Forestry Institute (ON) 188
Petroglyphs Provincial Pk. (ON) 186
Petrolia Discovery (ON) 124
Pheasantview Game Farm (MB) 96
Philip's Magical Paradise Mus. of Magic and Illusion (MB) 100
Point Pelee National Pk. (ON) 121
Pointe-à-Callière Mus. of Archaeology and History (PQ) 213
Police Dog Service Training Ctr. (AB) 56

Police and Military
(see also **Historic – Military**)

    Canadian Forces Communications and Electronics Mus. (ON) ... 170
    Citadel of Quebec (PQ) 228
    Comox Air Force Mus. (BC) 14
    Ft. Battleford National Historic Pk. (SK) 87
    Ft. Calgary Historic Pk. (AB) 52
    Maritime Command Museum (NS) 260
    Police Dog Service Training Ctr. (AB) 56
    Royal Canadian Mounted Police Centennial Mus. (SK) 74
    Wood Mountain Provincial Pk. (SK) 72

Politics and Politicians

    Ardgowan National Historic Pk. (PE) 279
    Bellevue House N.H.S. (ON) 169
    British Columbia Legislature (BC) 6
    Dalnavert P. and N.H.S. (MB) 101
    Diefenbaker Homestead (SK) 76
    Dundurn Castle (ON) 140
    Laurier House N.H.S. (ON) 180
    Louis S. St-Laurent N.H.S. (PQ) 224
    Mackenzie House (ON) 155
    Mackenzie King Estate (PQ) 205
    Manoir Louis-Joseph Papineau (PQ) 205
    Motherwell Homestead National Historic Pk. (SK) 79
    Parliament Hill (ON) 184
    Province House N.H.S. (PE) 278
    Rt. Hon. J. G. and Olive Diefenbaker Mus. (SK) 90
    Rt. Hon. J. G. Diefenbaker Ctr. Mus. and Archives (SK) 84
    Roosevelt Campobello International Pk. and
        Natural Area (NB) 244
    Rutherford House Provincial Site (AB) 64
    Sir George-Étienne Cartier House N.H.S. (PQ) 216
    Sir Wilfrid Laurier N.H.S. (PQ) 225
    Tilley House Mus. (NB) 248
    Woodside N.H.S. (ON) 129

Port of Vancouver Public Viewing Ctr. (BC) 21
Port Royal Habitation N.H.S. (NS) 259
Post House Mus. (PQ) 214
Prince Albert National Pk. (SK) 92
Prince Edward Island Marine Aquarium (PE) 281
Prince Edward Island Miniature Railway (PE) 274
Prince of Wales Ft. National Historic Pk. (MB) 113
Prince of Wales Northern Heritage Ctr. (NT) 301
Province House N.H.S. (PE) 278
Provincial Mus. of Alberta (AB) 61
Puck's Farm (ON) 147

Q

Quarry Pk. Provincial Heritage Site (MB) 109

R

Rankin Inlet (NT) 300
Reynolds–Alberta Mus. (AB) 58
Riel House National Historic Pk. (MB) 107
Rt. Hon. J. G. Diefenbaker Ctr. Mus. and Archives (SK) 84
Rt. Hon. J. G. and Olive Diefenbaker Mus. (SK) 90
Robert Service Cabin (YT) 312
Rocky Mountain House N.H.S. (AB) 58
Roosevelt Campobello International Pk. and
    Natural Area (NB) 244
Royal Botanical Gdns. (ON) 142
Royal British Columbia Mus. (BC) 9
Royal Canadian Mint (ON) 183
Royal Canadian Mounted Police Centennial Mus. (SK) 74
Royal London Wax Mus. (BC) 5
Royal Ontario Mus. (ON) 157
Royal Saskatchewan Mus. (SK) 75
Royal Tyrrell Mus. of Palaeontology (AB) 56
Rutherford House Provincial Site (AB) 64

S

Saguenay Marine Pk. (PQ) 237
Sam McGee's Cabin (YT) 314
Samuel de Champlain Provincial Pk. (ON) 189
Sandon Historic Site and Mus. (BC) 32
Saskatchewan Science Ctr. (SK) 74
Saskatoon Western Development Mus. (SK) 86

Science & Technology

    Alberta Science Ctr. (AB) 46
    Alexander Graham Bell National Historic Pk. (NS) 269
    Bell Homestead (ON) 132
    Brooks Aqueduct N.H.S. (AB) 45
    Canadian Forces Communications and Electronics Mus. (ON) ... 170
    David M. Stewart Mus.: Mus. of Discoveries (PQ) 216
    Hamilton Mus. of Steam and Technology (ON) 141
    Images of the Future (PQ) 220
    MacLachlin Woodworking Mus. (ON) 171
    Manitoba Mus. of Man and Nature (MB) 105
    National Mus. of Science and Technology (ON) 183
    Ontario Science Ctr. (ON) 161
    Reynolds–Alberta Mus. (AB) 58
    Saskatchewan Science Ctr. (SK) 74
    Science North (ON) 194
    Science World (BC) 18
    St. Catharines Mus. and Welland Canal
        Viewing Complex (ON) 139
    Thornhill Antique Clock Mus. (ON) 148

Science North (ON) 194
Science World (BC) 18

Serpent Mounds Provincial Pk. (ON)	166
Shaw Festival (ON)	138
Sherbrooke Village (NS)	266
Signal Hill N.H.S. (NF)	292
Simcoe County Mus. (ON)	198
Sir George-Étienne Cartier House N.H.S. (PQ)	216
Sir Wilfrid Laurier N.H.S. (PQ)	225
Six Nations Tourist Sites (ON)	132
SkyDome (ON)	158
Sloop's Cove N.H.S. (MB)	114
Sooke Region Mus. (BC)	10
Southern Newfoundland Seamen's Mus. (NF)	286

Space and Astronomy

Aero Space Mus. (AB)	51
Alberta Science Ctr. (AB)	46
David Dunlap Observatory (ON)	148
Dominion Astrophysical Observatory (BC)	4
Manitoba Mus. of Man and Nature (MB)	105
Montreal Planetarium (PQ)	221
National Mus. of Science and Technology (ON)	183
Pacific Space Ctr. (BC)	15
Royal Ontario Mus. (ON)	157
Science North (ON)	194
Spadina (ON)	159

Sports & Recreation

Algonquin Pk. (ON)	187
British Columbia Sports Hall of Fame and Museum (BC)	19
Canada Olympic Pk. (AB)	50
Canadian Football Hall of Fame and Mus. (ON)	139
Canadian Ski Mus. (ON)	178
Canada's Sports Hall of Fame (ON)	151
Gilles Villeneuve Museum (PQ)	226
Hockey Hall of Fame (ON)	155
SkyDome (ON)	158
Spruce Woods Provincial Heritage Pk. (MB)	97
SS Klondike N.H.S. (YT)	312
SS Moyie N.H.S. (BC)	31
St. Andrew's Blockhouse N.H.S. (NB)	245
St. Andrew's Rectory National Historic Pk. (MB)	111
St. Catharines Mus. and Welland Canal Viewing Complex (ON)	139
St. Roch N.H.S. (BC)	19
Ste-Marie Among the Hurons (ON)	197
Steele Narrows Provincial Historic Pk. (SK)	77
Stephansson House Historic Site (AB)	57
Stephen Leacock Mus. (ON)	196
Steveston Mus. (BC)	24
Storyland (ON)	185
Stratford Festival (ON)	128
Survival of the Acadians N.H.S. (NB)	250

T

Thornhill Antique Clock Mus. (ON)	148
Tilley House Mus. (NB)	248
Tivoli Miniature World (ON)	136
Todmorden Mills Heritage Mus. and Arts Ctr. (ON)	163
Toronto Stock Exchange (ON)	160
Toronto's First Post Office (ON)	159

Toys & Games

Bytown Mus. (ON)	176
Hamilton Children's Mus. (ON)	141
Mildred M. Mahoney Silver Jubilee Dolls' House Gallery (ON)	133
Old Strathcona Model and Toy Mus. (AB)	62
Trait-Carré Historic Site (PQ)	235

Transportation

Alberta Railway Mus. (AB)	63
Canadian Mus. of Rail Travel (BC)	29
Comox Air Force Mus. (BC)	14
J. Armand Bombardier Mus. (PQ)	224
Marine Mus. of Manitoba (MB)	110
Maritime Command Mus. (NS)	260
Maritime Mus. of the Atlantic (NS)	262
Moose Jaw Western Development Mus. (SK)	73
Nanton Lancaster Air Mus. (AB)	44
National Aviation Mus. (ON)	182
Prince Edward Island Miniature Railway (PE)	274
Reynolds—Alberta Mus. (AB)	58
SS Klondike N.H.S. (YT)	312
SS Moyie N.H.S. (BC)	31
St. Catharines Mus. and Welland Canal Viewing Complex (ON)	139
St. Roch N.H.S. (BC)	19
Trev Deeley Motorcycle Mus. (BC)	25
Yukon Transportation Mus. (YT)	315
Trev Deeley Motorcycle Mus. (BC)	25

U

Ukrainian Cultural Heritage Village (AB)	60
Ukrainian Mus. of Canada (SK)	83
Uncle Tom's Cabin (ON)	123
Underground Gold Mine Tour (ON)	190
Undersea Gdns. of Victoria (BC)	7
University of British Columbia Botanical Gdns. (BC)	16
Upper Canada Village (ON)	175

V

Vancouver Aquarium (BC)	17
Vancouver Mus. (BC)	22

Village historique Acadien (NB) 253
Village Mont-Carmel (PE) 276

W

Wanuskewin Heritage Pk. (SK) 82
Watson's Mill (ON) 176
West Edmonton Mall (AB) 59
West Point Lighthouse (PE) 274
Western Development Mus. (SK) 86
White Otter Castle (ON) 191
Whiteshell Laboratories (MB) 112
Wickaninnish Interpretive Ctr. (BC) 13
Wildcare Wildlife Rehabilitation Ctr. (ON) 145

Wildlife and Marine Life

   African Lion Safari (ON) 131
   Algonquin Pk. (ON) 187
   Biodôme (PQ) 218
   Calgary Zoo, Botanical Gdns. and Prehistoric Pk. (AB) .. 48
   Churchill, Manitoba "Polar Bear Capital of the World" (MB) ... 116
   Fisheries Mus. of the Atlantic (NS) 259
   Ft. Whyte Ctr. for Environmental Education (MB) 103
   Grasslands National Pk. (SK) 71
   Huntsman Marine Science Ctr. (NB) 245
   Kluane National Pk. Reserve (YT) 316
   Little Qualicum Spawning Channel (BC) 15
   Marineland (ON) 135
   Metro Toronto Zoo (ON) 164
   Mingan Archipelago National Pk. Reserve (PQ) 239
   Narcisse Wildlife Management Area (MB) 112
   Newfoundland Freshwater Resource Ctr. (NF) 289
   Ocean Sciences Ctr., Memorial University
      of Newfoundland (NF) 288
   Pheasantview Game Farm (MB) 96
   Point Pelee National Pk. (ON) 121
   Prince Edward Island Marine Aquarium (PE) 281
   Saguenay Marine Pk. (PQ) 237
   Undersea Gdns. of Victoria (BC) 7
   Vancouver Aquarium (BC) 17
   Wildcare Wildlife Rehabilitation Ctr. (ON) 145
   Yukon Wildlife Preserve (YT) 316

Winnie-the-Pooh Statue (ON) 193
Wood Buffalo National Pk. (NT) 303
Woodland Cultural Centre (ON) 133
Wood Mountain Provincial Historic Pk. (SK) 72
Woodside N.H.S. (ON) 129
World Whaling Capital AD 1550-1600 (NF) 295
World's Largest Smoking Pipe (MB) 99
World's Longest Suspended Footbridge (PQ) 223

Y

York Factory N.H.S. (MB) 115
Yorkton Western Development Mus. (SK) 80
Yukon Transportation Mus. (YT) 315
Yukon Wildlife Preserve (YT) 316

Z

Zuckerberg Island Heritage Pk. (BC) 29